Learning, Working and Living

Learning, Working and Living

Mapping the Terrain of Working Life Learning

Edited by

Elena Antonacopoulou

Peter Jarvis

Vibeke Andersen

Bente Elkjaer

Steen Høyrup

palgrave
macmillan

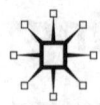

Selection and editorial matter © Elena Antonacopoulou,
Peter Jarvis, Vibeke Andersen, Bente Elkjaer and Steen Høyrup 2006
Individual chapters © contributors 2006

All rights reserved. No reproduction, copy or transmission of this
publication may be made without written permission.

No paragraph of this publication may be reproduced, copied or transmitted
save with written permission or in accordance with the provisions of the
Copyright, Designs and Patents Act 1988, or under the terms of any licence
permitting limited copying issued by the Copyright Licensing Agency,
90 Tottenham Court Road, London W1T 4LP.

Any person who does any unauthorised act in relation to this publication
may be liable to criminal prosecution and civil claims for damages.

The authors have asserted their rights to be identified
as the authors of this work in accordance with the Copyright,
Designs and Patents Act 1988.

First published 2006 by
PALGRAVE MACMILLAN
Houndmills, Basingstoke, Hampshire RG21 6XS and
175 Fifth Avenue, New York, N.Y. 10010
Companies and representatives throughout the world

PALGRAVE MACMILLAN is the global academic imprint of the Palgrave
Macmillan division of St. Martin's Press, LLC and of Palgrave Macmillan Ltd.
Macmillan® is a registered trademark in the United States, United Kingdom
and other countries. Palgrave is a registered trademark in the European
Union and other countries.

ISBN-13: 978–1–4039–4767–3 hardback
ISBN-10: 1–4039–4767–8 hardback

This book is printed on paper suitable for recycling and made from fully
managed and sustained forest sources.

A catalogue record for this book is available from the British Library.

Library of Congress Cataloging-in-Publication Data
Learning, working and living : mapping the terrain of working life learning /
    edited by Elena Antonacopoulou ... [et al.].
       p. cm.
    Includes bibliographical references and index.
    ISBN 1–4039–4767–8 (cloth)
    1. Organizational learning. 2. Employees—Training of.
    3. Learning. I. Antonacopoulou, Elena P.
    HD58.82.L43 2005
    658.3′124—dc22   2005051004

10 9 8 7 6 5 4 3 2 1
15 14 13 12 11 10 09 08 07 06

Printed and bound in Great Britain by
Antony Rowe Ltd, Chippenham and Eastbourne

Contents

List of Figures	x
List of Contributors	xi
Foreword	xiii
References	xvi

1. Learning, Working and Living: An Introduction   **1**
Elena P. Antonacopoulou

Rationale of the book	1
Organization of the book	2
Learning as a way of living	3
Learning and working	5
Learning and knowing in work organizations	7

Part I: Learning as a Way of Living

2. Organizational Learning and Workplace Learning – Similarities and Differences   **15**
Bente Elkjaer and Bjarne Wahlgren

Organizational learning	16
Workplace learning	22
Similarities and differences between OL and WPL	28
References	29

3. Two Logics of Learning   **33**
Per-Erik Ellström

Learning in organizations: reproduction versus development	34
Two logics of work and learning	35
The two logics presuppose different conditions of learning	38
Balancing the logics of performance and development	43
Concluding remarks	46
References	46

4. **Innovative Learning is Not Enough**   50
   Claus Elmholdt

   Situating the comparative study theoretically   52
   Situating the comparative study methodologically   54
   Workplace learning at yard   55
   Workplace learning at Web A/S   57
   Workplace learning at A-Soft   59
   Discussion   62
   Summary and conclusion   63
   References   64

Part II: Learning and Working

5. **Knowledge, Progression and the Understanding of Workplace Learning**   69
   Erik Laursen

   The concept of learning and modern work organizations   70
   Organizational learning viewed from three concepts
      of progression   74
   Learning situations – the interactional aspect of OL   78
   Learning as a perspective: what are we doing?   81
   References   82
   Notes   84

6. **Reflection in Learning at Work**   85
   Steen Høyrup

   Conceptual premises   85
   The root of reflection: the thinking of John Dewey   88
   Contributions from adult education   89
   The domain of problem solving   93
   Critical reflection   98
   Conclusions   99
   References   100

7. **How to 'Bridge the Gap' – Experiences in Connecting the Educational and Work System**   102
   Lennart Svensson and Hanne Randle

   Obstacles to workplace learning – two different systems
      that do not interact   102
   The complementarity of formal and informal learning   106

A flexible model for workplace learning	109
What strategy can be used?	113
Supportive structures are needed	114
Some final reflections	115
References	116
Notes	118

8. **The Workplace – a Landscape of Learning**   **119**
   Klaus Nielsen and Steinar Kvale

The landscape of learning at work	122
The personal learning horizon	132
Conclusion	134
References	134
Note	135

Part III: Learning and Knowing in Work Organizations

9. **Configuring Places for Learning – Participatory Development of Learning Practices at Work**   **139**
   Thomas Binder, Erling Björgvinsson and Per-Anders Hillgren

Machine setters on video	141
Self-produced video and everyday learning among intensive care nurses	144
Watching a colleague on video	147
Coming full circle	150
References	151

10. **Learning in and for Work, and the Joint Construction of Mediational Artefacts: An Activity Theoretical View**   **154**
    Reijo Miettinen and Jaakko Virkkunen

How the results of learning are preserved, accumulated, and transmitted	154
Joint creation of artefacts as a key to collective learning at work	156
The developmental contradictions of the labour-protection inspectors' work in the 1980s	158
Creating new instruments for inspection work within the Uusimaa Labour Protection District	160
Conclusions	165
References	167
Note	169

11. The Learning Processes in the Work Organization: From Theory to Design — 170
Annikki Järvinen and Esa Poikela

The case organization	171
Experience as a source of learning at work	175
Learning contexts in a work organization	176
Learning processes in the work organization	181
Conclusion	186
References	186

12. Conditions for Learning During a Period of Change. Dilemmas and Disturbances on the Production Floor — 188
Gun-Britt Wärvik and Per-Olof Thång

Analytical concepts	189
Gear	192
How to understand 'something different'	193
The production-planning meeting	193
Conclusions	198
References	200

13. A Context of Learning in the Workplace — 202
Hanne Dauer Keller

The concept of competence	203
Sense making in social work	204
Development of practical knowledge	206
Learning through being part of a community of practice	207
Learning as adaptation and renewal	208
A study of the development of social workers' competences	210
Some dilemmas of social work	212
The results	213
Developments of social practice	215
Conclusion	216
References	217

14. Non-learning in Multicultural Work Communities — 219
Marit Rismark and Jorun M. Stenøien

Theoretical framework	220
Object of study	222
Interviewing informants and analysing the material	223

	Filling the job at the nursing home ward	224
	Implications for workplace learning	230
	References	232
15.	**Working Life Learning: Learning-in-Practise**	**234**
	Elena P. Antonacopoulou	
	Introduction	234
	Learning, living, working as change routines	235
	Learning as a complex social system	239
	Inter-connectivity	240
	Diversity	241
	Self-organization/emergence	241
	Politics and power	243
	Learning-in-practise	244
	Conclusions	247
	Acknowledgements	248
	References	249
	Note	254

Index 255

List of Figures

7.1	The gap between the educational and work system	104
7.2	Competence as a result of reflective learning	107
8.1	Learning resources in the learning landscape	123
8.2	The apprentices' ladder of increasing responsibility	131
8.3	The personal learning horizon	132
10.1	The new instrumentality as a set of tools, actions and forms of collaboration	162
11.1	Learning in the context of an individual's work	177
11.2	Learning in the context of shared work	178
11.3	Learning in the context of an organization's work	180
11.4	The process model of learning at work	182
11.5	Processing initiatives (an example of a sub-process)	184

List of Contributors

Vibeke H. Andersen is Associate Professor at the Technical University of Denmark. Department of Manufacturing, Engineering and Management, Lyngby, Denmark.

Elena Antonacopoulou is Professor of Organisational Behaviour and Director of GNOSIS, University of Liverpool Management School and Fellow (UK) of the Advanced Institute of Management Research.

Thomas Binder is Director, PhD, Center for Design Research, Copenhagen Denmark.

Erling Björgvinsson is PhD student, School of Arts and Communications, Malmö University, Sweden.

Bente Elkjaer is Professor of Organizational Learning and Head of the Doctoral School of Organisational Learning (DOCSOL). The Danish University of Education. Department: Learning Lab Denmark, Denmark.

Per-Erik Ellström is Professor with special emphasis on work-related learning at Linköping University. Director of Centre for Studies of Humans, Technology, and Organization (CMTO), Sweden.

Claus Elmholdt is Assistant Professor at the University of Aarhus, Denmark.

Per-Anders Hillgren is PhD student, School of Arts and Communications, Malmö University, Sweden.

Steen Høyrup is Associate Professor at the Danish University of Education. Department: Learning Lab Denmark, Denmark.

Peter Jarvis is Professor of Continuing Education, University of Surrey, Guildford.

Annikki Järvinen is Professor at the University of Tampere, Finland.

Hanne Dauer Keller is Assistant Professor at the University of Aalborg, Denmark.

Steinar Kvale is Professor at the University of Aarhus, Denmark.

Erik Laursen is Professor of Sociology, University of Aalborg, Denmark.

Reijo Miettinen is Associate Professor at University of Helsinki, Department of Education, Center for Activity Theory and Developmental Work Research, Finland.

Klaus Nielsen is Associate Professor at the University of Aarhus, Denmark.

Esa Poikela is Professor at University of Tampere, Finland.

Hanne Randle is PhD student at the University of Karlstad, department of work science, and a Research assistant at APeL – R&D centre focusing on learning in working life.

Marit Rismark is PhD Research scientist at NTNU Adult Learning Research, Norwegian University of Science and Technology, Norway.

Jorun M. Stenøien is PhD Research scientist, NTNU Adult Learning Research, Norwegian University of Science and Technology, Norway.

Lennart Svensson is Professor at Linköping University, Director of research at APeL (a regional centre for research and development in workplace learning), Lindesberg, Sweden.

Per-Olof Thång is Professor in Workintegrated Learning, Göteborg University, Sweden.

Jaakko Virkkunen is Professor at University of Helsinki, Finland.

Bjarne Wahlgren is Professor of Sociology and Research Director of the Danish University of Education, Denmark.

Gun-Britt Wärvik is PhD in Education, Göteborg University, Sweden.

Foreword

This book draws together two important strands of study about the world of work: organizational and workplace learning. They are not the same conceptually or even linguistically but are brought together here because they are two sides of the same coin. However, it is necessary to see why they are two sides of the same coin and then to look at each side separately. The common word in these two terms is 'learning', a concept that conveys a sense of continuity and change, but especially the latter.

In order to try to capture the way that the world is changing, Bauman (2000) has introduced us to the concept of liquid modernity – a world of change, a place where people travel light and are flexible in the face of the forces of change. It is as if stasis has ceased to be and change is the norm of existence. It is endemic. This is a world that changes so rapidly that decisions have to be implemented before their possible outcomes can be properly tested – it is a risk society (Beck, 1992). What has caused such haste? Clearly this is a structural phenomenon and it might best be seen under the broad heading of globalization.

The world has changed drastically in the past half century as we have seen the emergence of the global village. In most villages, there is a central driving force (a core of institutions and people) and a periphery, and this is true of the global village too. Its driving forces are the economic institution and information technology and the people are those who control these institutions, such as directors of large organizations. Everything else is periphery. Moreover, the economic institution is the capitalist market in which the profit motive reigns supreme. In order to achieve this end there is both competition and mergers among the organizations, which means that they have each to be producing marketable commodities, many of which are in the (especially information) technology sector in the most efficient manner. But it is the information technology itself that is a major element in the rapidity of change: now communication is almost instantaneous and people can also travel freely and quickly around the village. Competition in the market means that every organization hastens to bring its commodities to the market as rapidly and as efficiently as possible. The speed of communication is essential to this process and new media are both part of the process but also commodities to be marketed. Consequently, new knowledge is at a premium, so that intellectual capital is now regarded as part of the capital of the economic institution and organizational flexibility is essential. We now live and work in a knowledge economy and we need a workforce that can function efficiently in this global village.

Knowledge itself does not really change, only our understanding of it and our recognition of its place in our society changes. In claiming this we are pointing to a very complex discussion that is well beyond the scope of this Foreword, and so we will focus only on some aspects of liquid knowledge. Even this discussion can be traced back to the 1920s when Scheler (1980 [1926], p. 76) suggested that even then knowledge changes every hour and that there were seven forms of knowledge: myth and legend; knowledge implicit in everyday natural language; religious knowledge; mystical knowledge, philosophic-metaphysical knowledge; positive knowledge – mathematics and the natural sciences and humanities; technological knowledge. For Scheler, this is a continuum from the least to the most artificial form of knowledge. Now it is not necessary to agree entirely with this typology but what it is trying to show is important for our understanding of knowledge today. The least artificial forms of knowledge, those that are embedded in societies' cultures, change slowly but the most artificial change rapidly and never have time to get embedded in culture before they have changed. In other words, they are liquid knowledge. Significantly, it is the two most artificial of Scheler's forms of knowledge that are crucial to the driving forces of the global village. They are the basis of the knowledge economy. Consequently, they have become the most dominant forms of knowledge in contemporary society to such an extent that they have become regarded as the truth by which everything else is judged. Nevertheless, it is these rapidly changing forms of knowledge that are central to our studies here of work and organization.

But there is one other significant element about the workplace and the marketplace. The commodities that are produced by the corporations need to be functional and the organizations themselves need to be seen to be efficient, so that the knowledge needs to have a practical basis. Traditionally, there have been three ways of legitimating knowledge: logical-rational; empirical; pragmatic. The first is based upon the ideas of rational argument that starts with a premise and develops the argument to its logical conclusion; the second states that knowledge is verified by empirical evidence, which is gained through our own senses; the third claims that knowledge is validated by its functionality, that is, that it works. It is this third approach that is important in a world where commodities have to be produced and sold in the consumer society. Knowledge important for liquid society is not only artificial but also it has to be practical.

Practical knowledge – 'knowledge *that*' was learned in educational institutions and people were equipped for work through learning 'knowledge *how*' in vocational educational institutions. In the latter the 'knowledge *how*' was sometimes converted into the *being able to* through the practical learning of the skills. Then it was assumed individuals would go into the workplace, often bureaucratically controlled and put into practice the knowledge (and skill) that had been learned. New members of the organization were expected to learn the established procedures and conform to its culture. Bureaucracies are the antithesis of the type of organization demanded by liquid society. In this society, organizations had to be sufficiently open as to incorporate change and its members had to be able to adapt to (learn) a continually changing organizational framework, or else the organization would appear outmoded and become increasingly dysfunctional and gradually entropy sets in. Organizations have to 'learn' to change in a liquid world, or become 'learning organizations', which meant that their members had to learn to change their roles within them.

But it is not only a matter of learning to adapt their roles, the work of producing efficiently new marketable commodities entails producing/ learning and using new knowledge and skills. Workers cannot always return to education in order to learn this new knowledge and skill, even if the educational institutions were equipped to provide these learning opportunities, which they are not! And so, workers also have to learn practical knowledge in the workplace. In order to be productive members of organizations functioning in a competitive market, workers themselves have to be competent and continue to remain competent in the changing work place.

Here, then, are the two sides of the same coin – organizational learning and learning in the workplace. Learning has become a very ambiguous word because it has been incorporated into such terms as 'lifelong learning', which can mean the process of learning throughout life, or the provision of opportunities to learn throughout life (in an institutionalized sense), or a set of policies about learning, and so on. It is also ambiguous because it is an individual process that has been used for another purpose, as in social learning, community learning, or even organizational learning, when learning relates in some way to the processes of change, flexibility and adaptation, that is, when it relates to the liquidity of contemporary society. Argyris and Schön (1978, p.18) suggest that it relates to changes in the theory-in-use in an organization brought about by individual members' learning. In a sense, organizational learning is not actually human learning but an intended or unintended outcome of several individuals' learning, individuals who are usually influential and powerful players. Human learning is a complex phenomenon that will almost certainly never be fully understood (see Jarvis and Parker, 2005).

Learning in the workplace is a form of experiential learning and is one of the sides of our coin. The workplace is a site in which learning occurs as it always has been, although much of the learning in the past has resulted in maintaining the organization rather than in developing it. Organizational learning is an outcome of its members' learning processes which is usually the outcome of one or more influential members' learning. This is a theory of change – the other side of the coin.

This book opens up a number of significant questions about organizational and workplace learning, which are important for both practitioners and students in contemporary society.

Peter Jarvis
March 2005

References

Argyris, C., & Schön, D. (1978). *Organizational Learning: a theory of action perspective*. Reading, MA: Addison-Wesley.
Bauman, Z. (2000). *Liquid Modernity*. Cambridge: Polity.
Beck, U. (1992). *Risk Society*. London: Sage.
Jarvis, P., & Parker, S. (eds). (2005). *Human Learning: a holistic perspective*. London: Routledge.
Scheler, M. (1980[1926]). *Problems of a Sociology of Knowledge* (edited by K. W. Stikkers). London: Routledge & Kegan Paul.

1
Learning, Working and Living: An Introduction

Elena P. Antonacopoulou

Rationale of the book

Learning and knowing have emerged in recent years as key issues in understanding work organizations. The popularization of ideas such as that of the 'learning organization' have contributed to the growing debate about the nature of learning at work. Identifying ways in which learning can be supported in the workplace has been a long-standing concern within the organization studies and education literatures alike. What perhaps is particularly interesting to note is that the debate has moved from a focus on formal and informal ways of supporting learning to ways in which learning can become a part of working life. Hence, the debate is not simply about new ways to improve workplace learning. It extends to the question of how we can achieve better sustainability and renewal of organizational resources at the same time as we allow learning to be the driving force behind a more human engagement with the challenges working life provides. Therefore, consistent with much current thinking about lifelong learning, it is critical that learning is central to life's journey and working is lived as a learning journey too.

The present book is the first to take this tone towards issues of learning at work. By addressing issues of learning and working as key elements in life, the book provides both the reflective stance so much needed in the fields of organizational learning and workplace learning. Fundamentally, however, it paves the way for a new repositioning of learning, working and living in the context of organizational complexity. The book acts as an accessible entry point into the theory and practice of learning as a way of living, which until now has not been readily available for students and practitioners.

Previously learning has been regarded as a way of fostering new forms of control to address the many political, social, cultural dynamics, which underpin the organizational priorities.

The book addresses the question of how does learning as a way of living provide a way of conceptualizing learning and knowing practices in work organizations. It suggests that it is through a focus on learning as a way of living that the needs of production can be reconciled with the needs of employees to have satisfying engagement with their work. Learning as a way of living becomes a key element in working life particularly as the image of the worker in new forms of organization also transforms to one of a lifelong learner.

The aims of the book are to:

- provide an understanding of the roles and purposes of learning as a way of living in work and organizations;
- build upon earlier perspectives and analyze ways in which earlier views of learning are challenged and extended by the view of learning as living promoted in this book;
- provide a rich empirical grounding for learning practices in a diversity of organizational contexts; and to
- integrate desperate discussions about learning, working and living across disciplines and contribute new conceptualizations of learning at work.

The book draws on the contributions of a diverse range of international authorities in the areas of management (human resource management, organizational behaviour, organizational development and management systems) and education (adult and vocational learning, experiential learning) as well as organizational psychology and sociology. A particular feature of the book is the way in which it crosses the boundaries of different disciplines and draws together views of learning to enable a secure grounding in academic thinking and working practice. The contributors are able to draw from their personal research in organizations as well as their experience and scholarship to ground discussion of learning in real settings and provide useful conceptual frameworks.

Organization of the book

The book is structured in three sections. The first section consists of three chapters under the heading *Learning as a Way of Living*. This section highlights why learning is important for organizations today and the different ways in which it is manifested. The second section, *Learning and Working*, consists of four chapters, which locate learning in relation to working not just workplace learning. The third section, *Learning and Knowing in Work Organizations*, consists of six chapters and focuses on locating learning and knowing as living, one may even say thriving, in work organizations.

All sections include a diverse set of theoretical, as well as, empirically informed ideas and provide case-based themes, which are grounded in examples of learning as a way of living in a variety of workplaces. The book concludes with a consolidating chapter by Elena Antonacopoulou, which draws together the themes of the book and identifies an agenda for reconceptualizing learning as a complex social system. The analysis examines the challenges facing learning research proposing future research directions exploring the unfolding nature of learning as part of living and working.

Learning as a way of living

In this section learning is conceptualized as an integral part of living and learning is seen as an essential human condition when we try to understand complex social arrangements such as organizations. Learning is a new form of labour and the concept of learning is applied as a lens through which organizational life and work are interpreted.

Learning is the daily ongoing process that is interwoven in and inseparably connected to the daily processes of work. Learning in this perspective is not institutionalized in formal educational settings or organized by external agents in terms of efficiency, but realized in complex organizations and the logics that prevail there. Learning this way is part of human existence and development in the social setting of work and organizational life and living. The adoption of facts and development of skills may be part of this learning but even more important is the construction of meaning, the construction of images of the world, the development of identities, collective practices and new perspectives of life.

The social setting, the complex work organization, might support or suppress the learning process, but can not cause its elimination. Learning as part of human existence will always flourish.

To think of learning as a way of living is opposed to a view of learning conceptualized in terms of performativity, efficiency and a narrowly defined instrumental means-end calculations. Learning as a way of living involves processes of exploring, questioning, reframing and transforming situations at work and in organizations, that is innovative or creative forms of learning. This kind of creativity mainly takes place in an informal organization in the work organization – unofficially behind the scenes. Thus, learning as a way of living meets fundamental human needs for creativity and development and constitute an important part of organizational life as a whole.

Learning as a way of living is important for organizations today for several reasons. Creative and innovative workplace learning are indispensable in late-modern flexible organizations for adaption and development. It constitutes in itself an important resource for the organization that management can support and try to balance in relation to other types of workplace learning.

The approach *learning as a way of living* makes explicit several fundamental themes dealt with in the three chapters. How can we in a learning perspective conceptualize the individual–environment relation, the unit constituted by individual and the social context? And what is the learning subject assumed to be in this connection? The learning subject can be the individual, the team or the organization. What does it mean that an organization is learning?

In chapter 2, by Elkjaer and Wahlgren, the focus is on theories of learning. Two broad research traditions – organizational learning and workplace learning – are compared. Although organizational learning and workplace learning originate in different fields of research, they nevertheless appear to share the same object: learning at work and learning related to organizations. Organizational learning is rooted in organization and management studies, where learning is regarded as a means to develop and manage enterprises as a whole. Workplace learning has its roots in adult education, with a clear focus upon the individual learner. Despite these differences in origin and focus, the authors show that there are more similarities than differences between the two fields. Thus, both attend to the issue of how the organization of the learning environment may help or hinder learning. One difference may be that more attention is paid to actual educational activities in the field of workplace learning, although the term 'interventionist practices' in organizational learning may be said to cover almost the same ground.

Chapter 3, by Ellström, addresses the important relation between levels of learning and conditions of learning in the organization. The starting point of this analysis is a distinction between two levels of learning: reproductive and developmental learning. It is argued that both levels of learning are needed, and that it is important to maintain a balance between the two. One of the difficulties in doing so, is that the two levels seem to require different conditions, and that there is limited knowledge concerning these conditions. The purpose of the chapter is to identify the conditions that are assumed to be critical for facilitating or constraining reproductive and developmental learning at work. Furthermore, based on an analysis of these conditions, a distinction is proposed between two logics of activity and learning. These two logics are viewed as patterns of practice that shape the conditions of learning in an organization, and, thus, also have a crucial bearing on the kind of learning that is dominant in different work situations.

The starting point for Chapter 4, by Elmholdt, is that creative and innovative workplace learning are important in late-modern flexible organizations. However, the value of creative and innovative learning may be questioned if this approval happens at the expense of reproductive or routine learning. Thus, the chapter adds a third dimension of learning at work and identifies three types of learning with respect to a balance between continuity and change in the workplace: reproductive, reconstructive, and innovative learning. Three case studies on workplace learning are compared: a shipyard, a web-design bureau, and a software production company. Different distributions of reproductive, reconstructive, and innovative learning are identified across the workplaces. The findings show harmful consequences for persons and organizations of overly reproductive learning environments with restricted access to engage in innovative learning. More surprisingly, the findings also indicate harmful consequences of overly innovative learning environments with limited access to participate in reproductive learning. The chapter suggests that reproductive, reconstructive, and innovative learning are to be understood as functionally complementary types of workplace learning.

Learning and working

This section locates learning in relation to working. The authors draw attention to the concepts of learning and knowing, learning situations and learning systems, and the meaning of these concepts in relation to working. A broad range of different types of learning processes is described and related to the contextual potentials and constraints of learning. The workplace is conceptualized in terms of options for learning. How can learning in and for work fruitfully be analyzed, and how are results of learning preserved, accumulated and transmitted?

There is no single way of understanding the relation between learning and working and no universal model of this relation exists. Against this background, different theoretical approaches are used as frame of reference: Organizational learning is viewed from different concepts of progression, a situated learning perspective and theories of reflection are brought into play.

Chapter 5, by Laursen, addresses the current tendency to use the concept of 'learning' when referring to activities and processes within our working lives that considered objectively could be referred to simply as change. Furthermore, both the individual employee and the entire organization are assumed to be *a priori* motivated for participating in learning processes. Laursen argues that an important criterion for perceiving change as learning should be the identification of some kind of progression of the behavioural change in question. The author discusses some of the problems concerning the understanding of the concept of 'progression' in a workplace context. A distinction is made between three ways of approaching organizational learning based on different perspectives on progression. The chapter concludes with a short discussion of the concept of 'learning situations' that sums up the possibilities for learning offered to members of organizations. Also, the possibilities of conceiving progression in organizational learning in the development of learning situations, is discussed.

In chapter 6, by Høyrup, three approaches to learning – adult learning, problem-solving and critical reflection theory – are used as different lenses for interpreting the questions: What is reflection and how is reflection related to learning? The author concludes that the fundamental role of reflection in learning is its potential for creating interaction between different kinds of experiences. Reflection contributes to the learning outcomes on several crucial dimensions of learning: expansion of the individual's potential for action, expansion of personal capability, and development of the individual's frame of reference and organizational learning. Reflection in learning thus becomes a fruitful approach to understanding learning at work.

Chapter 7 by Svensson and Randle adopts a critical perspective. Despite all of the rhetoric about lifelong learning and all the national programmes during the past decade in Sweden, the time for paid vocational training at work has actually diminished. The marked inequalities in learning provision among employees have in fact increased. One reason for the failure of lifelong learning is explained as a division – a 'gap' – between the educational and the work systems. A sociological analysis can explain the difficulties by integrating (formal) education with (informal) learning at work. A 'model' for workplace learning, which tries to connect these two systems, is presented. By making education work-based, flexible and accessible it can be attractive both to the employer and employees. Results from different case studies are presented. Different change strategies to 'bridge the gap' are discussed. A research and development centre (APeL) is presented, which tries to 'bridge the gap' by promoting workplace learning.

In Chapter 8, by Nielsen and Kvale, a landscape metaphor of learning is introduced in order to highlight different types of learning processes at workplaces. A situated learning perspective has inspired the presented assumptions of learning, focus being on the contextual potentials and constraints of learning. On the basis of interviews, participant observation and a questionnaire survey from the research project 'Learning in Modern Danish Vocational Training', a variety of learning resources in workplaces are described. Furthermore, novice learners' trajectories through the learning landscape at the workplace are discussed.

Learning and knowing in work organizations

The transmission of knowledge in the perspective of learning is the central theme for this section. The theoretical approach is that learning is a collective phenomenon, which implies that cultural knowledge is seen as locally preserved, shared and transmitted to members of the organization. The transmission of knowledge may also be across cultures, and might imply transformation of organizational routines.

How can we analyze and conceptualize problems and efforts in relation to transmitting knowledge and changing of practice – in the light of learning as a collective phenomenon, often in terms of participation and inquiry?

One position is that all forms of activity are passed on in the form of objects – termed artefacts – created by human beings for human beings. The embodiment of forms of human activity within artefacts – mediating objects – is the primary means of learning and transmitting human achievement. In these terms the significance of artefacts is obvious, knowledge can produce objects that congeal the knowledge into 'thingness'. In this way artefacts can have qualities of an affordance, a function or programme of action and goals. In these terms learning can be seen as collective investigation and collaborative retooling.

In some of the mentioned cases knowing may take the form of a new technical procedure enacted by professionals, or more complex and socially constructed nursing models, embedded in different cultures. Knowledge exchange in this way may involve a knowledge–cultural encounter. In these cases knowledge constitutes procedures that seem rational, but implies transmission of knowledge that is going to change work practice. This practice may be intertwined with established and conventional views of knowing, teaching and learning.

The section shows many facets of knowledge: knowledge that is separated from its creator and in some way takes on a life of its own, becoming objective knowledge. Knowledge that becomes reified constitutes artefacts. Knowledge does not reside exclusively in the individual. Knowledge may be situated in practice and organizational routines and culture. In this connection learning is conceptualized in different ways and models, but always as a collective phenomenon, involving sharing of processes, and as changes in complex systems.

Learning might be seen as social and reflective processes, happening simultaneously in individual, group and organization work contexts. A different approach is that learning is conceptualized as retooling that involves change in a complex activity system, and disturbances and dilemmas in and between activity systems are regarded as sources of learning.

In chapter 9, Binder, Björgvinsson and Hilgren show that participatory approaches to the development of new learning practices at work offers opportunities for exposing, articulating and reflecting upon practices of knowing and learning at the same time as participants may collaboratively probe for new learning possibilities. In this chapter, approaches and results from two participatory projects taking their point of departure in video documentation of 'best practices' are introduced and discussed. In the first project learning possibilities envisioned in the participatory process does not seem to find a place in the everyday life practice of work, partly due to the shift in connotations of learning in the transition from project to practice. In the second project a more sustainable change appear to have taken place as the workplace has more permanently adopted approaches of inquiry developed in the project. Even in this project, conventional notions of knowing, teaching and learning flow into the new learning practices indicating the volatility and vulnerability of the participatory process. The chapter ends by discussing the necessary sensitivity of participatory approaches towards the everyday configuring of places for learning.

Chapter 10, by Miettinen and Virkkunen, talks about the three dilemmas that have haunted the discussion concerning workplace learning: How to explain the retention of learning outcomes, how to understand the relationship between individual and collective learning as well as the relationship between learning and the development of work practices. They suggest that the appropriation, use and development of artefacts that mediate the joint activity is a key for understanding workplace learning and the development of work practices. They maintain, that this activity-theory-based explanation has several merits compared to the prevailing views that ascribe the retention of learning outcomes to changes in individuals' minds or body schemes or to shared practices and routines in work communities. They elaborate this idea by presenting a case example, in which the development of new instruments not only led to an expansive transformation of the work activity but also to a new, more effective form of individual and collective learning.

The starting point for Chapter 11, by Järvinen and Poikela, is that most of the workplace learning models view learning from either individual, group or organizational levels. In this chapter the authors have combined these levels, which means that learning is not happening at different levels, but simultaneously in individual, group and organization work contexts. Social, reflective, cognitive and operational processes combine these contexts. The authors describe the theoretical background for their process model and its application to the design process within a large construction enterprise. The phases of collaboration between researchers and practitioners are described as a shared development process. The goal of the development was to find the core processes and sub-processes producing learning and knowing in the organization. Three core processes were found and under each of them two to three sub-processes were recognized as the result of the collaboration. An example of a sub-process is given concerning the suggestion scheme (initiatives) of the construction enterprise.

The aim of Chapter 12, by Wärvik and Thång, is to discuss conditions for learning during a period of change. The point of departure is artefacts, developed by the management with the aim of transmitting their intentions to the production floor and also how these artefacts work on the production floor. The management describes difficulties to fully realize their intentions; they say that the workers 'don't want to learn'. To understand the situation, the authors have turned to activity theory and accordingly, the unit of analysis is the culturally and socially mediated activity system. Disturbances and dilemmas in and between different activity systems are regarded as sources for learning and change. They argue that this is not a story about workers who do not want to learn, it is a story about artefacts with different meanings in different activity systems. This means that the question of how the artefacts are historically developed is an important issue to understand the conditions for learning.

Chapter 13 by Keller deals with competence development of social workers. The author presents a perspective on competence as the staff members' pre-conscious understanding of their work task and work role and discusses the possibility for development of this competence. Staff members' community of practice stimulates competence development (i.e. learning) through the negotiation of meaning. However, the informal and incidental learning in a community of practice tends to lead to adaptation to the demands of the practice, that is, work environmental and organizational demands. Thus, in order to allow for the staff members' more reflective and critical learning as to their own practice, it may be necessary to establish a context for learning that is distanced from the immediate requirements of the practice performance. Such a context for learning, group supervision, was studied for its effect on staff members' competence development in two groups of social workers. The study indicated that to explicate the changes of staff members' competence it is not sufficient to analyze the outcome of the learning context isolated. In addition one must analyze how the psychosocial work environment influence the possibilities to apply the attained changes in competence in everyday work processes.

Chapter 14, by Rismark and Steinøyen, presents a case study of a very common situation around the world, namely multicultural staff working together in the joint production of goods and services. It is a study of the dynamics of shared duties in health ward practices with nurses embedded in two different nursing models working side by side. The analysis examines how Polish nurses and Norwegian health personnel have their own socially constructed nursing models – a 'medical' approach and an 'independent' approach to nursing. The different backgrounds and work experiences become an issue of mutual recognition, and it is evident that the potential for learning is not realized. Rather, we see a non-learning organization due to a power play through which the Norwegian staff preclude themselves from adding to their nursing practice. This study is important in the wider perspective of international agreements that aim to enhance knowledge exchange and promote mutual understanding between people and nations.

In the concluding Chapter 15, by Elena Antonacopoulou, the author states that learning is immensely rich and no single perspective is sufficient to capture fully the multiple connections and possibilities that it creates and from which it emerges. The author addresses the problem how to manage this complexity of learning. The discussion begins with an overview of the current approaches to learning. A broad range of classical learning definitions are presented and it becomes clear how different disciplinary perspectives underlines different – and narrow – aspects of learning, including behaviour, cognition, motivation, experience and action. It seems evident that these modes of thinking are limiting our capacity to fully understand and manage the complexity of learning as an integral part of living and working. To deal with this problem, references are made to themes and problems elaborated in the chapters of the book, for example the relation between learning and changing, and the influence of dominant logics of learning on space for learning at work.

The author takes further steps to reposition learning as a complex social system. In this thinking it is necessary to highlight dimensions as inter-connectivity, diversity, self-organization and power. Complexity science is presented and used as an approach to analyze these dimensions and a new conceptualization of learning as a complex social system is provided. The author reflects on future research in learning as a mode of living and working in organizations and recommend the notion of *learning-in-practise* as a new avenue for future research in learning.

Part I
Learning as a Way of Living

2
Organizational Learning and Workplace Learning – Similarities and Differences

Bente Elkjaer and Bjarne Wahlgren

When Zuboff wrote her seminal sentence in 1988 to coin the consequences of the application of information technology in enterprises: 'Learning is the new form of labour' (Zuboff, 1988, p. 395), she probably did not anticipate its more general applicability. The publication of Senge's book on learning organizations (Senge, 1990) as well as the revised publication in 1996 of Argyris and Schön's work from 1978 on organizational learning, is further evidence of an interest in applying the term 'learning' as a lens through which to view organizational life and work (Argyris & Schön, 1978, 1996). Marsick's edited book, *Learning in the Workplace* (Marsick, 1987a), Garrick's (Garrick, 1998) as well as the co-edited book by Boud and Garrick (Boud & Garrick, 1999) on 'learning at work' from the late 1990s, are all hallmarks of the interest in research – and practice – on workplace learning.

Researching learning in and with relation to work and organizations is, however, not new. There is nothing novel in focusing upon the 'human factor' or 'human resources' at work or on how to develop and change organizations. This happens all the time and has a long history attached to it (see, e.g., Hollway, 1991, for an overview). But the terms 'workplace learning' and 'organizational learning' have recently (within the last 10–15 or so years) attracted still more attention among both researchers and practitioners as 'tools to think with', that is as relevant concepts to guide understandings and practices of contemporary workplaces or organizations.

Thus, organizational learning (OL) and workplace learning (WPL) are two scholarly traditions apparently with the same object – learning at work as well as learning related to organizations. However, these two traditions originate in different research fields. Organizational learning is rooted in organization and management studies. Within this field, learning is regarded as a means to develop and manage enterprises as a whole – often, however, as we show in this chapter, by way of individuals. Workplace learning has its roots in adult education with a clear focus on the individual as the learner. Neither OL nor WPL are, however, unequivocal research traditions, but they reflect different definitions of learning and subsequently of what OL and WPL are, and how to make OL and WPL respectively happen in workplaces or organizations.

In this chapter, we present different perspectives on OL as well as selected issues within the WPL tradition. We show that although the term is organizational learning, it is difficult to avoid a starting point for learning that begins with individuals' learning in organizations. We also show that although the term applied is workplace learning, the classroom as a learning environment as well as some form of teaching activities to enhance learning at work are conspicuous issues in the WPL literature. By presenting the two traditions together, we hope to show that there are commonalities – the individual as learner is hard to escape in both traditions, and diversity, albeit more in degree than in kind. Thus, the attention to actual interventionist or educational practices as ways to support learning in and with relation to work and organizations are more visible in the WPL tradition than in the tradition of OL.

Organizational learning

Over the years there have been many attempts to define the field of organizational learning and it is not possible here to give a comprehensive review (for that, see, e.g., Dodgson, 1993; Easterby-Smith, 1997; Miner & Mezias, 1996). But the prevailing understanding is that OL happens through individuals' learning in organizational environments. There exists, however, a dividing line regarding the understanding of learning. Is learning primarily an issue of individuals' acquisition of skills and knowledge, or does learning embrace an ontological dimension by including learning as individuals' development and growth? Also, the degree to which the organizational context receives conceptual attention as a learning environment differs within the OL field (Elkjaer, 2003b).

There is, however, a movement within the OL field (as well as within organization studies as such, see, e.g., Law, 1994) to avoid focusing on individuals as the learning subjects of OL (Elkjaer, 1999, 2003a;

Gherardi, 2000a; Gherardi *et al.*, 1998). This trend may be called a social or a practice-based perspective on OL. The argument is that to regard the individual as the learning subject contributes to a dualistic thinking resulting in a separation of individuals and environments (see also Altman & Rogoff, 1987). This means that it is not possible conceptually (and subsequently, in practice) to comprehend the mutual constituency of individuals and environments in the organizational learning processes. This latter perspective on OL indicates that OL can only be understood as part of organizational actions and practices, events or situations. The problem with the perspectives that define OL as a process that happens through its individuals is how to transfer learning outcome from individuals to organizations, and the problem with the practice-based perspective on OL is that it is not obvious how to separate learning from other activities going on in organizations (Elkjaer, 2003c). In the following, we elaborate on these different perspectives on OL.

Organizational learning as individual knowledge acquisition

Literature on OL was first coined as theories of organizational behaviour within the field of management science (Cyert & March, 1963; Easterby-Smith, 1997; March & Simon, 1958). These early contributions to the emerging field of OL deal with ways for managers to enhance information processing and decision making in organizations. Organizational learning is in this understanding viewed as relevant because it is a way to help organizations through their managers' learning to adapt to changes in the environment. Thus, information processing and decision making in organizations is viewed as something done by individuals (managers) and as processes that can be enhanced by individuals' learning.

The process of abstraction is viewed as a necessary condition for OL in this early literature on OL; that is to be able to process information on a still more informed level based upon information and knowledge acquisition. Thus, to the learner, learning is the acquisition of a body of data, facts and practical wisdom accumulated by former generations of management; it is to come to know the organizational world and to learn about its practices. Learning is a process of knowledge delivery from a knowledgeable source to a target lacking that knowledge. The understanding of knowledge is that it is out there somewhere, stored in places (books, databases, minds) waiting to be transferred to and acquired by learners for future use. Organizational learning is assessed on the basis of the derived changes in the organizational routines and values, which are to be secured in the organizational memory (e.g. information systems, work descriptions and the like).

Organizational learning understood as individuals' knowledge acquisition, as enhancement of individuals' cognitive skills, is to occur through individuals' learning in organizations. This creates the problem of transferring individual learning outcome to the organization (see, e.g., Friedman, 2002; Kim, 1993; Mumford, 1991). The rationale seems to be that it is only a small number of organizational members, that is, managers, who have significant influence upon strategic decision making, which means that individual managers' learning will have an impact upon OL (Easterby-Smith *et al.*, 2000). When OL is thought of as involving employees other than managers, it is, however, necessary to solve the problem of transfer in another way. This following contribution to OL has done so by assuming that all organizational members act on behalf of the organization. Thus, in order for OL to take place in organizations, individuals must want it to. The organizational environment may, however, help further this, as we shall show in the next section of the chapter.

Organizational learning as individual development in organizational learning systems

The work of Argyris and Schön is also an example of OL based upon individuals' learning in organizations (Argyris & Schön, 1996). The scope is, however, wider than the view on OL as individual knowledge acquisition. Argyris and Schön's perspective on OL is based upon a wish to develop individual awareness of defensive ways of communicating in organizations, as this is what prevents OL from flourishing in organizations. Also, Argyris and Schön's contribution to OL includes an explicit conceptualization of the organization as that of a learning system. The organizational learning system is the learning environment in which individuals' learning and development takes place.

Argyris and Schön have an inclusive definition of OL, which implies that all organizations are learning. They define OL as a cumulative process reflecting an organization's acquisition of skills and knowledge. Learning is, however, done by individuals as:

> 'Organizational learning occurs when individuals within an organization experience a problematic situation and inquire into it on the organization's behalf' (ibid., p. 16).

A problematic situation can be a situation, for example, in which individuals experience a surprising mismatch between the expected and the actual results of the organizational activities currently in place. This is a situation that invites inquiry. It is a situation that can be defined as 'problematic', and as such subjected to the testing of hypotheses and experimentation and resolved for a time. If individuals make an inquiry, it can lead them to modify their picture and understanding of organizational activities and the organization as a whole. However, if the individual learning outcome is to become organizational, the results must become part of how other individuals picture and understand the organization. Individual learning outcome must, in other words, become embedded in organizational practices and stories.

In Argyris and Schön's theoretical world, individuals act on the grounds of their theories of action, which are mental models or representations of actions. There are two kinds of theories of action, the 'espoused' and the 'theories-in-use', which are respectively the theories of action that can be expressed in words and the theories of action that can only be identified from the observation of individuals' doings or actions. The theories-in-use may remain tacit because they are indescribable or undiscussable. They may be indescribable because the individual members who enact them are unable, rather than unwilling to verbally describe the knowledge embedded in their everyday actions, and the theories-in-use may be undiscussable because any attempt to reveal their incongruity with the organization's espoused theory would be perceived as threatening or embarrassing.

Argyris and Schön attempt to resolve the problem of transfer between individual and organizational learning by defining the organization as a political entity in which individuals act and learn on behalf of the organization. Individuals' decisions about when and how to act, in turn, depend on the organizational learning system. The organizational learning system consists, on the one hand, of structures that channel organizational inquiry, that is, communication and information systems; the spatial environment; procedures and routines for individual and joint inquiry as well as systems of incentives that influence the will to make inquiries. On the other hand, the organizational learning system is made up of the behavioural world of the organization, which is the habitual pattern of interaction among individuals within an organization:

> 'A key feature of the behavioural world of an organization is the degree to which organizational inquiry tends to be bound up with the win/lose behaviour characteristic of organizational games of interests and powers' (Argyris & Schön, 1996, p. 29).

Argyris and Schön argue on the basis of their many years of research and consulting that individuals are 'programmed with Model 1 theories-in-use', which means that all individuals have a wish to be in unilateral control and results in the prevailing defensive ways of acting and reasoning in organizations (Argyris & Schön, 1996, p. 106). Everybody wants to win and not to lose. The result of this 'programming' is that when individuals are faced with embarrassing or threatening issues, they act and reason in defensive ways. This enhances the organizational conditions for making mistakes and by doing so, inhibits individual learning. This individual way of acting and reasoning transmits into the organization, which then becomes dominated by organizationally defensive acting and reasoning inhibiting OL.

The way to change the Model 1 programming of individuals is to create interventions in which practitioners and researchers work together to overcome ways of thinking and acting that inhibit learning. They argue that this can be done by developing individual awareness of how Model 1 theories-in-use foster defensive reasoning and acting. Their methodology for doing so involves communication exercises in which individuals are to work with an actual or imaginary conversation, and with their thoughts and feelings produced by this conversation. The aim of the exercises is to reveal to individuals how they protect themselves when they experience real or potential threatening or embarrassing situations. A change in individuals' theories-in-use can only come about if individuals and organizations begin to reason and communicate in ways in which there is an open exchange of valid information. This involves public testing of the attributions and assumptions individuals ascribe to other individuals and their actions. It is by changing the individuals' Model 1 theories-in-use that a road to OL is paved. Thus, individuals' learning and development are prerequisites for organizational learning and development in Argyris and Schön's perspective on OL.

Organizational learning as ubiquitous

The last perspective on OL included in this chapter arises from a critique of OL as individual information and knowledge acquisition as well as the bifurcation between individuals' learning and organizational learning systems. This may be termed a social or a practice-based perspective on OL. According to this perspective on OL, learning is a result of everyday living and working. Learning cannot be avoided, as learning is ubiquitous. The inspiration for this understanding of OL derives from the work of Lave and Wenger and their theory of learning as 'legitimate peripheral participation in communities of practice', which is their attempt to define a situated world-view in which individuals, environment, and their doings, actions and thinking are connected (Lave, 1993; Lave & Wenger, 1991).

Thus, in this perspective on OL, learning is an integral part of the practice in everyday organizational life and work. Learning is not restricted to taking place inside individuals' minds but rather comprises processes of participation in the organizational practices. This view changes the locus of the learning process from the minds of individuals to the access and participation patterns for organizational members of organizations. This means moving learning into an area of conflicts and power. It means including the social structure of the organizational practice, its power relations and its conditions for legitimacy. Thus, one cannot talk of the relation between individuals and organizations or individuals and environment as individuals in an organization, but rather as individuals as part of a specific organizational practice as well as of patterns of access and participation in the organizational practices.

According to this perspective on OL, learners are social beings that construct their understanding and learn from participation in organizational practices. The role of individual learners is to be engaged in sense making, and to create knowledge within and among their trajectory of participation. The organization provides occasion for interpretations of what goes on in an organization (Richter, 1998). The individual learner is to become a practitioner who is skilled in and knowledgeable of the organizational practices. This means that learning is a practical rather than an epistemic accomplishment, and it is a matter of identity development. It is not only the individuals who solely retain knowledge; instead, knowledge is distributed within and among colleagues.

In sum, the field of OL shows a development beginning with a focus upon the individual, in fact the individual manager, and an attempt to help him or her make better decisions by way of still more informed information processing. This is to happen through individuals' information and knowledge acquisition. Argyris and Schön developed the field further to include not only individuals' knowledge acquisition but also individuals' general awareness of their defensive ways of communicating, that is, to include individuals' personal development, which is not only connected to specific situations but travels with the person from situation to situation (for elaboration of these different kind of skills, see e.g. Schoenfeld, 1999). Argyris and Schön also explicitly include the organization as a learning environment in their term 'organizational learning system'.

The organizational learning system is an environment consisting of certain structures and behaviours, and in which individuals act and reason. The two – individuals and environment – interact, they influence each other but they are not in this understanding mutual constituents as in a transactional relation in which both change at the same time (Altman & Rogoff, 1987; Bernstein, 1960; Dewey, 1933). The changes in Argyris and Schön's understanding are to happen by way of individuals' acting on behalf of organization, which, in turn, change the organizational learning system. The relation between individuals and environment is, in other words, understood in a sequential way.

The practice-based perspective on OL seeks to remedy this bifurcated and sequential understanding of the relation between individuals and environment by defining OL as taking place through legitimate peripheral participation in communities of practice. This throws light on aspects of organizational life that deal with power and legitimacy and questions the notion of individuals as the sole retainers of knowledge. Instead, the argument is that knowledge is distributed and inherent in the organizational structures and artefacts as well as between individuals. However, this tradition cannot fully avoid the 'individual standpoint' in OL as the authors talk about developing identities by developing membership of the organization as well as skilful practitioners.

Now we turn to the field of WPL, which is rooted in a humanistic tradition with a clear focus on the individual as the learner. We have chosen to highlight the issues of the workplace as a learning environment and the different methods for WPL (and, in fact, workplace education) that this environment affords and calls for, as these issues seem to be highly relevant in the WPL literature.

Workplace learning

Workplace learning, like OL, is neither a unified nor a clearly defined concept. In fact, it is difficult to talk about a single concept as the following concepts are applied indiscriminately in the literature on what we have chosen here to call 'workplace learning' (see also, e.g., Watkins, 1995): 'work-based learning' (Raelin, 1997), 'learning in the workplace' (Marsick, 1987b; Rowden, 1996) and 'learning at work' (Boud & Garrick, 1999). It is not possible here to provide a full overview of WPL (for that, see, e.g., Garrick, 1999; McCormack, 2000; Smith, 2003; Stern & Sommerlad, 1999). Essentially, WLP is about individual learning in the environment of work and workplaces, and although the importance of informal learning is stressed, WPL often involves some kind of deliberate and conscious learning activities by way of reflection on actual workplace experience (Marsick, 1987b; Raelin, 2000). One might say that it is by the intentional reflection and learning activities that the foundation in educational research is made evident, as education is always associated with some form of teaching or guidance.

In the following, we have chosen to focus upon two issues in the WPL literature, the contextual differentiation between the school and the WP as learning environments, and to elaborate on how WPL is to be deliberately supported at work and in workplaces.

The workplace as a learning environment

Because WPL is rooted in adult education, and educational researchers, often based in some form of school or university of education, carry out WPL research, the link to formal education in educational institutions is often made in the WPL literature. The differences between the school and the workplace as learning environments appear to be important in the WPL research tradition. Thus, in the early literature on WPL, the workplace is often viewed as a new learning environment, implying that it is the transfer of learning from schools to workplaces that is the novelty in WPL. This contextual movement, however, is more than a physical movement from the school or educational institution to the workplace as a learning environment. It is also regarded as a move from the behaviourist theory of learning prevailing in traditional vocational training to a new and emerging paradigm for learning. Quoting Marsick, she says that the focus upon WPL in a way is 'contrasting the current behaviourist paradigm for training with a newly emerging paradigm for learning in the workplace' (Marsick, 1987a, p. 199).

This development in the predominant theory of learning is regarded as an adequate answer to current societal development, globalization of the workplace, knowledge-based economies and the consequences for contemporary organizational life and work (Rowden, 1996; Torraco, 1999; Watkins, 1995). This development demands members of a workforce that are capable of taking care of their own learning and development and their employability, who are able to take part in innovative practices at work as well as in 'critical reflection' (Fenwick, 2001, p. 5) and who are 'strategic learners', that is, they can help 'organizations respond to their changing environments and to proactively change these environments' (Marsick, 2001, p. 9).

Thus, WPL is often related to the 'old' training paradigm, that is, the narrow vocational training of workers in order for them to fit into a specific job. The argument is that this way of training has become obsolete with the upsurge of the knowledge society and knowledge work, which means that new demands – continuous learning – are part of contemporary employees' and managers' everyday lives and work in workplaces or organizations. In that sense WPL becomes a relevant reaction to an old behaviourist training and education paradigm with its focus upon teaching fairly narrow skills and knowledge (see also Beckett, 1999; Billett & Rose, 1997).

The focus upon the workplace as a new context for learning as well as an emergent paradigm for learning is characterized by three recurrent perspectives included in the concept of WPL: (1) the meaning that is attached to informal or everyday learning; (2) an understanding of the workplace as a learning environment; and (3) the interest taken in the coupling between learning and competence development attached directly to working life and not least to the changes in working life (Ellström, 1996; Garrick, 1999).

The focus in WPL upon informal learning is linked with the experiential learning tradition represented by Kelly (1955), Kolb (1984) and Jarvis (1987). The crux of the matter here is that when learning is connected to workplaces learning is connected to work-related actions and the performance of employees. This is shown either in the form of the routinization of practice or in the form of reflection on actions or reflection on the results of actions related to a practice. The central issue is, however, the importance of learning that is not based upon teaching in a classroom or structured around giving lectures. Thus, Marsick and Watkins make an important distinction between informal learning and incidental learning by defining incidental learning as a sub-category of informal learning (Marsick & Watkins, 1990):

'... informal learning is a by-product of some other activity, such as task accomplishment, interpersonal interaction, sensing the organizational culture, trial-and-error experimentation, or even formal learning' (ibid., p. 12).

Most important in making this distinction is, however, the comment that incidental learning takes place 'although people are not always conscious of it' (ibid.). In that sense, WPL includes a hidden and tacit dimension of knowledge.

Understanding the workplace as a learning environment stresses several factors. One is that learning is connected to a specific learning context, the workplace. The other is that the learning environment is decisive for the learning going on, and that changes in this environment may have important impacts on the learning that can take place in the workplace. The third factor is that there is a coupling between on the one hand, production or mode of production and on the other hand, the possibilities the workplace offers for learning. Further, the importance of the workplace as a learning environment may be viewed as being connected to more formalized teaching activities (Boud & Garrick, 1999). The third focus, the coupling between workplace learning and competence development, is directly connected to changes in everyday life and work: 'Distinctions between life and work, between learning and production, communities and enterprise are becoming less firm' (ibid., p. 4).

This means that competences are not only viewed as being developed in schools or at work but in life as such. On a political level this is shown by the emphasis on including skills and knowledge, that is, competences learned in other contexts than educational institutions by finding ways of certifying and rewarding them in a working environment.

In sum, what appears to be a change in focus on environmental change – from school to work as an environment for learning is also a change in learning theory – from behaviourist training to developmental learning. This has brought forward an emphasis on informal learning and a wish to understand workplaces as learning environments as well as to include competence development other than in schools and workplaces. Next, we turn to the learning methods of WPL based upon the question of whether the workplace as a new environment for learning affords new ways of learning.

The methods of learning

An answer can be given from two angles to the question of whether the workplace and the focus upon WPL as being broader than behaviourist training affords other methods for learning. One regards WPL as informal learning as opposed to formal and institutional learning. From this angle, the 'methods' consist of organizing the social relations at work and the work processes in such a way that learning can take place. The other angle puts more emphasis upon interplay between some form of teaching methods and learning. From this angle it is possible to talk about 'methods' in a more traditional way, for example as systematic teaching, guidance, mentoring and supervision. These are all methods similar to school learning by way of establishing some kind of teacher–pupil relation.

When WPL is regarded as processes of informal learning it is important to ask what factors are guiding learning in the workplace. This question has been put forward in the field of WPL over the past 10 or so years, and the results hint at the complexity of the matter. Already in 1987, Marsick pointed to several factors that have subsequently been part of the discussion on WPL (Marsick, 1987a). These are: the importance of reflection, the importance of learning possibilities in connection with problem-solving and experiments, the importance of personal and not least social factors including support and supervision, and the importance of the combination of informal and formal learning.

Ellström, who is one of the leading Nordic researchers in the field of WPL, in 1996 pointed to the following six factors, which are 'of importance in order to further qualify learning in the workplace' (Ellström, 1996; see also Ellström, 2001). These factors are co-responsibility for the formulation of goals and planning of the work processes, a high potential for learning in the workplace, access to information and theoretical knowledge, possibilities for trying out different kinds of actions in problem solving, possibilities for exchange of experiences and reflection, and a workplace culture and an organization structure furthering learning (Ellström, 1996).

When WPL is regarded as interplay between teaching and learning, the task becomes how to plan learning in the workplace. It makes sense to use Billett's term 'workplace curriculum' (Billett, 1999). Thus, Billett constructs a model for a workplace curriculum on the background of his examination of the factors that influence workplace learning. This workplace curriculum, he argues, considers both the educational as well as the organizational factors of workplace learning. The purpose of a workplace curriculum is to ensure the unfolding of expertise through full participation of the employees in the workplace. Billett points to the following factors of importance in order to understand a workplace curriculum.

Employees must have full access to participate in relevant workplace activities and thus to be guaranteed a 'learning pathway', with reference to the work of Lave and Wenger and their notion of learning as a movement from peripheral to full participation in the working processes (Lave & Wenger, 1991). Also, employees should be given insight into the total production process and knowledge of the finished products, as one should be able to see oneself and one's work as part of a total production process. What is most important in Billett's understanding is, however, the emphasis he puts upon supervision, as there should be direct support or guidance from experts forcing the learner into potential learning situations, and there should be indirect support and guidance from other workers and the physical environment. Thus, in his model of a workplace curriculum, Billett emphasizes the structured and planned activities in workplace learning, which is why it is called a workplace curriculum. What is essential according to Billett is that WPL is not just something that happens by chance; rather, it consists of guided and supported activities, and systematic thinking as well as the linking of learning activities to current work processes are necessary.

Guidance is the pivotal point in WPL. Guidance should be understood in its broadest sense as a process in which another (e.g., a skilled expert, a teacher or a colleague) enters into a dialogue about the grounds for the workplace actions. Further, a systematic and guided process of reflection must be linked to the concrete actions to ensure that learning becomes conceptual. Thus, Billett and Rose argue that it is necessary to provide solid guidance if workplace learning is to develop a conceptual understanding of what goes on in the workplace (Billett & Rose, 1997). It is by way of a conceptual understanding that 'robust transfer' is to be ensured, that is, that an understanding can be transferred to and is valid for several situations other than that in which experience and knowledge are developed. Billett and Rose point to the useful coupling of systematic guidance to the informal or incidental learning that will initiate a conscious and guided process of conceptualization. It is interesting to note that while WPL stresses conceptual knowledge, OL stresses practice.

In sum, the point of departure for WPL is that it understands learning as strongly attached to the environment of which it is a part. However, the learning is at the same time an individual process. It is the individual who learns. It is the individual who acts, experiences, reflects and becomes competent for the work processes through the processes of learning. The learning is guided by the work process and by the more or less systematic possibilities for reflecting on that. Thus, the focus of WPL is the competence development of the individual. Learning is and continues to be individual and personal. The workplace is the environment for this individual learning. The methods of WPL stress both the organization of work and workplaces in order to further informal and incidental learning. Organizing the workplace in order to provide individuals with possibilities for informal and incidental learning may do this. Also, WPL stresses the necessity of guidance, of creating learning relations between experts or old-timers and novices or newcomers. This is where WPL draws upon its heritage from educational research to claim that abstraction and generalizations is important in learning – mere practice and action is not sufficient – learners also have to learn to think, to reflect in and on their practice (see, e.g., Elkjaer, 2000, for an elaboration on the continuity between action and thinking).

Similarities and differences between OL and WPL

In this chapter, we have presented three perspectives on OL. These perspectives embrace three understandings of learning – learning as individual knowledge acquisition, learning as personal development of awareness of defensive acting and reasoning, and learning as social based or practice based. The first perspective understands organizations as more or less equivalent to their managers, the second conceives of organizations as learning systems comprised by organizational structures and behavioural worlds. In the third perspective on OL, the organization is foregrounded as the contextual practices from which organizational membership and skilful professional expertise derives. The wish to transcend the individual–organization divide in the OL field is only partly successful in this third perspective, as it is difficult to avoid the fact that learning somehow has to do with individuals' learning and development, for example development of membership and identity. This perspective does, however, offer a much-needed critical gaze upon the implications of the different patterns of access and participation for different groups of management and employees and thus, for their individual learning possibilities as well as for the possibilities for OL.

Also, we have introduced two important issues within the WPL field. This was, first, the issue of the significance of moving learning out of the classroom and into the workplace, which we have shown to be not only a physical move but also a shift in the predominant theoretical understanding of how to acquire workplace-related skills and knowledge. Thus, we have shown that the introduction of the workplace as an environment for learning implied a shift from behaviourist training to the more encompassing notion of workplace learning. Second, we have pointed to the fact that change of learning environment not only requires new learning theories but also new methods of learning. The consequence of an understanding of WPL as mainly being informal or incidental learning is the paying of the utmost attention to how work and workplaces are organized so as to provide the best possible conditions for this. When WPL is regarded as a combination of teaching and learning, we showed that it is relevant to talk about a workplace curriculum and to create interplay between guidance of many sorts to support the learning of a workplace curriculum.

Regarding the task of pointing to the differences and similarities of these two traditions – apart from the fact that the researchers of each come from different research traditions, work in different institutions of higher education, publish in different journals and books, and apply different vocabulary – we have to admit that maybe the similarities are greater than the differences, and when there are differences, it might be more in degree than in kind.

Both traditions focus primarily upon the individual as the learner; in OL as a development from the individual (manager) as a container and processor of information and knowledge by way of the individual as oriented towards personal development towards development of membership and professional identity. In WPL it is possible to detect a development of the individual from a narrowly trained worker to a reflective worker, capable of participating in contemporary workplaces with its emphasis on knowledge and innovation. In the early days of OL, there was emphasis on abstraction and epistemology whereas today, ability to participate skilfully in the organizational practices is regarded as important. Within the field of WPL, there is alertness to the need for a conceptual understanding as opposed to narrow task performance, and there is much confidence in the potential of reflection to provide this conceptual understanding.

Both traditions – to a different extent and with slightly different descriptions – attend to how the organization of the learning environment, the workplace or the organization, may help further or hinder learning. In OL, the system perspective on organization is strong, and the notion of organizations as environments for distributed knowledge and skills plays a role in the contextual definitions as well as for the access and participation patterns of organizational members. In WPL, the workplace is particularly seen as providing opportunities for informal and incidental learning as well as a combination of these with more formal teaching and guiding activities.

So, are there any differences? We may point to at least one, namely the fact that there seems to be more attention to educational activities in the WPL tradition, that is, that educational activities may help further WPL. In OL, the term applied is interventionist practices, although it covers much the same ground in furthering actual learning in working life.

References

Altman, I., & Rogoff, B. (1987). World Views in Psychology: Trait, Interactional, Organismic, and Transactional Perspectives. In D. Stokols & I. Altman (eds), *Handbook of Environmental Psychology* (pp. 7–40). New York: John Wiley.

Argyris, C., & Schön, D. A. (1978). *Organizational Learning: A Theory of Action Perspective.* Reading, MA: Addison-Wesley.
Argyris, C., & Schön, D. A. (1996). *Organizational Learning II. Theory, Method, and Practice.* Reading, MA: Addison-Wesley.
Beckett, D. (1999). Past the guru and up the garden path. The new organic management learning. In D. Boud & J. Garrick (eds), *Understanding Learning at Work* (pp. 83–97). London and New York: Routledge.
Bernstein, R. J. (1960). *John Dewey. On Experience, Nature and Freedom. Representative Selections.* New York: Liberal Arts Press.
Billett, S. (1999). Guided Learning in Work. In D. Boud & J. Garrick (eds), *Understanding Learning at Work* (pp. 151–64). London: Routledge.
Billett, S., & Rose, J. (1997). Securing Conceptual Development in Workplaces. *Australian Journal of Adult and Community Education,* 37(1), 12–26.
Boud, D., & Garrick, J. (eds). (1999). *Understanding Learning at Work.* London: Routledge.
Cyert, R., & March, J. (1963). *A behavioral theory of the firm.* Englewood Cliffs, NJ: Prentice-Hall.
Dewey, J. (1933 [1986]). How We Think: A Restatement of the Relation of Reflective Thinking to the Educative Process. In J. A. Boydston (ed.), *The Later Works,* Vol. 8 (pp. 105–352). Carbondale and Edwardsville: Southern Illinois University Press.
Dodgson, M. (1993). Organizational Learning: A Review of Some Literatures. *Organization Studies,* 14(3), 375–94.
Easterby-Smith, M. (1997). Disciplines of Organizational Learning: Contributions and Critiques. *Human Relations,* 50(9), 1085–1113.
Easterby-Smith, M., Crossan, M., & Nicolini, D. (2000). Organizational learning: debates past, present and future. *Journal of Management Studies,* 37(6), 783–96.
Elkjaer, B. (1999). In search of a social learning theory. In M. Easterby-Smith, L. Araujo & J. Burgoyne (eds), *Organizational Learning and the Learning Organization. Developments in Theory and Practice* (pp. 75–91). London: Sage.
Elkjaer, B. (2000). The Continuity of Action and Thinking in Learning: Re-visiting John Dewey. *Outlines. Critical Social Studies,* 2, 85–101.
Elkjaer, B. (2003a). Social Learning Theory: Learning as Participation in Social Processes. In M. Easterby-Smith & M. Lyles (eds), *The Blackwell Handbook of Organizational Learning and Knowledge Management* (pp. 38–53). Malden, MA and Oxford: Blackwell.
Elkjaer, B. (2003b). *Organizational Learning: 'The Third Way'.* Paper presented at the Organizational Learning and Knowledge 5th International Conference, Lancaster University, Lancaster, UK.
Elkjaer, B. (2003c). Organizational learning with a pragmatic slant. *International Journal of Lifelong Education,* 22(5), 481–94.
Ellström, P.-E. (1996). Rutin och reflektion. Förudsättningar och hinder för lärande i dagligt arbeite. In P.-E. Ellström, B. Gustavsson & S. Larsson (eds), *Livslångt lärande.* Lund: Studentlitteratur.
Ellström, P.-E. (2001). Integrating Learning and Work: Problems and Prospects. *Human Resource Development Quarterly,* 12(4), 421–35.
Fenwick, T. (2001). Tides of Change: New Themes and Questions in Workplace Learning. *New Directions for Adult and Continuing Education* (92), 3–17.
Friedman, V. J. (2002). The Individual as Agent of Organizational Learning. *California Management Review,* 44(2), 70–89.

Garrick, J. (1998). *Informal Learning in the Workplace: Unmasking Human Resource Development.* London and New York: Routledge.
Garrick, J. (1999). The dominant discourses of learning at work. In D. Boud & J. Garrick (eds), *Understanding Learning at Work* (pp. 216–31). London and New York: Routledge.
Gherardi, S. (2000a). Practice-based Theorizing on Learning and Knowing in Organizations. *Organization,* 7(2), 211–23.
Gherardi, S., Nicolini, D., & Odella, F. (1998). Toward a Social Understanding of How People Learn in Organizations. The Notion of Situated Curriculum. *Management Learning,* 29(3), 273–97.
Hollway, W. (1991). *Work psychology and organizational behaviour. Managing the individual at work.* London: Sage.
Jarvis, P. (1987). *Adult Learning in the Social Context.* London: Croom Helm.
Kelly, G. A. (1955). *The Psychology of Personal Constructs,* vols 1 and 2. New York: Routledge.
Kim, D. H. (1993). The Link between Individual and Organizational Learning. *Sloan Management Review,* 35(1), 37–50.
Kolb, D. A. (1984). *Experiential learning. Experience as The Source of Learning and Development.* Englewood Cliffs, NJ: Prentice-Hall.
Lave, J. (1993 [1996]). The practice of learning. In S. Chaiklin & J. Lave (eds), *Understanding practice. Perspectives on activity and context* (pp. 3–32). Cambridge: Cambridge University Press.
Lave, J., & Wenger, E. (1991). *Situated Learning: Legitimate Peripheral Participation.* Cambridge: Cambridge University Press.
Law, J. (1994). *Organizing Modernity.* Oxford and Cambridge, MA: Blackwell.
March, J., & Simon, H. A. (1958). *Organizations.* New York: Wiley.
Marsick, V. J. (ed.). (1987a). *Learning in the Workplace.* London, New York, and Sydney: Croom Helm.
Marsick, V. J. (1987b). New Paradigms for Learning in the Workplace. In V. J. Marsick (ed.), *Learning in the Workplace* (pp. 11–30). London: Croom Helm.
Marsick, V. J. (2001). *Informal Strategic Learning in the Workplace.* Paper presented at the Second Conference on HRD Research and Practice Across Europe, University of Twente, Enschede, The Netherlands.
Marsick, V. J., & Watkins, K. E. (1990). *Informal and Incidental Learning in the Workplace.* London: Routledge.
McCormack, B. (2000). Workplace learning: a unifying concept? *Human Resource Development International,* 3(3), 397–404.
Miner, A. S., & Mezias, S. J. (1996). Ugly Duckling No More: Pasts and Futures of Organizational Learning Research. *Organization Science,* 7(1), 88–99.
Mumford, A. (1991). Individual and organizational learning – the pursuit of change. *Industrial and Commercial Training,* 23(6), 24–31.
Raelin, J. A. (1997). A Model of Work-Based Learning. *Organization Science,* 8(6), 563–78.
Raelin, J. A. (2000). *Work-Based Learning. The New Frontier of Management Development.* Upper Saddle River, NJ: Prentice-Hall.
Richter, I. (1998). Individual and Organizational Learning at the Executive Level. Towards a Research Agenda. *Management Learning,* 29(3), 299–316.
Rowden, R. W. (1996). Current Realities and Future Challenges. *New Directions for Adult and Continuing Education* (72), 3–10.

Schoenfeld, A. H. (1999). Looking Toward the 21st Century: Challenges of Educational Theory and Practice. *Educational Researcher*, 28(7), 4–14.

Senge, P. M. (1990). *The Fifth Discipline. The Art & Practice of the Learning Organization*. New York: Doubleday Currency.

Smith, P. J. (2003). Workplace Learning and Flexible Delivery. *Review of Educational Research*, 73(1), 53–88.

Stern, E., & Sommerlad, E. (1999). *Workplace Learning, Culture and Performance*. London: Institute of Personnel and Development.

Torraco, R. J. (1999). Integrating Learning with Working: A Reconception of the Role of Workpace Learning. *Human Resource Development Quarterly*, 10(3), 249–70.

Watkins, K. E. (1995). Workplace Learning: Changing Times, Changing Practices. *New Directions for Adult and Continuing Education* (68), 3–16.

Zuboff, S. (1988). *In The Age of the Smart Machine. The Future of Work and Power*. New York: Heinemann.

3
Two Logics of Learning
Per-Erik Ellström

A recurrent theme in critical studies of adult education, lifelong learning, and, in particular, work-based learning is their alleged instrumental character. A common point of departure for a lot of this criticism is the principle of performativity (Lyotard, 1984), that is, the idea that education is subjugated to a managerialist discourse of efficiency and instrumental means-end calculation. The principle of performativity is argued to have a predominant influence on the educational system at large, and, thereby, also on systems for promoting lifelong learning (Halliday, 2003) and learning at work (Garrick & Clegg, 2001). As argued by the latter authors, in 'performative times' being a good learner is equal to being a good performer.

Undoubtedly, there is a certain degree of truth in this argument. Learning has traditionally to a large extent been defined in instrumental terms, for example, in terms of how to acquire or improve a subject's capacity for dealing with situations in which problems and other parameters are given (or taken for granted). However, this is not the whole story. For quite a long time, researchers have also conceptualized forms of learning that seemingly represent a break with performativity and instrumental rationality. In these forms of learning, there is a focus on exploring, questioning, reframing and transforming a situation, rather than simply adapting to a predefined reality. To conceptualize these types of learning, Argyris and Schön (1978) make a distinction between single and double-loop learning, and Bateson (1987) distinguishes between 'lower' and 'higher' levels of learning. Reinterpreting the levels of learning proposed by Bateson (1987) and Engeström (1999) makes a distinction between reproductive, productive and expansive or innovative learning.

Considering empirical evidence, there is strong support for the predominance of single-loop and reproductive forms of learning in many contexts (e.g., Argyris, 1993; Davidson & Svedin, 1999; Ellström & Gustavsson, 1996; Gustavsson, 2000). However, as clearly indicated by these and other studies there are also a range of examples that support and exemplify the existence of more creative and innovative forms of learning (e.g., Barley & Kunda, 2001; Brown & Duguid, 1991; Hirschorn, 1984; Zuboff, 1988). One prominent example is Hirschorn's (1984) demonstration of the unofficial and unacknowledged development work ('second-order work') performed in various work contexts to tackle unexpected problem situations that arise. What these examples all have in common is that they show how in practice there is significant creativity in carrying out many types of practical jobs. At the same time these studies show that this creativity mainly takes place unofficially as a part of what happens 'behind the scenes', that is, in an organization's non-canonical practice (Brown & Duguid, 1991), and that it thus is not made visible and given recognition.

The purpose of this chapter is to identify and discuss some of the conditions that are assumed to be critical for facilitating or constraining reproductive and developmental learning at work. This is done by exploring two different, although complementary, logics of work and learning, called the logic of performance and the logic of development. These two logics are viewed as patterns of practice that, intendedly or unintendedly, shape the conditions of learning in an organization. Thus, the actual balance between these two logics in an organization is assumed to have a crucial bearing on the available space for reproductive and creative learning respectively. However, before going into a discussion of the two logics, it is necessary first to make a few additional comments on the concept of learning used here.

Learning in organizations: reproduction versus development

The focus of this chapter concerns learning in organizational settings. As noted above, much research on learning in organizations has underlined the necessity to distinguish between at least two qualitatively different forms or levels of learning which I prefer to call adaptive (reproductive) and developmental (creative) learning, respectively (Ellström, 1992, 2001).

As already indicated, the notion of adaptive or reproductive learning has a focus on a subject's adjustment to and mastery of certain, specific tasks or situations. This is in contrast with developmental learning, where the focus is on transforming rather than reproducing a prevailing situation. This means there is emphasis on exploring and questioning existing conditions, solving ambiguous problems, and developing new solutions. The notion of developmental learning used here has links to Dewey's (1933) model of problem solving and reflective learning, as well as to such different traditions as Engeström's (1987) activity-theory-based model of expansive learning and Argyris' *et al.* (1985) model of investigative organizational learning.

In order to clarify this distinction, three additional points should be made. First, the distinction between adaptive and developmental learning does not concern two forms of learning that are in some sense mutually exclusive. They rather represent two complementary levels of learning, where one level or the other can be dominant or relatively inconspicuous, depending on which conditions prevail in the specific situation. Second, it is possible to define one or more 'middle forms' of learning representing more incremental forms of transformation between reproduction and radical transformation. One example is the notion of productive learning proposed by Engeström (1987) and used also by Ellström (1992, 2001). Another example of such a 'middle form' is the notion of reconstructive learning proposed by Elmholdt (this volume). However, for the purposes of this chapter, it is sufficient to use only the two main categories of adaptive and developmental learning. Third, although adaptive learning might be perceived as having mainly negative connotations, for example, focusing on people adjusting themselves to a perhaps aversive reality, the significance of this kind of learning should not be depreciated. Newcomers' socialization to a new workplace and their attempts to master existing norms, cultural practices, and routines can be mentioned as prime examples of the importance of this form of learning (Elmholdt, this volume; Fenwick, 2003). Conversely, developmental or creative learning, although the connotations are positive, may nevertheless entail negative aspects. For example, too strong an emphasis on flexibility, transformation of prevailing practices, and the creation of new solutions might create negative stress and feelings of anxiety and insecurity. In this perspective, it is important to maintain a balance between adaptive and developmental learning. One of the difficulties in doing this is that these forms of learning, at least to some extent, seem to require different conditions (see below).

Two logics of work and learning

A basic assumption in this chapter is that the two levels of learning distinguished above – reproductive and developmental learning – can be understood as integral aspects of two idealtypic patterns (logics) of practice in organizations, referred to as the logic of performance and the logic of development, respectively. The two logics of work and learning distinguished here are assumed to reflect not only different ways of viewing learning at work, but also different ways of organizing for work-related learning in practice.

What, then, is a more precise meaning for each of these two logics? Somewhat simplified, one could say that the logic of development has a focus on fostering new ideas and solutions through a process of developmental learning starting from current practice. The logic of performance, however, focuses rather on the implementation of new ideas, that is, on transforming new ideas and knowledge into practice through processes of adaptive learning. Of course, in principle, these two logics presuppose each other. However, in practice, there is in many organizations a significant risk for a lack of balance between them. In the text below, I take a closer look at the respective meanings of the two logics.

The logic of performance

This logic has a focus on promoting efficient and reliable action that, as far as possible, is also relatively stable over time. In order to accomplish this it is necessary to *reduce variation* in thought and action patterns, within and between individuals, in an organization, that is, to promote homogeneity. In line with this orientation, the logic of performance puts a strong emphasis on goal consensus, standardization, stability, and avoidance of uncertainty. In several respects, this logic comes close to what March (1991) refers to as processes of exploitation in organizational learning characterized by a focus on refinement, production, efficiency, and execution. Of course this thinking is also recognizable in Taylorist models for organizing work, but the logic of performance may be said to transcend the boundaries of the Taylorist model and it is in certain respects more general than this model. Also, in some respects it has affinities with the principle of performativity (Lyotard, 1984) that was referred to in the introductory section of this chapter.

In terms of learning, the logic of performance presupposes (reproductive) learning processes, with a focus on establishing and maintaining well-learned and routinized action patterns, that is, eliminating errors, as rapidly as possible (cf. Argyris & Schön, 1978). Problems are handled through the application of given rules/instructions, that is, one learns to follow certain prescribed rules or procedures for handling a certain problem. Thinking and reflection, although in practice an integral aspect of many work processes (Hirschorn, 1984; Schön, 1983), are in this logic officially valued primarily to the extent that they are instrumental in supporting and promoting efficient action. The predominance of routine action becomes a way to manage the daily flow of events, problem situations and contradictory demands, and at the same time maintain a feeling of security and stability (Klein et al., 1993).

A problem, of course, is that excessive routinization can play devastating tricks by placing on us blinkers, which impede our detection and management of changes. We tend to reinterpret and, by the same token, ignore or misinterpret changes in our surroundings, so as to maintain existing structures and patterns of thought and action (Gersick & Hackman, 1990; Levitt & March, 1988). However, at the same time routinized action can relieve the burden on individuals and free mental resources for other purposes (Dreyfus & Dreyfus, 1986). In this sense, routinization can be viewed as a precondition for generating the freedom and variation of action associated with creativity and developmental learning.

The logic of development

Similar to what March (1991) refers to as processes of exploration, the logic of development has a focus on flexibility, discovery and innovation. Accordingly, in this perspective, it is not a matter of reducing variation and attaining uniformity but, rather, of *creating and handling variation and diversity* in thought and action, that is, of promoting heterogeneity. The logic of development, interpreted thus, entails action and learning that calls for the taking of risks and acceptance of failures, a capacity for critical reflection, together with sufficient scope and resources for experimenting with and testing alternative ways of acting in different situations.

Contrary to the logic of performance, this logic requires analytical thinking based on individuals' reflection on previous experience and available knowledge of the task or situation at hand. In this sense, it involves a movement away from a routinized level of action towards a knowledge-based or reflective level of action (Ellström, 1992, 2001). As used here, reflection means a capacity for distancing, alternative thinking and critical analysis of the objectives and underlying premises of action, including the organizational and social contexts of action.

In terms of learning, this logic presupposes developmental learning as a primary driving force. Thus, there is a strong emphasis on the subjects' capacity for self-management and their preparedness to question, reflect upon and, if necessary, transform established practices in the organization into new solutions or ways of working (cf. Dewey, 1933; Engeström,

1999). In this view, conflicts and ambiguity are not potential threats to learning or to efficient performance, but rather potentials for triggering innovative learning processes.

To conclude this section, it is important to underline that the two logics distinguished above are understood here as ideal types, that is, as reconstructions of actual practices that will not be found in pure form in real life. In an empirical perspective, the two logics will rather appear as more or less conspicuous patterns in the flow of practice within an organization.

The two logics presuppose different conditions of learning

As is clear from the descriptions of the two logics given above, they both involve learning as a basic mechanism for furthering, in the one case, efficient performance, and in the other case innovativeness. The two logics also presuppose different organizational conditions and practices, which are assumed to constrain or facilitate learning. In this way the two logics are assumed to shape the conditions of learning that prevail in a certain organization at a particular time. Thus, depending on the balance between the logic of performance and the logic of development, there will be different preconditions for adaptive and developmental learning.

In this section, I identify and discuss several factors that, based on previous research, have proved to be significant conditions for learning in organizational settings. As shown, it is also possible, for each of these factors, to distinguish between learning conditions that are consistent with and support the logic of performance and the logic of development respectively. As it is used here, the term 'learning conditions' refers to factors in an organization that constrain or facilitate learning at an individual or organizational level. These factors may be of a structural character, that is, linked to the material, cultural or social structures that prevail in the organization at a particular time, or they may relate to the actors' backgrounds and subjective resources.

The learning potential of the task

Research on the conditions of learning in organizations has long emphasized the crucial importance of different task characteristics (see, e.g., Davidson & Svedin, 1999; Kohn & Schooler, 1983). As an umbrella term for task characteristics that promote learning, one may refer to the 'learning potential' of a task or job (Ellström, 1992, 2001). Generally, the learning potential of a task may be said to be a function of its complexity, autonomy and competence requirements. One important precondition for anything but purely reproductive learning is the existence of 'objective' autonomy, that is, individuals' scope for defining the task, its content, and the criteria for what constitutes a well-executed task. A newly published study also supports the existence of a relationship of this kind between autonomy and learning (McGrath, 2001). According to this study, developmental learning (exploratory learning) presupposed substantial autonomy for the project groups in terms of interpreting and defining objectives and tasks; conversely, reproductive learning was favoured by limited autonomy and by clearly specified tasks/goals.

The 'objective' autonomy of a task may be seen as a necessary but not sufficient precondition for learning at work. In addition, individuals or groups need to have the subjective capacity required to make use of the autonomy afforded by their jobs. This in turn is related to, for example, not only previous experience with similar tasks and the individual's knowledge and understanding of the task (Sandberg, 1994), self-confidence (Bandura, 1977), but also factors relating to occupational identity (Lave & Wenger, 1991; Thunborg, 1999). These subjective factors are separately, but even more so in combination, crucially important to an individual's or group's scope for utilizing the learning potential of a particular task. As an umbrella term, we may refer to these factors as subjective learning resources. I return to this discussion below.

Autonomy versus standardization of tasks and work processes

Formalizing work processes through written rules and instructions is a traditional way of seeking standardization in the performance of a task and, accordingly, reduced variation in its performance both for a single individual over time and between individuals. This is a method we associate particularly with bureaucratic and Taylorist models of work organization (Mintzberg, 1979), but it is also included as a main element in neo-Taylorist models (e.g., ideas of democratic Taylorism, Adler, 1993). When it comes to the relationships between standardization and learning, it has long been assumed that standardization inhibits developmental learning – by reducing autonomy and, by the same token, variation in work performance – but that standardization may simultaneously promote reproductive learning. There is also substantial support for this assumption (Campbell, 1993; Staw, 1990). Recent empirical support is given in the study by McGrath (2001) cited above. This study also included measures of the project groups' autonomy in relation to work performance ('supervision autonomy'). The results indicated a relationship corresponding to that for task-related autonomy, that is, high autonomy tends to promote developmental (exploratory) learning.

Subjective and cultural factors

Subjective factors, such as individuals' attitudes towards and motivation for learning, have a major bearing on their propensity to take part in various types of learning activities at a workplace (e.g., Helms Jørgensen and Warring, 2002; Gustavsson, 2000; Rönnqvist, 2001). Shaping the work in such a way as to require individuals' competence and facilitate learning in various ways may be described as a necessary, but hardly sufficient condition for individuals' participation in learning activities at the workplace. As shown in a recent study by Fenwick (2003), certain subjective factors appear to be at least as important as favourable objective conditions. Specifically, her findings point to the importance of employee 'awareness' of the learning opportunities that are encountered as part of the daily work, combined with 'self-awareness' of their own way of handling these learning opportunities. Other subjective factors included perceived 'space' for experimentation and 'permission' to view goals as fluid and tentative.

In many cases, subjective factors such as those observed by Fenwick (2003) appear to be related to characteristics of the cultures that exist at a workplace, and the obstacles that these may pose to competence development and learning at a workplace. Examples of cultural aspects that may serve as obstacles are norms that depreciate abstract tasks, further education, qualifications, careers and individual assumption of responsibility at work (Björkman & Lundqvist, 1992). Woven into many worker cultures as well as the society at large are also gender-related notions of 'masculinity' and 'femininity' that might influence individuals' notions of the kinds of activities – such as teamwork and learning activities – that are more or less compatible with one's own identity as, for example, a male wage earner (e.g., Eldh, 2001).

What then would characterize a culture that may be expected to promote developmental learning at work? Several studies indicate that such a learning-oriented culture would have a number of characteristic features, notably a climate that encourages questioning and critical reflection on what is taking place in the work process, and what is attained and not attained. Other characteristics would include an emphasis on action, initiative and risk-taking as well as tolerance towards disparate views, uncertainty and incorrect actions (Weick & Sutcliffe, 2001).

Organizational objectives – consensus versus conflict

One fundamental assumption in many contexts is that the existence of clearly formulated and distinct objectives is a basic condition of individuals' and groups' action and, by the same token, also of opportunities for learning from this action. Specifically, clear and distinct objectives are viewed as a key precondition for feedback – information on the outcome of one's actions – which has, in turn, been regarded as a key condition for both learning and motivation (Annett, 1969; Frese & Altmann, 1989). Questions of contradictions, conflicts and power have frequently, in this perspective, been regarded as barriers to learning, rather than as fundamental conditions of an activity that may also be driving forces for learning and change. However, there are good reasons to question the consensus and harmony perspective that has traditionally characterized research on learning in organizations. Today, fairly comprehensive research exists indicating that contradictions and conflicts regarding the objectives of an activity do not necessarily hinder learning. On the contrary, developmental learning is assumed to require questioning and discussion of an activity's ends and means (Dewey, 1933; Engeström, 1987, 1999). Gustavsson (2000) also finds support for such a view by showing the importance of contradictions as opportunities for learning – for example, contradictions between formal and informal production and quality targets. These and other contradictions paved the way for initiatives and provided scope for active testing of new ways of working. Thus, there appears to be a contradiction between two different views of objectives and their significance for learning in organizations. Both views may nevertheless be correct. Somewhat simplified, one might say that while ambiguity and conflicts regarding objectives are obstacles to reproductive learning, they are at the same time (with appropriate support) potential catalysts for developmental learning.

Transformation pressure

Developmental learning entails a departure from established routines and habit patterns (Ellström, 1992, 2001). However, for this to occur, we often need to face demands for change in the form of some new problem situation that we have never encountered before. There are also various other factors that may result in our abandoning a routine. For example, that we reach a natural breaking point, a milestone, or that we meet demands for change in terms of, for example, the tasks we perform, our occupational role or the work organization to which we belong (Gersick & Hackman, 1990). In line with this, several studies of learning and competence development in organizations indicate that the initiation of such processes very often requires external pressure. Examples of such external pressure include a modified competitive situation, rapid technical development, increased quality requirements, or changing demands from customers or clients, colleagues or management (see, e.g., Lundvall & Nielsen, 1999).

At the same time, it seems to be the case that a strong transformation pressure may be a necessary, but hardly a sufficient, precondition for departing from established routines, and for initiation of developmental learning. Changes that are either too big or too small both tend, for different reasons, to result in avoidance. It is, for example, a well-known phenomenon that in crises or situations we perceive as threatening, we tend to fall back on habitual routines (Ellström, 2002). Evidently, it is often not enough to see learning and change as a result of a 'departure' from habitual patterns of thought and action, that is, what Kurt Lewin termed 'unfreezing'. Various types of support and resources for learning are also required. The purpose of these are, in particular, to create the security and trust needed to balance the uncertainty and anxiety that every more thoroughgoing change involves for individuals and collectives (Schein, 1988).

Management support, employee participation, and other learning resources

A range of studies indicates the importance of active management support and encouragement for the promotion of developmental learning at work (Davidson & Svedin, 1999; Ellström & Gustavsson, 1996; Rönnqvist, 2001). The importance of management lies, in particular, in its ability to undertake measures that foster long-term development of the organization and of the employees' jobs, to involve employees in development activities, and to integrate measures for technical, organizational and competence development in the organization (Davidson & Svedin, 1999). Not least, employee participation appears to be a crucial factor for promoting developmental learning. As shown in several studies, problems and disturbances that arise in day-to-day work are potential sources of learning (Frese & Altman, 1989; Gustavsson, 2000; Norros, 1995). However, this presupposes that employees actually might and can assist in the management and solution of emerging problems (Davidson & Svedin, 1999; Kock, 2002; Norros, 1995).

Another pivotal management function is to generate the material resources – including, not least, time – necessary to bring about learning activities at the workplace. Besides time, access to attractive and legitimate forums for exchange of experience and ideas appear to be a key factor for success (Lillrank *et al.*, 1998). One way of dealing with this is to create, alongside the 'activity flow,' parallel structures of shorter or longer duration to which work on development issues is assigned. The advantage of such more or less temporary parallel structures is that they enable us to distance ourselves from the ongoing workflow, thereby making it easier to pay attention to and deal with developmental issues. However, in order to support informal learning at work such arrangements are hardly sufficient. In addition, it appears necessary to support informal learning at work with different measures, including formal learning arrangements (Ellström, 1992; Fenwick, 2003; Rönnqvist, 2001).

In this section, several factors were identified as important conditions of learning in an organization. These conditions are related to the work organization (e.g., autonomy, degree of standardization), the culture of the workplace and subjective resources for learning, organizational objectives, transformation pressure, management support, employee participation and available material resources for learning.

Depending on how we design the learning environment of a workplace with respect to these factors, we can expect a situation where there would be more or less scope for adaptive (reproductive) and developmental learning respectively. If the organization is designed and managed in such a way that is likely to reduce variation and promote stability in its practices, that is, if it is designed according to the logic of performance, we would expect an emphasis on adaptive learning and only quite a limited scope for developmental learning. If, however, the organization is designed and managed to promote variation and heterogeneity, that is, if it is designed according to the logic of development, we would expect a scope also for developmental learning. Of course, in reality we hardly encounter a simple either/or situation with respect to these two logics, but rather a more complex situation that is likely to be based on a mix of different learning conditions. To what extent, then, is it possible in practice to try to find a balance between the logic of performance and the logic of development, and, thereby, also a balance between adaptive and developmental processes of learning? This question is dealt with below.

Balancing the logics of performance and development

The relationship between the logic of performance and the logic of development is viewed here not as mutually exclusive, but, rather, as complementary patterns of practice. That is, both are regarded as necessary for the long-term continuation and development of an organization. However, this does not prevent the two logics, in the short term and the medium term, from being contradictory in that they entail different ways of using available resources in an organization. In this perspective, the challenge is to find a suitable balance and assign priorities between measures that bring about stability, efficiency and short-term results in accordance with the logic of performance, and to promote long-term development and innovation in accordance with the logic of development.

Here we touch on a tension between time for production and time for learning, exploration and innovation that has long attracted the attention of researchers who have studied learning in organizations (e.g., March, 1991; March & Simon, 1958). As used here, time for production refers to time set aside for value creation through utilization of existing knowledge and competence. Time for learning relates, instead, to the time allocated for the exploration of alternative views and testing of alternative ways of working in order to create new knowledge and competence that can form the basis of, for example, product development. One way of handling this tension is to focus on the material conditions under which an activity is carried out and resources that are allocated within these limits to promote developmental learning. This may be said in the light of substantial research backing the contention that developmental learning actually requires special resources and even a certain redundancy ('slack') in order not to be driven out by the demands of more routine activity (Axelsson, 1996; March, 1991; March & Simon, 1958).

Of course, as underlined by March (1991), one difficulty in establishing these priorities is that the value of learning activities in terms of increased innovativeness and long-term survival is both more remote in time and less reliable than the more easily calculated value of measures to boost day-to-day production. Furthermore, the decisions made when it comes to allocating resources for work-related learning are highly related to prevailing views concerning management strategies and leading actors' perceptions of the possible, desirable and, for the time being, appropriate way of conducting an activity (Davidson & Svedin, 1999; Ellström & Gustavsson, 1996).

Considering this line of reasoning, it could be argued that it is limited by its underlying chronological conception of time as 'clock-time', and that it might prove more fruitful to adopt a notion of subjective time or 'event time' (cf. Antonacopoulou & Tsoukas, 2002; Hassard, 2002).

Using a notion of time as experienced and socially constructed, it would be possible to move from a focus on the allocation of 'clock-time' between production and learning activities, to a focus on peoples' temporal structuring of their work. From this perspective, time is defined by organizational members and is the product of prevailing beliefs and cultural practices in the organization. By implication, a change in the use of time in an organization would, from this perspective, be viewed as a result of a collective learning process, rather than a consequence of a management decision to change the allocation of time.

In fact, such a view is supported by the findings of Fenwick (2003) cited above. According to her results, an increased subjective awareness of the learning opportunities encountered in daily work, and how these learning opportunities were handled, proved more important than the allocation of 'objective' learning time for the promotion of learning from everyday activity. Thus, these subjects appeared to 'learn how to learn' from their own practice, and, thereby, also how to find the time for this learning. From this perspective, the first priority of management should not be to allocate time for learning separate from everyday practice, but rather to put development and learning issues on the agenda, and to ensure that the organizational members have the necessary knowledge and skills to be able to identify and deal with these issues as an integral part of ongoing activities.

In line with this view, as noted already in the introduction to this chapter, several studies have shown that there is, in practice, substantial creativity in many kinds of work processes (Barley & Kunda, 2001; Hirschorn, 1984; Zuboff, 1988). The logic of development thus seems to be required *de facto* in many work processes in order to support and compensate for the contradictions and shortcomings that often exist. Hence, seeking a better understanding of how developmental learning takes place in practice – despite the dominance of a performance logic that is characteristic of many activities – becomes a key research task.

This would demand, among other things, a better understanding of how developmental learning can be supported by, for example, being made 'visible' and part of the official canonical practice of the activity concerned. One interesting approach in this context would be to take the notion of improvisation as a starting point (Weick, 2001), and seek to formulate a 'logic of improvisation' in the tension between what we have termed the logics of performance and development.

Concluding remarks

The point of departure for this chapter was the alleged instrumental and reproductive character of much workplace learning. For many researchers this seem to be *a priori* a truth justified by philosophical considerations along the lines of, for example, the performativity principle as suggested by Lyotard (1984). Although there is much empirical evidence of the predominance of instrumental and reproductive learning in many work processes, there are, as indicated by the studies reviewed in this chapter, in many contexts also considerable scope for and examples of creative, developmental learning.

A main point made in this chapter is that these seemingly contradictory observations may be explained by the conditions of learning that prevail in a certain situation, and that these conditions, in their turn, are shaped by the overall pattern of practice that characterizes the work system. Specifically, a distinction was made between two patterns of practice: the logic of performance and the logic of development.

Considering the complementarity between these two logics as well as between the two levels of learning entailed by these logics, another point made concerns the need for striking a balance between the two logics in actual work processes. By implication, this balance and the relative strength of the two logics in the daily flow of practice will also determine the available scope for both reproductive and developmental learning. Thus, depending on how we, intentionally or unintentionally, shape the workplace as a learning environment we might be able to challenge the alleged predominance of the performativity principle. Whether or not this means that there is also an 'emancipatory potential' (Garrick & Clegg, 2001) for the person at work in this context is, of course, another question. However, this should not be ruled out *a priori*. On the contrary, this question requires and deserves profound empirical inquiry, not least studies along the lines indicated in this chapter.

References

Adler, P. S. (1993). The learning bureaucracy. In B. M. Staw & L. L. Cummings (eds), *Research in Organizational Behavior*, 15, 111–94. Greenwich, CT: JAI Press.

Annett, J. (1969). *Feedback and human behavior*. Baltimore: Penguin.

Antonacopoulou, E., & Tsoukas, H. (2002). Time and Reflexivity in Organization Studies: An Introduction. *Organization Studies*, 23(6), 857–62.

Argyris, C. (1993). *Knowledge for action. A guide to overcoming barriers to organizational change*. San Francisco: Jossey-Bass.

Argyris, C., & Schön, D. A. (1978). *Organizational learning.* Reading, MA: Addison Wesley.
Argyris, C., Putnam, R., & McLain Smith, D. (1985). *Action Science. Concepts. Methods, and Skills for Research and Intervention.* San Francisco: Jossey-Bass.
Axelsson, B. (1996). *Kompetens för konkurrenskraft.* [Competence for competition]. Stockholm: SNS Förlag.
Bandura, A. (1977). Self-efficacy: Toward a unifying theory of behavioral change. *Psychological Review,* 84, 191–215.
Barley, S. R., & Kunda, G. (2001). Bringing work back in. *Organization Science,* 12(1), 76–95.
Bateson, G. (1987). *Steps to an ecology of mind.* Northvale, NJ: Jason Aronson.
Björkman, T., & Lundqvist, K. (1992). 'Smart Production' – *processindustrins framtidsmodell? En studie av Berol Nobel.* Stockholm: KTH/Castor.
Brown, J. S., & Duguid, P. (1991). Organizational learning and communities of practice. Towards a unified view of working, learning, and innovation. *Organization Science,* 2(1), 40–57.
Campbell, D. T. (1993). Blind variation and selective retention in creative thought as in other knowledge processes. In G. Radnitzky & W. W. Bartley III (eds), *Evolutionary Epistemology, Rationality, and the Sociology of Knowledge* (pp. 91–115). Chicago: Open Court.
Davidson, B., & Svedin, P. O. (1999). *Lärande i produktionssystem. En studie av operatörsarbete inom process-och verkstadsindustri.* [Learning in production systems: A study of operator works in highly automated process and manufacturing industry]. Unpublished doctoral dissertation, Linköping University, Sweden.
Dewey, J. (1933). *How we think. A restatement of the relation of reflective thinking to the educative process.* Boston: D. C. Heath.
Dreyfus, S. E., & Dreyfus, H. L. (1986). *Mind over Machine.* Oxford: Blackwell.
Eldh, C. (2001). 'Remember all racing at own risk!' – föreställningar om risk och teknik i konstruktionen av maskulinitet. *Fronesis* (8), 44–56.
Ellström, P.-E. (1992). *Kompetens, lärande och utbildning i arbetslivet: Problem, begrepp och teoretiska perspektiv.* [Competence, learning and work-based education: Problems, concepts and theoretical perspectives]. Stockholm: Publica.
Ellström, P.-E. (2001). Integrating Learning and Work: Conceptual Issues and Critical Conditions. *Human Resource Development Quarterly,* 12(4).
Ellström, P.-E. (2002). Time and the Logics of Learning. *Lifelong Learning in Europe,* 2, 86–93.
Ellström., P.-E., & Gustavsson, M. (1996). Lärande produktion – erfarenheter från ett utvecklingsprogram för processoperatörer. [Learning production – Experiences from a development programme for process operators]. In P.-E. Ellström, B. Gustavsson & S. Larsson (eds), *Livslångt lärande.* [Lifelong Learning]. Lund: Studentlitteratur.
Engeström, Y. (1987). *Learning by expanding: An activity theoretical approach to development research.* Helsinki, Finland: Orienta Konsultit.
Engeström, Y. (1999). Innovative learning in work teams: Analyzing cycles of knowledge creation in practice. In Y. Engeström, R. Miettinen & R.-L. Punamäki (eds), *Perspectives on activity theory* (pp. 19–38). New York: Cambridge University Press.

Fenwick, T. J. (2003). Professional Growth Plans: Possibilities and Limitations of an Organization wide Employee Development Strategy. *Human Resource Development Quarterly*, 14(1), 59–77.
Frese, M., & Altmann, A. (1989). The treatment of errors in learning and training. In L. Bainbridge & S. A. Ruiz Quintanilla (eds), *Developing skills with information technology* (pp. 65–86). Chichester: John Wiley.
Garrick, J., & Clegg, S. (2001). Stressed-out Knowledge Workers in Performative Times: A Postmodern Take on Project-based Learning. *Management Learning*, 32(1), 119–34.
Gersick, C. J. G., & Hackman, J. R. (1990). Habitual Routines in Task-Performing Groups. *Organizational Behaviour and Human Decision Processes*, 47, 65–97.
Gustavsson, M. (2000). *Potentialer för lärande i processoperatörers arbete. En studie av operatörers lärande och arbete i högautomatiserad processindustri*. [Potentials for learning in process operator work. A study of learning and work in highly automated processing industry]. Linköping: Linköping Studies in Education and Psychology, Linköpings Universitet.
Halliday, J. (2003). Who Wants to Learn Forever? Hyperbole and Difficulty with Lifelong Learning. *Studies in Philosophy and Education*, 22, 195–210.
Hassard, J. (2002). Organizational Time: Modern, Symbolic, and Postmodern Reflections. *Organization Studies*, 23(6), 885–92.
Helms Jørgensen, C., & Warring, N. (2002). Læring på arbejdspladsen. In K. Illeris (ed.), *Udspil om læring i arbejdslivet*. Roskilde: Roskilde Universitetsforlag.
Hirschorn, L. (1984). *Beyond Mechanization: Work and Technology in a Postindustrial Age*. Cambridge, MA: MIT Press.
Klein, G. A., Orasanu, J., Calderwood, R., & Zsambok, C. (eds). (1993). *Decision Making in Action: Models and Methods*. Norwood, NJ: Ablex.
Kock, H. (2002). *Lärande i teambaserad organisation*. [Learning in teambased organizations]. Linköping: Linköping Studies in Education and Psychology, Linköpings Universitet.
Kohn, M. L., & Schooler, C. (1983). *Work and personality: An inquiry into the impact of social stratification*. Norwood, NJ: Ablex.
Lave, J., & Wenger, E. (1991). *Situated Learning: Legitimate Peripheral Participation*. Cambridge: Cambridge University Press.
Levitt, B., & March, J. G. (1988). Organizational learning. *Annual Review of Sociology*, 14, 319–40.
Lillrank, P., Shani (Rami), A. B., Kolodny, H., Stymne, B., Figuera, J. R., & Liu, M. (1998). Learning from the Success of Continuous Improvements Change Programs: An International Comparative Study. *Research in Organizational Change and Development*, 11, 47–71.
Lundvall, B.-Å., & Nielsen, P. (1999). Competition and Transformation in the Learning Economy. Illustrated by the Danish Case. *Revue D'Économie Industrielle*, 88(2), 67–89.
Lyotard, J.-F. (1984). *The postmodern condition: a report on knowledge*. Manchester: Manchester University Press.
March, J. G. (1991). Exploration and exploitation in organizational learning. *Organization Science*, 2, 71–87.
March, J. G., & Simon, H. A. (1958). *Organizations*. New York: Wiley.
McGrath, R. G. (2001). Exploratory learning, innovative capacity, and managerial oversight. *Academy of Management Journal*, 44(1), 118–31.

Mintzberg, H. (1979). *The structuring of organizations*. Englewood Cliffs, NJ: Prentice-Hall.

Norros, L. (1995). An orientation-based approach to expertise. In J.-M. Hoc, P. C. Cacciabue & E. Hollnagel, *Expertise and technology: Cognition and human-computer interaction* (pp. 141-64). Hillsdale, NJ: Erlbaum.

Rönnqvist, D. (2001). *Kompetensutveckling i praktiken – ett samspel mellan ledning, yrkesgrupper och omvärld*. [Competence development in practice – interactions between management, occupational groups and context]. Linköping: Linköping Studies in Education and Psychology, Linköpings Universitet.

Sandberg, J. (1994). *Human competence at work: An interpretative approach*. Göteborg, Sweden: BAS Förlag.

Schein, E. H. (1988). *Organizational Psychology*. Englewood Cliffs, NJ: Prentice-Hall.

Schön, D. A. (1983). *The Reflective Practitioner: How professionals think in action*. London: Temple Smith.

Staw, B. M. (1990). An evolutionary approach to creativity and innovation. In M. A. West & J. L. Farr (eds), *Innovation and Creativity at Work*. New York: John Wiley.

Thunborg, C. (1999). *Lärande av yrkesidentiteter. En studie av läkare, sjuksköterskor och undersköterskor*. [Learning professional identities at work: A study of doctors, nurses and assistant nurses]. Unpublished doctoral dissertation, Linköping University, Sweden.

Weick, K. E. (2001). *Making Sense of the Organization*. Oxford: Blackwell.

Weick, K. E., & Sutcliffe, K. M. (2001). *Managing the Unexpected: Assuring High Performance in an Age of Complexity*. San Francisco: Jossey-Bass.

Zuboff, S. (1988). *In the age of the smart machine: The future of work and power*. New York: Basic Books.

4
Innovative Learning is Not Enough
Claus Elmholdt

Major transformations have occurred in work and organization of work since the advent of what is called the post-industrial society (Bell, 1973), and more recently the innovation economy (Saperstein *et al.*, 2002). These transformations have obviously influenced the conditions of workplace learning. The physical exertion, manual dexterity, and endurance of industrial work have been increasingly displaced by knowledge work that requires attentiveness and the ability to analyze problems and make decisions (Stehr, 1994). A fundamental characteristic of the new innovative economy is a market-driven demand for flexibility and change that has put (innovative) learning high on the agenda. Workers must be willing to and able to engage in lifelong learning – flexibility has become a core requirement of workers (Sennett, 1998).

The concept of a 'learning organization' has emerged in recent years, as a strategic answer to the increasing demands of flexibility and change (Senge, 1990; Watkins & Marsick, 1993; Marquardt, 1996). The learning organization is defined as an organization that learns continually and has the capacity to transform itself (Watkins & Marsick, 1993). The learning organization is characterized by people continually expanding their capacity to create the results they truly desire, where new and expansive patterns of thinking are nurtured, where collective aspirations are freed, and where people are continually learning how to learn together (Senge, 1990, p. 3). The strategic interests of the learning organization is to develop more effective practices, which implies a principal focus on what is here called innovative learning, involving a breach of harmony and discontinuity in the workplace. The opposite of innovative learning is called reproductive learning, involving stability and continuity in the workplace.

Management approaches to organizational learning as a means to increase competitiveness in the global market mostly ignore reproductive learning. Reproductive learning, if mentioned, is usually described as an outdated and oppressive type of learning, related to monotonous and exploitive industrial production, 'the black school', and traditional apprenticeship. Such a perspective is reflected in the argument that education should be a liberating project, pointing out that 'the animal training as cumulative learning is going to disappear due to the declining needs for production of active adjustment qualifications' (Illeris, 1974, p. 76; my translation). However, the liberating capacities of (innovative) learning have recently been questioned by scholars, who relate the contemporary learning euphoric to the needs of a neo-liberal market. For instance, Contu and Willmott argue that organizational learning (OL) is part of an all-embracing liberal learning discourse where certain governing variables such as those which guide the individual to serve rather than to subvert the organization, remain unexamined (Contu & Willmott, 2003, p. 936). A related point is made by Kvale (2003), who argues that lifelong learning liberates primarily to more consumption, satisfying the neo-liberal consumer society's demands of flexibility and change.

This chapter accepts the governing variables of a neo-liberal society, but questions whether recent decades' dramatic changes of work and workplaces have lessened the importance of reproductive learning. In other words, whether or not a discursive focus on creative and innovative learning matches the needs of contemporary organizations. The chapter explores this question empirically through a comparative discussion of three case studies on workplace learning: a shipyard (Yard) (Elmholdt & Winsløv, 1999), a software production company (A-Soft) (Elmholdt, 2003), and a web-design bureau (Web A/S) (Elmholdt, 2001).

The empirical discussion challenges the notion of fundamental discontinuity between traditional (bureaucratic) organizations of the industrial society (Yard) and post-bureaucratic 'learning' organizations of the knowledge society (Web, A-Soft). The findings show that all three types of learning – reproductive, reconstructive, and innovative – exist across traditional bureaucratic (Yard) and post-bureaucratic (Web, A-Soft) types of organization. However, the findings also reveal huge differences in distribution of the three types of learning across the compared workplaces. The empirical discussion points out harmful consequences of an overly reproductive learning environment at Yard, with restricted access to engage in innovative learning. More surprisingly, the findings indicate harmful consequences of an overly innovative learning environment at Web with limited access to participate in reproductive learning. The chapter challenges the notion of reproductive learning as unproductive in contemporary organizations, and suggests an understanding of reproductive, reconstructive, and innovative learning as functionally complementary types of workplace learning.

Situating the comparative study theoretically

The chapter takes theoretical outset in a situated understanding of learning as the changing participation in changing communities of practice. The community of practice is defined as 'a set of relations among persons, activity, and world over time and in relation with other tangential and overlapping communities of practice' (Lave & Wenger, 1991, p. 98). The community of practice is a mid-level category between the person and the formal structures of organization. The situated perspective understands learning as a social and relational process that exceeds the individual mind. The metaphor of a workplace landscape of learning (Nielsen & Kvale, 2003) refers to a methodological focus on describing the social-physical environment and which contributes to shape the generative processes of workplace learning.

The chapter develops the concepts of reproductive, reconstructive and innovative learning as a means to analyze how different types of workplaces support and constrain different types of learning. The situated notion of learning as the changing participation in changing communities of practice implies a changed relation between the person and the community/organization. It is the quality of this change that is described by the concepts of reproductive, reconstructive, and innovative learning. In particular, the concepts elaborate on the situated notion of interplay in learning between 'social competence and personal experience', which 'combines personal transformation with the evolution of social structures' (Wenger, 2000, p. 227). The personal experience and the social competence (shared repertoire) always stand in a relation from divergent to convergent. The concept of shared repertoire refers to the totality of distributed competences in a community of practice or an organization, not to competences shared among all individual members.

A divergent relation between personal experience and shared repertoire of competence may result in learning that creates a higher degree of congruence through a process of personal adaptation to the shared repertoire, which is continued. This type of learning is called reproductive. When an apprentice welder engages in learning that aims toward reproducing the shared repertoire of welding, it is a process of reproductive learning. Reproductive workplace learning does not imply organizational learning, defined as a collective process leading to the changing of organizational behaviour (Swieringa, 1992, p. 33). However, reproductive learning can be said to imply (re)learning of organizational behaviour, as it continues the shared repertoire of competences in the community of practice.

Two types of discontinuing learning that expand and/or exceed the shared repertoire are identified in this chapter. Reconstructive learning expands the community's shared repertoire of competences, by adding to, without fundamentally changing, its basis. Reconstructive learning implies that both the person and the shared repertoire of the community/organization are changed. When an apprentice welder engages in learning that expands the shared repertoire of foot placements during welding, it is reconstructive learning, as it does not fundamentally change the basis for learning in the community.

Innovative learning exceeds and extends the community's shared repertoire of competences – breaking fundamentally with the basis of the former practice. When an apprentice welder engages in learning that extends the shared repertoire of welding pipelines, it is potentially innovative learning. In order to qualify as 'truly' innovative, the new method must be integrated as an aspect of the shared repertoire to be handed down by reproductive learning until it is eventually overtaken by new changes. The latter constraint implies that discontinuing learning, which is not accepted in the working community, does not qualify as 'truly' innovative.

The concepts of reproductive, reconstructive, and innovative learning are not sharply demarcated categories, but depict a continuum of learning that either reinforces the status quo or changes some aspects of the workplace. The human subject is always changed in the process of learning, even though the social-physical landscape of the workplace may be continued. The concept of continuing reproductive learning is similar to single-loop learning where 'we learn to maintain the field of constancy by learning to design actions that satisfy existing governing variables' (Argyris & Schön, 1974, p. 19), and discontinuing innovative learning is similar to double-loop learning where 'we learn to change the field of constancy itself' (ibid.). A difference is that Argyris and Schön did not recognize the middle-form of reconstructive learning. Another distinctive feature is that the concepts of reproductive, reconstructive, and innovative workplace learning are not hierarchically related or valued. Any of the three types of learning may be a good thing or a bad thing, depending on the circumstances of the concrete situation. In order to communicate the main argumentation of the chapter clearly, the case studies focus on the extremes of reproductive and innovative workplace learning.

Situating the comparative study methodologically

The analysis of workplace learning at Yard, Web A/S, and A-Soft is based on separate case studies conducted by the author, who used research designs that combined participant observation with interviews.

Yard was, until it went into bankruptcy in autumn 1999, a traditional heavy industry production plant operating in a highly competitive business sector. In earlier years, Yard competed mainly with shipyards in Europe, but latterly the biggest threat came from Asian shipyards that are highly competitive on prices. When analyzing these market conditions, the board came up with a plan indicating that Yard should focus on quality, precision, flexibility towards new technology, and niche production (Sonne *et al.*, 1995). Yard had no tradition of flexibility; on the contrary, it had a tradition of continuity. Yard was a highly union controlled organization, in which the majority of workers stayed in the same job throughout their working life.

The case study at Yard was conducted over a two-year period 1997–99, focusing on the workplace-based training of welding apprentices. Trades education in Denmark is structured as a dual system combining school and workplace training. Four welder apprentices and one skilled welder were interviewed. One of the apprentices was observed on the job and interviewed twice during the two-year period.

Web A/S is a high-technological company producing websites, intranet, extranet, and e-commerce solutions to the private and the public sector. It was established by two business degree students in 1996. The company expanded rapidly until it amalgamated in 2000. Web A/S is a fast changing company in a fast changing world – employees, products, tools, economy, customers, technology – everything changes at a high speed.

The Web A/S case study was conducted over a three-month period in autumn 1999 and in which the author participated as an observer in the everyday working life of the organization. The company had 50 employees at this time. The study was designed as a broad analysis of organizational learning. Nine employees (newcomers and old timers), one department manager, and one board member, were interviewed about everyday learning at work.

A-Soft is a software producing company with 400 employees. The company is part of a 200-year-old corporation that began to take an interest in software production in the late 1970s, and founded A-Soft as an independent unit in the early 1980s. Over the past twenty years, A-Soft has become one of the world's leading developers and suppliers of software solutions within its business area.

The case study at A-Soft was conducted over the two-year period 2001–02, which included two periods of three months in the field. The case study focused on the company's service division, which has 100 employees. The first research period focused on the training of newcomer supporters, the second period focused on the everyday work practice of support. Formal interviews were conducted with 16 employees and one manager by the end of the first research period, and follow-up interviews were conducted in the second research period.

The following empirical analysis shows how diverse types of work and organization of work across the three workplaces are related to various distributions of reproductive, reconstructive, and innovative learning. Selected interview statements and observational data are represented in order to illustrate the characteristics of organization, work, and learning in each of the cases.

Workplace learning at yard

The majority of employees at Yard were craftsmen who had completed apprentice training in the organization and been employed ever since.

Reproductive learning through observation – scaffolding – rehearsal

Welder apprentices' learning proceeds largely from observation, over scaffolding, to rehearsal. The first step is to observe how the skilled welder carries out a task, a learning mechanism which Bandura (1977) studied and described as observation and model learning. The following quote illustrates how small interruptions and breaks in the daily work routine are used for observational learning.

> 'If there is a quiet moment, if for example, the welder goes to pick up something, and you can see someone welding something special, you go to watch how he is doing it. When you walk around you snatch tricks here and there' (Ib, welder apprentice, first year).

The second step in the typical learning process is that the apprentice carries out the task under scaffolding by a skilled welder. Scaffolding refers to situations where the more experienced helps the less experienced to accomplish tasks that they do not yet master on their own. The concept of scaffolding is inspired by Vygotsky's concept of the zone of proximal development (Hansen & Nielsen, 1999). Scaffolding can take place as guided participation (Rogoff, 1990), which is described in the following statement:

> 'I was welding when the skilled welder passed by, glanced at me, and said; no, you are holding it completely wrong. Then he showed me how to hold it... he taught me how to hold a welding machine' (Ib, welder apprentice, first year).

The less experienced is guided through the task by the more experienced. Scaffolding can also take place by making the task simpler and gradually add on complexity. What is common in both types of scaffolding is that the skilled worker is in close interplay with the apprentice's learning removes the scaffold.

The third step is rehearsal. The apprentice carries out the assignment on his own, again and again, until he 'can sit and weld with his back towards what he is doing and still make the whole thing perfect', as Ib describes the skills of mastery. These three steps describe the typical learning process of handing down existing practice forms to the new generation of employees at Yard.

Strike as generator for experimenting practice – innovative learning

The following interview statement, describing a situation where the skilled worker went on strike, exemplifies literally that innovative learning was not an everyday occurrence at Yard:

> 'When we put up the big pipes at the ships, we once used wooden blocks to stabilize the whole thing. I have found out that it is much easier to use line instead. Using line, you can easily make adjustments, which are faster than hammering wooden blocks under the pipes.'
> I: 'How did you find out?'
> 'Actually, it was during the period when the skilled workers went on strike. The cabinetmakers' workshop was closed, so we did not have access to wooden blocks. That forced us to think on our own. I figured out that we could try with some line and weld on some iron. We did, and it worked very well. We have kept on using it ever since, and we can now see that others start using it' (Ib, welder apprentice, third year).

The statement illustrates innovative learning as the consequence of a strike, allowing Ib to experiment and invent a line pulling system. The strike created a situation where order and disorder were juxtaposed. Only these kind of situations render organizational learning possible argue Weick and Westley, who see organization and learning as essentially antithetical (Weick & Westley, 1996, p. 445). The solidness of this argument very much depends upon how learning and organization are conceptualized. Yard was well adapted to support continuation of routine through reproductive learning while innovative learning occurred only occasionally and mostly on the outskirts of the established organization. As such, the case illustrates that organization is not antithetical to learning *per se*, but indicates that innovative learning is restricted by the bureaucratic structures of traditional industrial production. The next case, describing the post-bureaucratic organizational structures at Web A/S, shows that neither is innovative learning antithetical to organization *per se*. Yard's problem was not in lacking ability to learn but the inability to transform the organization into supporting discontinuing types of learning. As such, Yard may be characterized as reproductively skewed.

Workplace learning at Web A/S

Most employees at Web A/S have a formal academic education at the time of employment. The training of newcomers takes place through participation in everyday work, as at Yard, but the organization that supports and restrains learning is highly different.

Learning starts with practice – observation is something you grasp

A characteristic difference between learning at Yard and Web A/S is that newcomers' work and learning are less structured and monitored at Web A/S. The three-step learning process, which was 'compulsory' at Yard, is also found at Web A/S but it is less formally structured. It is primarily individual learners' responsibility whether or not they want to follow the three-step progression of observation, guided participation, and rehearsal. The workplace landscape of learning does not push hard in this direction. Actually, the pressure often goes in the opposite direction: towards the newcomer being requested to start with rehearsal by 'playing' with software programs. It is rarely possible for newcomers to observe the problem solving of experienced employees. The following statement illustrates observation and modelling as highly constrained resources for learning:

> 'Sitting right next to the programmers, looking down at the graphic designers and having an ear at the doors of the project managers, I continuously hear and see things that I can use' (Vibeke, web-designer).

Observation is not an acceptable work activity, but something you snatch by peeping from your desk.

Experimenting practices – try out and use the Internet

The message to newcomers at Web A/S is largely 'try out' and ask only if you cannot find help on the Internet. Poul, head of the programmers department, points out that 'we encourage newcomers to use the Internet, it booms with online information out there, but many newcomers do not use it'. The experimenting culture at Web A/S is emphasized by the fact that employees often refer to situations of reconstructive and innovative learning as situations of 'play'. This is described in the following statement by Knud, in which he explains how he learns to use new software by 'playing' with it. 'If I need to learn how to use a new piece of software, I will sit down and start playing with it. I will test it and examine what you can actually do with this piece of software' (Knud, graphic designer).

Limited access to observation and imitation

Web A/S is characterized by a flexible work practice with unconditional access to the Internet and limited access to observation and imitation of working experts. Landscapes of learning with these characteristics are criticized by Dreyfus (2001), who argues that access to observe and imitate working experts of flesh and blood is fundamental for the development of expertise. This claim seems to suggest that innovative learning needs attachment in reproductive learning, in order to end up with genuine expertise and 'true' innovations in the working community. Empirical support for this may be found in the story about Carl, a novice web designer who failed to engage in reproductive learning ahead of innovative learning.

> 'Now, after Carl has quit, I have rewritten up to 80% of his codes. It has cost us a lot to have him employed for six months. I am sure we would have been better off had we given him US$ 50,000 and asked him to stay away' (Kenneth, programmer).

The result, as described by Kenneth, was that Carl's creative experimentation exceeded and expanded the shared repertoire; however, it did not qualify as 'truly' innovative learning, as it was not integrated in the community's shared repertoire. Carl's work did not live up to the community's shared standards; the codes were poor and full of mistakes.

The story about Carl indicates that reproductive workplace learning is a prerequisite for innovative workplace learning. This interpretation is based on the precondition that organizational learning is always directed towards the achievement of certain outcomes, not just any outcome, but outcomes that secure the survival and competitiveness of the organization. This is pointed out as one rarely examined governing variable in organizational learning literature (Contu & Willmott, 2003, p. 936). If we accept that innovative workplace learning is always limited and directed, the problem of Web A/S is that its organization supports flexibility and change through innovative learning, but fails to secure a solid attachment in reproductive learning. Innovative workplace learning without attachment in reproductive workplace learning has no limitation or direction, and that hampers the organization's ability to secure continual production of high quality products. In the light of these arguments, Web A/S may be characterized as innovatively skewed.

Workplace learning at A-Soft

A-Soft is a division of a 200-years-old company that has changed in adaptation to the market conditions from industrial fabrication of mechanical products towards computer-based fabrication of software products. The organization of A-Soft supports and constrains a balanced distribution of reproductive, reconstructive, and innovative learning as compared to the cases of Yard and Web A/S.

Reproductive learning as prior to innovative learning

New employees' first year at A-Soft is educationally structured in order to support reproductive learning. Newcomers are not allowed to work on their own before they are able to put to use the basic skills of a software supporter. Employment begins with a four-month introductory course: starting with 'department external' classroom teaching on theoretical knowledge and simulated problems, and ending with 'department internal' classroom teaching on specific knowledge and authentic problems. During this period, the amount of formal classroom teaching decreases, whereas the amount of participation in the everyday work practice increases. The contexts of formal education and the contexts of everyday practice all support newcomers to engage in reproductive learning in advance of innovative learning. The following interview statement expresses a newcomer's perspective on the process of becoming a competent supporter in the community of practice. When asked what is necessary in order to participate on equal terms with his colleagues, Bjarne says:

> 'I need more experience in this job. I need access to follow my colleagues from the sideline; observe how they talk to customers. I learn a lot just from sharing the office with more experienced colleagues. You hear how they address the customers on the phone, how they get a new release sold to the price they do. What you really need is observational experience – if you can call it so – of what they do' (Bjarne, key account manager, four months).

Bjarne finished the introductory course and began to take part in everyday work practice. He shares an office with two experienced colleagues from whom he learns a lot through observation and modelling. The interview statement expresses respect for the shared repertoire, and an understanding of the primary importance of learning this repertoire in order to become a skilled supporter in the community of practice. The work task of supporting A-Soft's products is highly complex. Becoming a skilled supporter involves a prolonged training period. Employees are still mostly orientated towards reproductive learning after two years of employment, as described by Hans in the following statement:

> 'Where I am right now, I think it is more important for me to gain experience with the A-Soft products than keeping updated on third part products. I could easily bring in new knowledge, but would it be the right knowledge? I cannot know this before I know more about A-Soft. In my opinion, bringing in new knowledge should primarily be the responsibility of the more experienced supporters' (Hans, support, two years).

While acknowledging the importance of reconstructive and innovative learning for the community as a whole, Hans points out that his energy is better used on reproductive learning. The humility and respect for the task of reproductive learning, which is reflected in the interview statement, is typical for newcomers between one and two years of seniority. 'The first 1½ years you are only confirmed in how much you still need to learn. I would not say "how ignorant you are", but you feel ignorant' (Pia, support, two years).

The skilled supporter is a good learner and teacher

The everyday reality of A-Soft requires constant engagement in reconstructive and innovative types of learning by all employees. This is emphasized in the following interview statement by Julian:

'The reality at A-Soft Service is that immediately when you have learned the latest upgrade you need to realize that three other releases are on their way. Learning is an ongoing process' (Julian, support, 12 years).

Every new software release includes minor or major changes that the employees must learn to support. New software releases are a destabilizing factor that requires reconstructive and innovative learning. The act of engaging in reconstructive and innovative learning is regarded as important and prestigious in the working community of supporters. One aspect of this practice, namely the sharing of knowledge through formal teaching of colleagues in classrooms and informal instruction in everyday practice, is highly valued by the management, but somewhat less prestigious in the working community of supporters. Most prestigious in the working community is the core job function of technical problem solving. The leading metaphor in describing the skilled supporter used to be 'someone whom you can throw out in a parachute with his toolbox and he will fix the problem' (Doris, manager, 14 years). The skilled supporter is still primarily associated with the good problem solver; however, in recent years this characteristic has extended to include being a good learner and a good teacher. The latter is reflected in the following statement by Rikke, describing the job as a supporter:

'The primary task is to solve problems for your customers, and to help your colleagues. Secondly, it is to become more skilled – but that happens automatically when you work on customer assignments. It is rare to have the same assignment twice – unusual to be that lucky. Thirdly, it is to teach colleagues, I am for instance teaching the newcomers tomorrow' (Rikke, support, two years).

The workplace landscape of learning at A-Soft is characterized by (1) a balanced distribution of reproductive, reconstructive, and innovative learning; (2) organizational structures that secures innovative learning an attachment in reproductive learning; and (3) an external environment that demands continual innovate learning. The organizational structure of A-Soft supports reproductive learning without rendering innovative learning impossible, indicating that (innovative) learning is not antithetical to organization. A-Soft does neither share Yard's problem of creating flexibility and adaptation to environmental changes nor Web's problem of securing continual production of high quality products, indicating that innovative learning is not enough but needs to be balanced by reproductive learning. Moreover, the educational structures of A-Soft secures innovative learning a solid attachment in reproductive learning, indicating that reproductive learning is a prerequisite of 'truly' innovative learning – guided towards securing the survival and competitiveness of the organization.

Discussion

In contrast to the management literature on 'learning organizations' that mostly focuses on promoting discontinuing innovative workplace learning, some academic writings on organizational learning argue for the importance of balancing continuing and discontinuing types of workplace learning (e.g. March, 1991; Ellström, 2002). March argues for balancing processes of exploitation (reproductive learning) and exploration (innovative learning). Ellström differentiates adaptive (reproductive) from developmental (innovative) orientated types of learning, and argues that it is important for persons and organizations to maintain a balance between the two types. Adaptive learning is understood as necessary in order to carry out routine and habitual actions, whereas developmental learning is supposed a driving force in change and innovation.

March's and Ellström's arguments for balancing continuing and discontinuing types of learning share similarities with this chapter's argument for the complementary values of reproductive, reconstructive and innovative workplace learning. However, some noticeable differences are present. One is that March focuses on avoiding the harmful effects of too much continuity of routine through reproductive learning, whereas the present empirical findings show that too much discontinuity through innovative learning may also have harmful consequences. Another difference is that neither March nor Ellström conceptualize the middle form of reconstructive learning. A third difference is that neither argues for the interrelatedness of reproductive and innovative learning. On the contrary, Ellström describes continuing and discontinuing workplace learning as two separate logics (2002, p. 88). The logic of production emphasizes adaptive (reproductive) learning oriented towards the mastery of procedures and routines, and the logic of development emphasizes development orientated (innovative) learning. The empirical findings of this chapter cannot support the claim of separate logics of production and development. All cases focused on workplace learning through everyday productive work, and in all cases were found – although highly diverse distribution – the existence of reproductive, reconstructive, and innovative learning. Contrary to the idea of separate logics, the present findings show that everyday work practice integrates the logics of both production and development.

Summary and conclusion

This chapter compared the organization work and learning of one traditional (bureaucratic) organization of the industrial society (Yard) and two post-bureaucratic 'learning' organizations of the knowledge society (Web, A-Soft). The findings supported the generally accepted notions of reproductive learning as particularly related to traditional bureaucratic organization and industrial production, and innovative learning as particularly related to post-bureaucratic organization and knowledge production. However, the findings challenged the notion of fundamental discontinuity between traditional bureaucratic (reproductive) organizations of industrial society and post-bureaucratic (innovative) 'learning' organizations of the knowledge society. All cases focused on learning in everyday productive work, and all cases reported the existence of reproductive, reconstructive, and innovative workplace learning – although in highly different distributions.

The case of Yard showed harmful consequences of too much reproductive learning, hampering the organization's ability of flexibility and adaptation to environmental change. The case of Web A/S revealed harmful consequences of innovative learning without a solid attachment in reproductive learning, hampering the organization's ability of continual production of high quality products. The case of A-Soft displayed a balanced distribution, taking primacy in routine through reproductive learning as the ground for flexibility through innovative learning, overcoming the described problems of Yard and Web A/S. These findings indicate that innovative learning is not enough but needs the functional complementarity of reproductive learning in order to direct workplace learning towards survival and competitiveness of the organization. Reproductive learning seems to play an important role in guiding the outcome of innovative learning also in post-bureaucratic organizations of the knowledge society. If these findings are solid, we may conclude that a discursive focus on creative and innovative learning does not match the needs of contemporary organizations.

References

Argyris, C., & Schön, D. (1974). *Theory in practice: Increasing professional effectiveness.* San Fransisco: Jossey-Bass.
Bandura, A. (1977). *Social learning theory.* Englewood Cliffs, NJ: Prentice-Hall.
Bell, D. (1973). *The Coming of Post-Industrial Society: A Venture in Social Forecasting.* New York: Basic Books.
Contu, A., & Willmott, H. (2003). Re-embedding situatedness: The importance of power relations in learning theory. *Organization Science*, 14(3), 283–96.
Dreyfus, H. (2001). *On the Internet.* London: Routledge.
Ellström, P. E. (2002). Time and the Logics of Learning. *Lifelong Learning in Europe*, 2, 86–93.
Elmholdt, C. (2001). Læring som social praksis på arbejdspladsen – et feltstudie af læring mellem person, informationsteknologi og organisation. *Psykologisk Studieskriftserie*, 4(2), 1–175.
Elmholdt, C. (2003). *Landscapes of learning in the ICT world – learning as an aspect of change in social practice.* PhD thesis, University of Aarhus, Department of Psychology, Aarhus.
Elmholdt, C., & Winsløv, J. H. (1999). Fra lærling til smed. In K. Nielsen & S. Kvale (eds), *Mesterlære – læring som social praksis* (pp. 103–13). København: Hans Reitzels Forlag.
Hansen, J. T., & Nielsen, K. (1999). *Stilladsering – en pædagogisk metafor.* Aarhus: Klim.
Illeris, K. (1974). *Problemorientering og deltagerstyring: Oplæg til en alternativ didaktik.* København: Munksgaard.
Kvale, S. (2003). Frigørende pædagogik som frigørende til forbrug. Pædagogikken som kritisk instans – myte eller virkelighed? NFPF 31st Congress, København.
Lave, J., & Wenger, E. (1991). *Situated Learning: Legitimate Peripheral Participation.* Cambridge: Cambridge University Press.
March, J. G. (1991). Exploration and exploitation in organizational learning. *Organizational Science*, 2(1), 74–87.
Marquardt, M. (1996). *Building the Learning Organization.* New York: McGraw-Hill.
Nielsen, K., & Kvale, S. (eds) (2003). *Praktikkens læringslandskab – at lære gennem arbejde.* København: Akademisk Forlag.
Rogoff, B. (1990). *Apprenticeship in Thinking: Cognitive Development in Social Context.* New York: Oxford University Press.
Saperstein, J., Rouach, D., & Harney, M. (2002). *Creating Regional Wealth in the Innovation Economy: Models, perspectives, and best practices.* Upper Saddle River, NJ: Financial Times Prentice-Hall.
Senge, P. (1990). *The Fifth Discipline: The Art and Practice of the Learning Organization.* London: Century Business.
Sennett, R. (1998). *The Corrosion of Character: The personal consequences of the new capitalism.* New York: W.W. Norton.

Sonne *et al.* (1995). *Aarhus Dockyard Ltd. 1945–95.* Aarhus: Aarhus Dockyard Ltd.
Stehr, N. (1994). *Knowledge Society.* London: Sage.
Swieringa, J. W. A. (1992). *Becoming a Learning Organization.* Wokingham: Addison-Wesley.
Watkins, K., & Marsick, V. (1993). *Sculpturing the Learning Organization.* San Francisco: Jossey-Bass.
Weick, K. E., & Westley, F. (1996). Organizational Learning: Affirming an Oxymoron. In S. Clegg, C. Hardy & W. Nord (eds), *Handbook of Organizational Studies* (pp. 440–58). London: Sage.
Wenger, E. (2000). Communities of practice and social learning systems. *Organization,* 7(2), 225–46.

Part II
Learning and Working

5
Knowledge, Progression and the Understanding of Workplace Learning
Erik Laursen

For at least the past fifteen years at least there has been a growing and largely positive interest for topics such as organizational learning (OL) and workplace learning (WPL) in the economically most advanced parts of the world – including Scandinavia. This interest has been an important part of a broader complex of themes, topics, ideas and collective representations concerning knowledge, information, learning, information technology (IT) and even globalization.

The foundation of this set of collective representations is the idea, that today we are living in an information society, based on a knowledge economy, in which the crucial advantages in the competition between private enterprises (and public institutions) that are created by the access of the organization to important knowledge or information. As expressed by Charles Leadbetter, '...in the next century the driving forces behind growth will be the process, through which an economy creates-, uses- and develops values from knowledge' (Leadbeater, 1998).

Some of the central premises concerning the belief in the existence of a knowledge society have been questioned by several observers, most recently by Abrahamsson, Abrahamsson and Johansson (2003).[1] It certainly represents a 'zeitgeist' we all seem to share and which structures our overall perspective on the social world in one way or another. As a consequence of this perspective knowledge and learning are not seen as boring, but (alas) necessary elements of life. Rather they are represented as important and sexy like money or designer objects.

The premise, that knowledge is of fundamental importance for the economy and for the society at large, might have found its ultimate expression in the organizational development concept the *learning organization*.[2]

This concept offers a management tool for developing the organization by developing the competencies of the employees (Elkjaer, 1999) and the learning systems of the organization (see Senge, 1990), neatly described by Steen Hildebrandt, among others, by listing several tasks that a 'learning organization' should be good at, such as performing a systematic problem-solving, experimenting with new approaches to the performance of task and learning from self-made experience (see Hildebrandt & Brandi, 1998; Senge, 1990; van Hauen, 1995).

If the learning organization is the solution, it is tempting to ask, 'what is the problem?' One type of answer refers to the ever-growing speed of change in society, making it necessary to develop a high potential for flexibility in the organization to match the turbulence of the environment. Another possible answer refers to the high growth rate of knowledge, making constant updating of the competencies of the employees necessary. A third possible answer is produced by the claim that innovative knowledge is becoming more and more important in the fierce competition of the market. A fourth answer could be that this tool offers the management a good opportunity to control, even the unplanned and unintentional learning in the workplace (Abrahamsson et al., 2003). In most presentations of the learning organization we find some interesting *normative assumptions*:

(1) The organization is *per se generating important knowledge*, owing to the way its employees are performing normal duties.
(2) To a great extent *the organization is learning from itself*. To put it in other words: There is a balanced relationship between the organization's own production – and its import of knowledge.
(3) The organization *is appreciating quality, knowledge, expertise and innovation*.
(4) It is possible to make management requirements for flexibility and positive attitudes towards behavioural change *converge* with the employees' requirement for *real competence development* and personal development.

Here it is important to point out, that a balance of this kind, between the interests of the employees and those of the management, depends on a developed consensus concerning the *standards* of the work and the related competences (see Boud, 1998).

The concept of learning and modern work organizations

Viewed as an expression of a set of collective beliefs concerning the overall importance of information and knowledge, the present interest for OL and WPL contains four important tendencies, which relates to a broader reorganization of knowledge and skills in modern societies. Learning seems to be:

- Encompassing almost every kind of behavioural change, which is evaluated as positive.
- Changing in focus from teaching towards learning, and learning processes.
- Changing in focus of learning contexts from formal education towards informal, work integrated learning processes.
- Changing in focus of learning results from qualifications, seen as general objectified and explicit knowledge, towards context related, more or less tacit knowledge.

If the social organization of knowledge is conceived as a set of structured social relations between the teacher, the learner and the content (the 'didaktical triangle'; see Künzli, 1998), it is possible to make the following observations:

- Activities and arrangements such as education and teaching, involving asymmetrical relations of authority and knowledge, with a formalization of the role of teacher, are largely ignored in some of the research on WPL.
- It is often ignored that WPL in most cases takes place in more or less established hierarchies of skills, status and authority in the workplace.
- In contrast to this, knowledge is assumed to be distributed and reproduced in symmetrical social relations 'facilitating' the acquisition processes of the individual learner.
- The *content*, that is, the knowledge and the skills, which are to be learned, is largely *undefined* as an objectified goal of the learning processes. This implies, that learning and the evaluation of learning, is based on tacit, context-specific conceptions of 'what is called for to solve a given task in a satisfactory way'.
- The question of who is in control to select the content, and through which processes and which criterion this selection is done, is frequently not asked.

This understanding of modern WPL puts a heavy burden on the concept of *learning*, making it the central element in a theoretical understanding of OL and WPL. Because of this, I shall shortly discuss the concept here.

It is well known that the concept of 'learning', like other important concepts of the behavioural sciences, has been the object of a diversity of alternative definitions, reflecting very different ontological, epistemological premises. I do not wish to go into a discussion of this rich semantic field. Instead, I want to focus on the aspects most of the definitions seem to share.

In doing this, I make the observation that, in general, the concept of 'learning' refers to behavioural change, taking place in interactional processes between the actor and environment. This process of change can be perceived as a response on the environment, but it must contain an aspect that goes beyond sheer reaction. It is this aspect that is referred to as 'learning'. Furthermore, the 'new' behaviour must hold some greater adaptable value, when compared to the 'old' behaviour. To characterize it further, a process must possess three qualities to be considered 'learning':

- It produces *behavioural change*. That is, 'learning' is considered a process generating behavioural change (the *change criteria*).
- This behavioural change can be considered as a change 'for better' according to one or more criteria that could be listed for the behaviour (the *progression criteria*).
- The phenomenon itself includes a change in the *knowledge*, enabling the behavioural change (the *knowledge criteria*).

So learning refers to a process that includes changing knowledge, thereby causing another type of change, namely in behaviour, which can be described as progressive, according to a given criteria. In summary, *learning is a process, transforming the knowledge base in a certain field of behaviour, producing a progressive change of behaviour*, where 'change of behaviour' also includes changes in ways of perceiving, feeling, thinking and knowing.

Clearly this definition does not concern the 'how' and 'why' of the process. It is aimed at defining the necessary conditions for categorizing a behavioural change of a special kind as learning. Furthermore, the definition is focused on 'knowledge', because this perspective makes it possible to make a distinction between 'learning' and other kinds of behavioural change, which could be conceived as 'progressive' according to a given criteria.

Obviously this aspect of the definition raises more questions than it answers – especially how the concept of 'knowledge' is to be understood. And what is meant by 'transforming the knowledge base'? On these rather complex matters, I make a few (hopefully) clarifying remarks.

It is important to stress that according to many observers, knowledge contains two central aspects. On the one hand, knowledge can be described as 'knowing-what', or considered as a product, a result, an object, which can be used and distributed in an explicit form. On the other hand, it can be seen as 'knowing-how', related to actions, intentions, relations and contexts, and generally conceived as something, which exists in an implicit form (Baumard, 1999; Polanyi, 1966; Nonaka & Takeuchi, 1995).

Following the last aspect, I focus on 'knowing', 'how people "do" their knowing' and on what could be described as the 'infrastructure of knowing' (Blackler et al., 1999, p. 208), including the methods, social relations, concepts, tools and technologies used in the process. The concepts of 'learning situations' and 'learning systems', which are presented later in this chapter, are attempts to develop this idea a bit further in relation to organizational learning.

Finally, this definition of the concept includes an analytical distinction between the two aspects of the learning process – the change of behaviour and the change of knowledge, offering two possibilities to determine the possible progressive element in the behavioural change; namely, the adaptive value of the changed behaviour and the transformation of the knowledge base, enabling the behavioural change.

For both approaches, the concept of 'quality' is central in defining progress. It is necessary to relate to some standards of quality if 'change' is to be constructed as 'progression'. For knowledge-based definitions, it is a question of the quality of the knowledge-in-use, while adaption-based definitions focus on the quality of performance. It is important to point out that 'quality' and 'progression' are ways of perceiving change, based solely on the judgement of the actors involved.

Finally, I would like to add a third possible way to define 'progress'. Progression might also refer to the development of *learning skills*, that is, the development in the ways 'people do their knowing' or to the 'infrastructure of knowing'. As pointed out in the following section, it is not an easy task to decide on usable criteria of progression in relation to organizational learning. The concept of progression, based on a notion of quality relating to the knowledge in use, and the idea, that actions can be improved by 'better knowledge', requires the existence of a social consensus on how to evaluate different elements of explicit knowledge. However, the behaviour and adaptation orientated concepts of progression are often very task- and context-specific, making it hard to relate to the overall development of the organization as a whole. This situation makes it important to construct a third way of approaching progression in organizational learning, based on the development of the 'infrastructure of knowing and learning' of the organization as a whole.

Organizational learning viewed from three concepts of progression

Organizational learning is a complex concept that can be considered from numerous perspectives. Comparing some of the central efforts that have been made in defining organizational learning (see, e.g., Dixon, 1994), I think it would be relevant to classify them in accordance to the way they approach the question of progression. My point is that the perspective on progression of a certain theory or analytical approach gives us a fairly accurate picture of what the theory holds as important concerning the learning processes of the organization. Examples of alternative ways of classifying approaches to OL are found in Shrivastava (1983), who used the content of the learning process as a criterion, and Elkjaer (1999), who focused on the process of acquisition. The three perspectives outlined in this section are based on the three possibilities for defining progression, mentioned above.

Perspective 1: Organizational learning as the aggregated learning of the employees (the competence container)

An obvious interpretation of the 'organizational learning' concept is letting it refer to *all processes, developing the employee competences*, as the sum of these competences is an asset making up the company's total capacity of performance. So we are looking at a very wide and in principle immeasurable field in which 'employee competences' are simply referring to the knowledge at the company's disposal in one way or another.

According to this point of view, the organization as such becomes 'wiser' or 'more proficient' when its total volume of competence has been increased. But how are we to understand an 'increased volume of competence'? In general, there is no connection between the wisdom of an organization and the volume of the competence of its members if this knowledge is either irrelevant or cannot be made operative in relation to the organization's central fields of effort.

Obviously this perspective on OL must be based on a *knowledge-based* approach to learning, describing the progression against a 'curriculum', that is with a reference to an established volume of objectified knowledge. An important part of organizing such a corpus of knowledge is the distinction made between different categories or types of knowledge, based on selected differences in the semantic fields, the complexity, the status or even the sacredness of the content (see, e.g., Berger & Luckmann, 1966; Bourdieu & Passeron, 1977; Durkheim, 1968; Bernstein, 1971). This set of differences is not only used to organize a system of classification, it also makes it possible to construct a *hierarchy* of knowledge types as well. A hierarchy, to be used in the social construction of the curriculum, mapping out the various trajectories the learner must follow to be a competent master of the knowledge in question. Together with the relevant corpus of knowledge, a curriculum is reproduced and controlled by one or several *communities practices* or – *knowledge*, such as vocational groups, educators, etc. (see Lave & Wenger, 1991).

In principle, here the idea of progression is based on a notion of quality relating to the knowledge, and not of the performance in itself. The performance is of course important as evidence of knowledge, but a brilliant performance is often valued as next to worthless if it is based on 'imitation' and not on 'real' (or even 'critical') understanding of the knowledge base.

Fiol and Lyles (1985) have developed a more sophisticated version of this type of definition, according to which, 'Organizational learning is defined as the process of improving actions through better knowledge and understanding'.

The important part here is the idea that actions can be improved by 'better knowledge'. As discussed above, the question of progression of knowledge is difficult. Fiol and Lyles' definition only makes sense if there exists a *consensus* in the organization and its environment, that is, between the management, the employees and the customers or users on the criteria of 'good knowledge and quality performance'. This consensus often only exists in a very fragile or momentary sense.

Perspective 2: The organization as the adaptable learner ('survival of the wisest')

Another way to answer the question of how to ascertain whether the competences of an organization have 'been developed' in a way to have made it more 'proficient' or 'clever', is to take a closer look at when the organization's 'performance power', including its 'competitive power' have been 'enhanced'.

This perspective on progression emphasizes the element of *behaviour* and describes the progression against the enhanced adaptative value of the changed behaviour compared to the requirements, opportunities or expectations posed by the learner's environment. Organizations need to learn in order to adapt successfully to the environment.

According to classic learning theories or contingency theories, a behavioural change should generally be understood as a response to a preceding response of the environment to the behaviour of the learner (Bateson, 1973). The decisive factor in this process is the response of the environment and the learner's appraisal of these responses. In this case, the sense of progression is based on the adaptive value of the changed behaviour. Generally (leaving the theoretical frame of classical behaviourism), the adaptive value of behaviour is closely related to the intentions of the actor.

According to this approach, the organization is typically understood as an 'integrated' system, interacting with its environment and acting, learning and reflecting in ways comparable with an individual player (Bateson, 1973). Examples of this perspective are presented by, for example, Hedberg:

> 'Organizational learning includes both the processes by which organizations adjust themselves defensively to reality and the processes by which knowledge is used offensively to improve the fits between organizations and their environments' (Hedberg, 1981).

The interesting and even problematic part of this approach to WPL is embedded in the relation between the learning processes of the individual and of those of the organization. The question is 'What makes the correction of individual behaviour a case of OL?' The answer might be that it is exactly the organization of the interplay between the individual level and the organizational level of behavioural change that makes the learning processes 'organizational'.

Perspective 3: Organizational learning as the development of learning opportunities in the organization

> 'A central aspect in presentations of "the learning organization" is the development of a range of structured social situations, which I will denote as opportunities for learning, drawing on a range of contextual resources. As mentioned above they could be described situations structured as "learning systems"' (Salomon & Perkins, 1998).

It is possible to understand the development of these social situations as developing the organizational *capability of learning*, or in other words, their development is a manifestation of the fact that the organization is *learning to learn* (Bateson, 1973), as they are offering the individual a set of resources for understanding and evaluating the feedback of the environment. There are several examples on this approach in the literature on organizational learning: 'A learning company is an organization that facilitates the learning of all its members and continuously transforms itself' (Pedler et al., 1991).

Pedler et al. hold as progression for 'learning enterprises' the developments in the social arrangements inside the organization, which enable the employees to learn. This approach of course leaves the question of whether or not the content of what is learned by the employees is doing them or the company any good unanswered. What matters is not progression in relation to defined fields of knowledge. What matters is the question of flexibility of the organization, that is, its resources in 'continuously transforming itself'. Senge (1990) makes the same point:

'[learning organizations are] organizations where people continually expand their capacities to create the results they truly desire, where new and expansive patterns of thinking are nurtured, where collective aspirations is set free, and where people are continually learning how to learn together'.

It is interesting that Senge leaves it to the individual employee to decide how the job shall be done, and how quality performance should be defined. Hardly a realistic premise, even in a 'learning organization'. Apart from this, Senge defines organizational learning as the development of contexts that enables innovation and learning competences. Argyris and Schön (1978) present the last example of this approach:

'Organizational learning is a process in which members of an organization detects errors and anomaly and correct it by restructuring organizational theory of action, embedding the results of their inquiry in the organizational maps and images'.

Argyris and Schön's book *Organizational Learning: A theory of Action Perspective* (1978) was based on Bateson's ideas of adaptional learning and a distinction between learning through correction of errors (Type I) and learning through re-contextualization of the interactional sequences. However it is not the organization as such that is doing the learning, it is the individual employee. The 'organizational' aspect of the learning processes is the social frame developed by the organization as a context for the error detections and corrections made by the employees. The interesting point for Argyris and Schön is if this frame is broad or tolerant enough to allow more expansive reflections (Type II), or if it only allows the detection of errors in its most limited and instrumental sense (Type I). Consequently, progression is conceived by Argyris and Schön as a development of the quality of the social contexts for individual learning in the organization.

Learning situations – the interactional aspect of OL

In each of the three perspectives on OL listed above, one of the following qualities is emphasized:

Perspective 1: The existence of one or more *sets of externalized knowledge*, hierarchical classified according to one ore more criteria of value.
Perspective 2: The existence of a set of *feedback relations* integrated in the interactive relations between the organization and the environment, in which the responses of the environment to the efforts of the organization have an *adaptive* meaning for the organization.
Perspective 3: The existence of an organizational infrastructure of learning and knowing, through which knowledge is produced, acquired, evaluated and transformed in social relations.

Considered as three possible perspectives for doing research on organizational learning, the third perspective stands out as the most inclusive, as it covers the social construction of a hierarchical structured knowledge base, as well as the organization of a feed back system, related to organizational behaviour. As a point of departure for doing research on WPL, I think that this perspective should stress the following aspects of organizational knowing:

- The formation of a social consensus, concerning what is 'knowledge', and the hierarchical classification of this knowledge base.
- The social differentiation concerning status, power and knowledge, which is the condition for the social construction of hierarchical ordered knowledge base.
- The adaptive feedback processes, through which the organizational processes of knowing are tested and the knowledge implied is evaluated.
- The distinction between stored knowledge, accessible knowledge, and actually used knowledge, as well as the distinction between elements of knowledge, which can be remembered, reproduced and which is transferable to other fields of practice, and those elements that can not be recycled.

As previously mentioned, it is possible to conceptualize knowledge, both as an externalized, objectified structure, and as well as an ongoing activity, embedded in an interactional and relational process of knowing. Following this last perspective, knowing can be conceived as a *situated activity* (Layder, 1997), that is, social interaction taking place in 'focused gatherings' of social actors (Goffman, 1961). What we have in mind, might be conceived as processes of social interaction, reproduced over time, taking place in a context of recognizable social settings and drawing on *contextual resources* (Layder, 1997, p. 80).

These 'learning situations' could be defined as social episodes (see Goffman, 1961; Giddens, 1984; Layder, 1997) of knowing, in which knowledge is produced, reproduced, acquired and used in symmetrical or asymmetrical relations between 'teachers' and 'learners', where somebody is learning something *from* or *with some* 'other'.

As previously mentioned, we refer to the structural components of these situations as the 'infrastructure of knowing' (Blackler *et al.*, 1999), 'learning systems' (Salomon & Perkins, 1998) or 'contextual resources' (Layder, 1997).

The key structural elements linked to the processes of social interaction are tools, techniques, concepts, discourses, procedures, norms and social structures (Blackler *et al.*, 1999; Giddens, 1984; Engeström, 1987). Furthermore the structure is seen as both *enabling* and *constraining* actions (Giddens, 1979, p. 69), like a tool that makes it possible to carry out certain actions and fulfilling certain goals, but at the same time enforces its user to carry out the task in a specific way that is embedded in the structure of the tool. Relations to 'teachers' can make information and techniques stored by the organization accessible and even usable for the 'learners'. At the same time, an asymmetrical relation between teacher and learner might reduce the range of possible alternatives open for the learner.

Learning situations include the evolving of distributed, collective knowledge in social networks, in which the relation between the learner(s) and the teacher(s) mediate between the collective stored knowledge and the competences actually used by the individual.

In focusing on the *control* of the persons involved in relation to the contextual resources, Layder (1997) makes a distinction between three types of resources – 'material resources' such as tools, and physical materials, 'dominative resources' related to power, status and influence in relation to other persons, and 'cultural/discursive resources', 'including practical, technical and interpersonal knowledge and skills' (ibid., p. 81). Combining these types of resources makes it possible to describe and analyze a concrete mix of enabling and constraining elements involved in the learning situation. To sum up, learning situations can be defined as social episodes of interaction, structured by a set of contextual resources, through which the knowledge base of the learners involved is transformed, producing progressive changes of behaviour.

These situations can be described and analyzed, referring to three groups of parameters:

(1) The *frame* of the situation, including (a) the integration – separation between knowledge and behaviour; (b) the organization of the feedback relations between actions of the learners and the response from the environment; (c) the control of the learners and teachers involved in relation to the situational factors such as action, selection and evaluation of knowledge (Bernstein, 1971).
(2) The *relations between 'learners' and 'teachers'*, concerning symmetrical, asymmetrical and reciprocal distribution of contextual resources (such as knowledge, power, status) and functional roles (Bateson, 1936).
(3) The *transformation of the knowledge base*. Including (a) transformations between different forms of knowledge, especially transformations between explicit, objectified forms of knowledge and implicit, practice-embedded forms of knowing, or personal knowledge and collective knowledge (Polanyi, 1966; Nonaka & Takeuchi, 1995; Baumard, 1999). Both Nonaka and Takeuchi, and Baumard are making an important distinction between two central concepts: *knowledge modalities* (for instance, explicit and implicit knowledge) and *ways of transformation*, for the converting of knowledge from one modality to another – like 'awareness', converting individual, implicit knowledge into individual, explicit knowledge, or 'extension', which is converting individual, explicit knowledge into collective knowledge (Baumard, 1999, p. 29); (b) the distinction between learning, which is more or less in harmony, with already existing ways of seeing, doing and knowing, in contrast to processes of learning, which establish some kind of breakdown and reconstruction of established knowledge (Piaget, 1954; Glasersfeld, 1995).

In theories of OL, this distinction has often been conceptualized as a distinction between two levels or contexts of learning, referred to as '*reproductive-* and *developmental* learning' (Ellström, 1992, 2002), '*single-* and *double-loop* learning' (Argyris & Schön, 1978) or 'reproductive and expansive learning' (Engeström, 1987, 2003), all more or less explicitly referring back to Gregory Bateson's well-known distinction between '*Learning I* and *Learning II*' (Bateson, 1973). While the context of reproductive learning is the correction of errors in order to accomplish predefined results by already known methods and solutions, the context of developmental learning is the development of new methods, solutions and even results or goals (Ellström, 2002).

Previously I made an effort to include some of these elements in a model, differentiating between six types of learning situations, half of which include either symmetrical role relations between learners or reciprocal relations between learner and teachers, while the other half include asymmetrical role relations. The other main parameters are explicit–implicit knowledge, and the control to select and evaluate the knowing (Laursen, 2000; Dahl et al., 2001).

Using the model to analyze storytelling in an private enterprise, in order to implement a set of new values in the organization (Laursen, 2005), I did not primarily focus on the question of whether the value was actually implemented at all by this kind of activity. Rather, I was interested in asking 'What kind of learning situation was this storytelling event? Who was controlling the content of the stories? Who decided which stories should be rewarded by applaud, and which should be killed be an awkward silence? And why were most of the stories, rewarded by a positive feedback so dull? What kind of knowledge transformation was the storytelling? Some produced a new story from selected fragments of personal memory, other retold and transformed already existing, 'classical' old stories, which had already been circulating inside the enterprise for ages. Adapting them to this new context, how is it that some of the learners were smoothly included by the task of storytelling, easily offering stories, that turned out to be both entertaining and having value relevance as well? And why were others almost naturally excluded, having no interesting material to offer, and being unable to construct and tell a story? And most importantly: was the learning of how to organize and to perform a storytelling event to be conceived as OL at all? What were the possibilities of transferring the developed knowledge of how to organize such an event to intentions and projects other than the implementation of new values?'

Learning as a perspective: what are we doing?

A group of employees giving mutual collegiate supervision. A consultant encouraging a group of employees to illustrate a certain value. An employee evaluating the ability of her department to implement a set of standards laid down by management in relation to the service rendered to customers. What are we actually doing?

The obvious answer on this question is that we are 'learning', that is, developing knowledge and skills both as persons and as organizations. In many ways this answer is subjectively meaningful and hence satisfactory, while still covering a large number of interesting agendas. In this chapter I have focused on the content of the learning process and especially the different ways of establishing a sense of progression in WPL. The bottom line of OL and WPL seems to be that the companies wants to grow richer and more flexible, while the employees want to grow more competent. It is not impossible that the development of the competencies of the employees sometimes becomes economically rewarding for the company, but in a situation where the content of competencies are defined by standards for doing the job well, controlled by the management, this is not always the case.

References

Abrahamsson, K., Abrahamsson, L., & Johansson, J. (2003). From over-education to under-learning: Qualification structures, changing job skill requirements and work place learning. In *Work and Lifelong Learning in Different Contexts*. Tampere: University of Tampere.

Argyris, C., & Schön, D. A. (1978). *Organizational Learning: A Theory of Action Perspective*. Reading, MA: Addison-Wesley.

Bateson, G. (1936[1958]). *Naven*. Stanford: Stanford University Press.

Bateson, G. (1973). *Steps to an Ecology of Mind*. London: Paladin.

Baumard, P. (1999). *Tacit knowledge in organizations*. London: Sage.

Berger, P. L., & Luckmann, T. (1966). *The Social Construction of Reality*. Garden City, NY: Doubleday.

Bernstein, B. (1971). *Class, Codes and Control*. London: Routledge & Kegan Paul.

Blackler, F., Crump, N., & McDonald, S. (1999). Organizational Learning and Organizational Forgetting: Lessons from a High Technology Company. In M. Easterby-Smith, L. Araujo & J. Burgoyne (eds), *Organizational Learning and the Learning Organization. Developments in Theory and Practice* (pp. 194–216). London: Sage.

Boud, D. (1998). Enhancing learning through Self Assessment. In P. Jarvis (ed.), *The Theory and Practice of Learning*. London: Kogan Page.

Bourdieu, P., & Passeron, J.-C. (1977). *Reproduction. In Education, Society and Culture*. London: Sage.

Dahl, P., Jørgensen, K. M., Laursen, E., Rasmussen, J., & Rasmussen, P. (2001). *Perspektiver på organisatorisk læring*. [Perspectives on Organizational Learning]. Aalborg: Videncenter for Læreprocesser, Aalborg Universitet. VCL-serien, 2001, nr. 28.

Dixon, N. (1994). *The Organizational Learning Cycle. How we can learn collectively*. London: McGraw-Hill.

Durkheim, E. (1915[1968]). *The Elementary Forms of the Religious Life*. London: Allen & Unwin.

Elkjaer, B. (1999). In search of a Social Learning Theory. In Easterby-Smith *et al.* (eds), *Organizational Learning and the Learning Organization*. London: Sage.

Ellström, P.-E. (1992). *Kompetens, lärande och utbildning i arbetslivet: Problem, begrepp och teoretiska perspektiv.* [Competence, learning and work-based education: Problems, concepts and theoretical perspectives]. Stockholm: Publica.

Ellström, P.-E. (2002). *Time and the Logics of Learning. Lifelong Learning in Europe,* 2, 86–93.

Engeström, Y. (1987). *Learning by expanding: An activity theoretical approach to development research.* Helsinki: Orienta-Konsultit.

Engeström, Y. (2003). New Forms of Learning in Co-configuration Work. In *Work and Lifelong Learning in Different Contexts.* Tampere: University of Tampere.

Fiol, C. M., & Lyles, M. A. (1985). Organizational Learning. *Academy of Management Review,* 10(4), 803–13.

Gibbons, M. (1994). *The New Production of Knowledge.* London: Sage.

Giddens, A. (1979). *Central Problems in Social Theory.* London: Macmillan.

Giddens, A. (1984). *The Constitution of Society.* Cambridge: Polity Press.

Glasersfeld, E. von (1995). *Radical Constructivism. A way of knowing and learning.* London: Falmer Press.

Goffman, E. (1961). *Asylums.* Harmondsworth: Penguin.

Hedberg, B. (1981). How Organizations Learn and Unlearn. In P. Nystrom & W. Starbuck (eds), *Handbook of Organizational Design.* New York: Oxford University Press.

Hildebrandt, S., & Brandi, S. (1998). *Lærende organisationer – erfaringer fra danske virksomheder.* [Learning Organizations – Experiences from Danish Companies]. København: Børsen.

Künzli, R. (1998). The Common Frame and the Places of Didaktik. In B. B. Gunden & S. Hopmann (eds), *Didaktik and/or Curriculum: an international dialogue* (pp. 29–43). New York: Peter Lang.

Laursen, E. (2000). Billeder af læring – og udvikling af læringsadfærd i organisationer. [Representations of Learning – and the development of Learning Practices in Organizations]. In A. Christensen (ed.), *Det lærende perspektiv.* [The Learning Perspective]. Aalborg: Aalborg Universitetsforlag.

Laursen, E. (2005): Kan man lære af artige historier? [Is it possible to learn from polite stories?]. In K. M. Jørgensen & P. Rasmussen (eds). *Læring i organisatoriske forandringsprojekter* [Learning in projects of organisational development]. Aalborg: Aalborg Universitetsforlag.

Lave, J., & Wenger, E. (1991). *Situated Learning: Legitimate Peripheral Participation.* Cambridge: Cambridge University Press.

Layder, D. (1997). *Modern Social Theory.* London: UCL Press.

Leadbetter, C. (1998). Welcome to the Knowledge Economy. In I. Hargreaves & I. Christie (eds), *Tomorrow's Politics.* London: Demos.

Nonaka, I. & Takeuchi, H. (1995). *The Knowledge-creating Company.* New York: Oxford University Press.

Pedler, M., Burgoyne, J., & Boydell, T. (1991). *The Learning Company.* New York: MacGraw-Hill.

Piaget, J. (1937[1954]). *The Construction of Reality in the Child.* New York: Basic Books.

Polanyi, M. (1966). *The Tacit Dimension.* London: Routledge & Kegan Paul.

Salomon, G., & Perkins, D. N. (1998). Individual and Social Aspects of Learning. In P. David Pearson & Ali Iran-Nejad (eds), *Review of Research in Education,* 23, pp. 1–24.

Senge, P. M. (1990). *The Fifth Discipline.* New York: Doubleday.

Shrivastava, P. (1983). A typology of organizational learning systems. *Journal of Management Studies*, 20(2), 7–28.
van Hauen, F., *et al.* (1995). *Den lærende organisation*. [The Learning Organization]. København: Industriens Forlag.

Notes

1 In their article, Abrahamsson *et al.* criticize the empirical basis of the so-called 'the more, the better' presumptions of contemporary 'educational expansionists' by pointing out, most convincingly, that over-education and under-qualification seem to operate in parallel, but in different segments of the labour market.
2 In the following I discriminate between the 'learning organization' as a concept for organizational development and 'organizational learning' which in short means a focus on the learning activities within a given organization (see, e.g., Elkjaer, 1999).

6
Reflection in Learning at Work
Steen Høyrup

Workplaces are important sites of learning, and the understanding of learning at work is a field of great interest for both universities and enterprises and which is dealt with in the fields of education, management, psychology, sociology, human resource management, etc. When workplaces are sites of learning it is important to understand that learning is a complex and multifaceted phenomena. The learning involved can be related to knowledge and skills that are demanded by the employer in the specific job function. This can be the basis for creating new work practices and forms of production and for developing increased productiveness and effectiveness of the firm. Learning also involves personal development, which may spill over into civic life and personal lives.

The field of learning theories often accentuates two kinds of learning in the workplace: *implicit* learning and *experiential learning* (Woerkom, 2003). In this perspective, many theories give reflection a crucial role – *reflection is the key to learning from experience* (Kolb, 1984; Boud *et al.*, 1985; Woerkom, 2003). Therefore, our main questions are 'What is reflection and how does reflection contribute to the process of learning at work?' Answers to these questions could form an important basis for fostering reflection and learning at work, recognizing the power and importance of workplaces as sites of learning.

Conceptual premises

The concept of learning
We must criticize the position that considers learning to be a very general and comprehensive concept – integrated in and not separated from thinking and social practice – and possibly superfluous as an

implication of this. We agree that learning should not be objectified as a separate activity that excludes other important and related activities. But instead of merging the concepts with thinking, action and practice, it should be possible on an analytical level to distinguish between thinking, action, social practice and learning as aspects of complex activities. According to Lave, learning is captured as an aspect of social practice. Lave expresses the opinion, that if you conceptualize all social practice as learning, implying that everything is learning, or conceptualize all learning as social practice, implying that everything is practice, then learning has no specific meaning. And that would be an unacceptable loss (Lave, 1997).

Merriam and Clark offer this outline of a learning concept, which makes important cornerstones in the *learning processes* explicit – learning involves: *separation, initiation and return* (Merriam & Clark, 1993). *Separation* is differentiation on an inner level (e.g. identity) and an external level (e.g. attending to new features of the social world). *The initiation* into the new requires finding different ways of structuring meaning, of perceiving the self and the world and social relations and work relations (Merriam & Clark, 1993, p. 130). *Return* is the integration of the whole at a higher level of understanding, and re-engagement with the world in a new way. Learning thus involves taking apart and putting together a structure that is important for our actions, relationships, work and life. Thus, *learning outcomes* may involve:

- expansion of the individual's potential for action, conceptualized in terms of changed possibilities of participation in social practice/ organizational life;
- expansion of personal capability (knowledge, skills and abilities);
- expansion of sense of self and relatedness in relation to the social field; and
- expansion of life perspective, understanding of life or work in general. This is a change in the individual's *frame of reference*, the very basis for the construction of meaning in the individual's experiences.

Learning related to the process of work may be dealt with in two different approaches. First, *formal learning*, in which learning is institutionalized and has become subject to organization for efficiency. Learning is intended and deliberate – people know they are here to learn. Learning may be based on experience, but in often the experience is secondary – semantically transmitted – experience (Jarvis, 1996, p. 77).

The second approach to work-related learning is defined by Woerkom as *the natural learning process*, which is interwoven in the daily work process (Woerkom, 2003, p. 11). Terms often used are 'informal' and 'incidental' learning. We may learn from our experiences without being aware of doing so. Informal learning may be planned or unplanned and the individual may be conscious or unconscious of the learning that takes place. What is crucial to the learning process in this setting is that the most important sources of learning are the challenges of work itself, organization of work and social interactions with other people in the workplace.

The chapter addresses both learning settings: institutionalized learning and natural learning related to work.

Experiential learning

As reflection is often seen as a process facilitating experiential learning, there should be a brief mention here about what seem to be the shortcomings in experiential learning (Woerkom, 2003, p. 37).

Learning outcomes often have the structure of tacit knowledge with characteristics of being personal and context-specific, implying problems of formalizing and communicating, as well as transfer of learning. Learning is usually relearning – a reorganization of prior learning. However, the prior learning may be outdated, no longer correct or even superstitious, and because it has the structure of tacit knowledge, it may be resistant to change.

If tacit knowledge remains unquestioned, learning processes may be supported – through mechanisms of anxiety and defences – in the form of confirmation of misconceptions and prejudices, and learning of errors in performing work tasks. Experiential learning may lead to mere reproduction of existing practice.

How are processes of reflection related to these pitfalls and challenges in experiential learning?

The concept of reflection: first steps in defining the concept

Mezirow understands reflection as an assessment of *how* or *why* we have perceived, thought, felt, or acted (Mezirow, 1990, p. 6). Michael Reynolds contrasts the concept of critical reflection with the more familiar concept of reflection. While reflection focuses on the immediate, presenting details of a task or problem, the hallmark of critical reflection is in terms of *the questioning of contextual taken-for-granted aspects – social, cultural and political – within which the task or problem is situated* (see Reynolds, 1998, pp. 184, 189). As a preliminary definition, I quote here Van Bolhuis-Poortvliet and Snoek from Woerkom:

> Reflection is a mental activity aimed at investigating one's own action in a certain situation and involving a review of the experience, an analysis of causes and effects, and the drawing of conclusions concerning future action (Woerkom, 2003, p. 40).

The root of reflection: the thinking of John Dewey

In Dewey's terms, reflective thought is an active, persistent, and careful consideration of any belief or supposed form of knowledge in the light of the grounds that support it, and the further conclusions to which it tends. It includes a conscious and voluntary effort to establish belief upon a firm basis of evidence and rationality (Dewey, 1980[1916]). Dewey's notion of reflection should here be related to the chosen learning concepts: *Separation, Initiation* and *Return*.

Separation. In Dewey's notion we find two important processes in this category. A necessary precondition for reflection is the *inhibition of action*. Habit does not work with implications of feelings of disturbance and uncertainty. When we act in routinized ways we do not reflect. A second process in separation is *postponement of immediate action*, which is an internal control of impulses. This postponement gives the individual the space to put ends together: the peculiar relation between the active elements of experience – trying and inquiry – and the passive elements, we suffer the consequences of changes caused by our actions; as Dewey puts it.

Initiation. In Dewey's thinking, we see two processes – (1) *defining the problem*, that is *Construction of a tentative concept*. The process of reflection starts with the individual's attempt to define what is wrong in the situation. The individual defines the problem by constructing a tentative conception of the difficulty. The basis for this concept construction is the individual's observations and the individual's investigation of both the situation and the conditions of the situation. The conceptualization of the problem influences further acquisition of knowledge and thinking: (2) *Formation of a guiding idea for action* is the second process of initiation. The analysis and diagnosis of the situation leads to a working hypothesis formed as a tentative guiding idea for action: the individuals elaborate a plan of action.

Return. Two processes belong to this category. *Elaboration of the meaning of ideas in relation to each other*. The tenability of the working hypothesis can be tested in an experiment on the level of thinking, and in this individuals can apply and integrate the available knowledge in their memory. The union of observation and memory is to Dewey the heart of reflection. Reflection thus becomes a conscious and voluntary effort to establish belief upon a firm basis of evidence and rationality. *Testing of the guiding idea in action. Feedback processes are processes of return too.* Here the guiding idea is tested in action by trying to realize it in practice. This is really a process of return. Embedded in the practical testing of the guiding idea is a reconstruction of the situation, that is, the individual-environment relationship. The testing of the hypothesis makes learning possible. It creates a link between the consequences of action and changes created by action on the one hand, and the presuppositions in the hypothesis on the other hand.

Reflection and the outcomes of the learning process

Returning to our concept of learning, the following categories of learning outcome are important:

- Expansion of the individual's potential for action conceptualised in terms of changed possibilities of participation in social practice. This is a learning outcome. According to the theory, the initial problem that initiates reflection becomes resolved by the reconstruction of the situation, and the individual gains increased control over his activity.
- Expansion of personal capability. This is the other main outcome – production of knowledge and beliefs upon a firm basis of evidence. It is the construction of meaning and the construction of new concepts that can be used by the individual in the elaboration and solution of forthcoming problems.
- Development of the individual's *frame of reference*. We also find learning at this deep level in Dewey's notion of reflection. In the elaboration of the meaning of ideas in relation to each other, a coherent system of new knowledge is made and this functions as a new basis for framing new problems.

Contributions from adult education

David Boud gives a thorough account for reflection in learning and is chosen here as a representative for the approach of adult education (Boud *et al.*, 1985). We are in the domain of *deliberate and intentional learning*, where learners are aware that they are learning. Reflection is a form of response from the learner to experience. After the experience, a processing phase occurs – this is the area of reflection (ibid., p. 19.). *Reflection* is conceived as the intervening processes that constitute the link between *experiences*, including elements of behaviour, ideas and feelings, and *outcomes*, including new perspectives on the experiences, commitment to action and readiness for application. Boud *et al.* give this conceptualization:

> 'Reflection is an important human activity, in which people recapture their experience, think about it, mull it over and evaluate it. Reflection in the context of learning is a generic term for those intellectual and affective activities in which individuals engage to explore their experiences in order to lead to new understanding and appreciations' (Boud *et al.*, 1985, p. 19).

Boud points to three elements that are important in the reflective process:

- Returning to experience
- Attending to feelings
- Re-evaluating experience.

Reflection is the learner's elaboration on his experience – typically with the help and support of other learners in the same learning situation – to create what is learning within this frame of reference: new perspectives on experience, readiness for application, commitment to action and change in behaviour. Experience consists of the total response of a person to a situation or event: what he or she thinks, feels, does and concludes at the time and immediately thereafter (Boud *et al.*, 1985, p. 18).

What role do these reflective processes play in learning? According to our conceptual structure of the learning process, we find important elements of *separation*. One is *returning to experience*. In this the individual stands back from the immediacy of the experience – creating a distance to it – and reviews it with the leisure of not having to act on it in real time, recalling what has taken place. It is a split of thinking and action. This is to many authors a crucial process: *Putting experience at a distance enables individuals to be made sense to them.*

Returning to experience can be seen as an important function in learning because it counteracts a serious shortcoming in experiential learning. We can make false perceptions, false implications and in the end false learning. Through this process of reflection, false perceptions can be detected and the learner can view the experience from other perspectives and have the opportunity to look at the event in a wider context compared to the more concrete context in which it was situated. The latter is a clear process of *initiation*. These new perspectives on experience constitute learning.

Another important process of initiation is *attending to feelings*. This process of reflection has two aspects – utilizing positive feelings and removing obstructive feelings. The removal of obstructive feelings is related to learning in the way that it is a necessary precursor to a rational consideration of events. With negative feelings the individual cannot make a thorough examination of the experience. Awareness of positive feelings are important to learning as they can provide the learner with the impetus to persist in what might be very challenging situations and they might facilitate the learner's freedom in moving to different perspectives on his experience. Contrary to this, negative feelings can fix the learner at a single perspective – *return*. This category involves *re-evaluating experience* too, which according to Boud *et al.* is the most important of the three components of reflection in learning. Boud *et al.* describe this important component of reflection thus:

> 'Re-evaluation involves re-examining experience in the light of the learner's intent, associating new knowledge with that which is already possessed, and integrating this new knowledge into the learner's conceptual framework. It leads to an appropriation of this knowledge into the learner's repertoire of behaviour. This can involve a rehearsal in which the new learning is applied mentally to test its authenticity and the planning of subsequent activity in which this learning is applied in one's life' (Boud *et al.*, 1985, p. 27).

We can distinguish between two important functions of reflection in relation to learning. First, reflection implies that old and new knowledge are being integrated in the individual's conceptual framework. The learning consists of a changed conceptual framework in relative harmony. The second function is reflections connection to action. The new knowledge can be the basis for planning of subsequent activity, the learning being applied and tested. Boud states that some benefits from reflection may be lost if they are not linked to action. And it is important that the learner makes a commitment of some kind on the basis of his learning.

What seems to give reflection its distinctive character in relation to learning is the way that it is embedded in thinking and action. On the one hand reflection may involve a split between thinking and action that gives the individual optimal opportunities – through examining his experiences – to change his conceptual frame of reference. But on the other hand reflection also involves commitment to action and testing the new frame of reference through action. Reflection in this way is a dialectic process.

It looks inwards at our experiences, feelings and conceptual frame of reference, and outwards at the situation in which we are going to act. When we consider the interaction of the internal and the external, our reflection orients us for further thought and action. Reflection in this way is a kind of meta-thinking where we consider the relationship between our thoughts and understandings and our actions in a context. At the same time reflection is a social process. This presents us with the possibility of learning.

Learning outcomes influenced by reflection

One outcome is expansion of the individual's potential for action through readiness for application and commitment to action. The other is expansion of personal capability through new perspectives on experience.

We recognize that the concept of reflection developed in the realm of adult education is different from Dewey's concept but also has similarities when compared with this concept. The main differences are the trigger of the reflection process and how action is captured in the complex processes that constitutes reflection. Reflection in adult education is not triggered by an ill-structured situation in which habits do not work. It is a deliberate process that can be initiated and controlled by the teacher in collaboration with the students. And a main point is not the framing of a problem in which action, trying, anticipatory thinking and receiving of feedback are crucial elements. The main process in reflection in the realm of adult education is, as we have seen, *re-evaluating experience* and integration of new knowledge, that is, linguistic transmitted secondary experience into the learner's conceptual framework – a reconstruction of knowledge. The reconstruction of knowledge may involve correction of earlier false knowledge, updating of old knowledge and new perspectives on knowledge. The next step in the learning process is to connect this new cognitive structure to action. In short, the process of reflection is first cognition and then action. Although among these differences we can also see crucial similarities, the concepts of separation, initiation and return work as a way of structuring the processes in both concepts.

The domain of problem solving

Problem solving in this connection should be seen in the perspective that the individual accommodates to a life of continual and rapid change, and most of what is learned in life is the result of our efforts to solve problems. In our thinking, problem solving is a means of constructing, organizing, indexing and extending knowledge (Billett, 1996). Knowledge is constructed by engaging in problem solving activities encountered as part of everyday workplace activities.

Mezirow

Mezirow adds to our understanding of reflection in two ways. First, through his transformative learning concept, and, second, through his description of different kinds of reflection. In Mezirow's *theory of transformative learning*, to learn is very close to *making meaning*. And to make meaning is to make sense of an experience, and to make an interpretation of it. The relation between making meaning and learning is posed this way:

> 'When we subsequently use this interpretation to guide decision making or action, then making meaning becomes learning... Learning may be defined as the process of making a new or revised interpretation of the meaning of an experience, which guides subsequent understanding, appreciation, and action' (Mezirow, 1990, p. 1).

The interpretation – the construction of meaning – takes place in the meeting between the individual's frame of reference and the experience of the individual. The frame of reference is constructed by two psychological structures – meaning *schemes* and meaning *perspectives*. Meaning schemes are sets of related and habitual expectations governing if-then, cause-effect and category relationships as well as event sequences (Mezirow, 1990, p. 2). Meaning perspectives are made up of higher-order schemata, theories, propositions, beliefs, prototypes, goal orientations and evaluations (ibid., p. 2). Meaning perspectives provide principles for interpretation and are, for the most part, uncritically acquired in childhood through the process of socialization (ibid., p. 3). Meaning perspectives seem more complex than meaning schemes and exist in the deepest levels of the personality in terms of being closely connected to the identity of the individual. Mezirow defines reflection:

> 'Reflection is the process of critically assessing the content, process or premise(s) of our efforts to interpret and give meaning to an experience' (Mezirow, 1991, p. 104).

Reflection involves 'stop and think'. The pause may only be a split second in a decision-making process, for example a pause to reassess by asking, 'What am I doing wrong?' Or reflection may involve an *ex post facto* reassessment, to check the decisions we have made. Reflection is what we do when we 'stop and think' about what we do or have done (ibid.). And the relation between reflection and learning this way is:

> 'Reflection enables us to correct distortions in our beliefs and errors in problem solving. Critical reflection involves a critique of the presuppositions on which our beliefs have been built' (ibid., p. 1).

Content reflection and process reflection

In *content reflection*, focus is on the content of the problem or the description of the problem. This is reflection on *what* we perceive, think, feel or act upon (ibid., p. 107). In *process reflection*, focus is on the process, strategy or method followed in problem solving. Process reflection is an examination in *how* we perform these functions of perceiving, thinking, feeling or acting and an assessment of our efficacy in performing them (ibid., p. 108). Content reflection and process reflection can go on in the course of taking action and sometimes afterward (ibid., p. 104). Process reflection can also focus on complicated questions such as, 'Is the logic sound, is the evidence convincing, is the action consistent with my values?' etc.

These two kinds of reflections allow us to assess consciously what we know about taking the next step in a series of actions and consider whether we will be 'on course in doing so' (ibid., p. 117). In relation to the learning process, Mezirow states that content- and process reflections are the dynamics by which our beliefs – meaning schemes – are changed, that is, become reinforced, elaborated, created, negated, confirmed or identified as problems and transformed (ibid., p. 111).

Premise reflection

Premise reflection, equal to critical reflection, is reflection on premises. Premises are special cases of assumptions, of presuppositions. The critique of premises or presuppositions pertains to problem posing as distinct from problem solving. Problem posing involves making a taken-for-granted situation problematic, raising questions regarding its validity (ibid., p. 105).

Ex post facto *reflection on prior learning*

A special kind of premise reflection is *ex post facto* reflection on prior learning. Mezirow points to *ex post facto* reflection – reflecting back on prior learning to determine whether what we have learned is justified under present circumstances – as a crucial learning process, often ignored by learning theorists. In relation to the learning process Mezirow states that premise reflection is the dynamic by which our belief systems – meaning perspectives – become transformed. Premise reflection leads to more fully developed meaning perspectives, that is, meaning perspectives that are more inclusive, discriminating, open and integrative of experience (ibid., p. 111).

What then is the role of reflection in learning?

In the learning process *separation* gets the form of 'stop and think' often caused by an orientation dilemma. *Initiation* is composed of several elements on different psychological levels – *the perceptual level*. Through reflection, the individual pays attention to the situation in which he/she is going to act. What are the important features, what constitutes the problem in the situation in which the individual is going to act? This is giving meaning to the situation, the process of interpreting and re-interpreting the situation at hand, and the premises involved in this. In *self-awareness and feedback processes*, the individual pays attention to his or her own actions and especially the outcomes of the actions, the feedback on actions – 'What am I doing and what are the effects of my actions? What am I doing wrong?' The analysis and understanding of faults can constitute a strong impetus for insight and learning. With regard to *corrections of actions through decision making*, reflection involves 'stop and think' and decision-making is an integrated part of reflection. Decision is the process that links thinking to action. The individual can look back and check the quality of his or hers decisions and the individual can decide how to perform in order to solve the problem. Reflection in this way can be both reactive and proactive in its directness. In *recalling resources*, reflection allows the individual to clarify what he/she knows about the problem, his/her concepts and knowledge and experience of relevance for the problem at hand. What does he/she know about taking the next step in a series of actions, and 'Will I be on course in doing so?'

Return

Reflection gives the individual the opportunity to correct distortions in beliefs and changes to the individual's frame of reference, his/her prepositions and assumptions by which he/she meets the world. The central function of reflection is that of validating what is known. This is learning at the level of meaning schemes in Mezirow's terms. This learning influences the individual's construction of meaning and interpretation of his world in the future.

Learning outcomes

Reflection contributes to learning at different levels:

- *Expansion of personal capability.* Learning is realized on this level. Through reflection the individual validates his/her knowledge, he/she can correct his/her meaning schemes, knowledge and beliefs uncritically acquired in childhood through the process of socialization, and later acquired knowledge. Skills are improved through correction of actions through decision making.
- *Expansion of the individual's potential for action.* Learning takes place on this level because the validated and corrected knowledge is the basis for the individual's actions, and the individual's interpretation of the situation (content reflection), improvement in performance (process reflection) and insight in premises and 'taken for granted' in the situation at hand (premise reflection).
- *Expansion of sense of self and relatedness in relation to the social field.* This goes on through 'recalling resources' and correction and validation of beliefs.
- *Expansion of life perspective, understanding of life or work in general or a more specific and localized understanding.* This is a change in the individual's *frame of reference*, the very basis for the construction of meaning in the individual's experiences. According to Mezirow, reflection may imply validation and construction of knowledge, but critical reflection may cause learning at a more deep level. Critical reflection gives the individual a opportunity to change his/her frame of reference in terms of change in meaning perspectives. This learning constitutes a change in the very fundamental psychological mechanisms by which new learning is constructed and deals with systems and values embedded in the individual's identity.

Schön

Schön's concept of *reflection in action* extends our understanding of the processes of reflection in two crucial areas. The first is the character of the knowledge on which professionals rely when they act in problem situations. The essence of Schön's view is that the application of theoretical knowledge is not essential in professional practice. He rejects the technical-rational paradigm, where professionals' practice takes the form of applied scientific theory. Professionals in their problem solving rely heavily on 'knowing-in-action' (a kind of tacit knowledge) and reflection, especially reflection-in-action. Schön thus coined the term *reflection-in-action* to describe the way various professionals deal with situations of uncertainty, instability, uniqueness and value conflict. These demands and characteristics are those met in most workplaces today. Professionals respond to the problem situation by turning their thoughts back to the process of knowing implicit in their action. *When acting in problem solving the individual attends to a kind of knowledge that is embedded in action.* The knowledge can be conscious or tacit. Schön's theory involves this intimate relationship between knowing and action (Schön, 1983).

How is reflection initiated? When something does not accord with expectations, when we are surprised, we might respond through the activity of *reflection-in-action that occurs at the time of the action*. This is the second main point. In the previous theory's 'stop and think', a split between thinking and action was a cornerstone in reflection. Reflection-in-action is an on-the-spot process of surfacing, testing and evaluating intuitive understandings – sometimes not conscious – which are intrinsic to experience. Reflection-in-action serves to reshape what we are doing while we are doing it.

An empirical investigation tested Schön's main point of view that professionals' problem solving does not have the character of application of theoretical-rational (scientific) knowledge. The result of the investigation was that Schön is not quite right and not quite wrong. Professionals typically use both methods – the rational-empirical paradigm and practice as reflection-in action (Cheetham & Chivers, 2000).

This result is of great importance to our conception of reflection in adult education and problem-solving situations. It seems that two very different kinds of knowledge exist side by side in the individual: a codified language knowledge including theoretical and fact knowledge and a not codified body embedded implicit knowledge. The individual uses both as the recourse basis for action. In this light, reflection can be seen as connecting the two realms of knowledge explicated in the concept of re-evaluating experience, the main process of reflection according to Boud.

Critical reflection

Critical reflection involves a critique of the presuppositions on which our beliefs have been built (Mezirow, 1990, p. 1). In critical reflection, the individual challenges the validity of his presuppositions. In this way, critical reflection is not concerned with the *how* or the *how to* of action but with the *why*, the reasons for and consequences of what we do (ibid., p. 13). Mezirow states that critical reflection may imply learning at a deep level, transformational learning:

> 'Uncritical assimilated meaning perspectives, which determine what, how and why we learn, may be transformed through critical reflection. *Reflection on one's own premises can lead to transformative learning*' (ibid., p. 18).

Critical reflection involves awareness of *why* we attach the meanings we do to reality, especially to our roles and relationships – meanings often *misconstrued* out of the uncritically assimilated half-truths of conventional wisdom and power relationships (Mezirow, 1981, p. 11). Our frame of reference *can be wrong*; individuals can be caught in an uncritical acceptance of distorted meaning perspectives. We make misconstructions of meaning, we can make wrong interpretations of experiences, because we live and make experiences in a culture with a lot of taken for granted.

Reflection may imply reconstruction of knowledge, but critical reflection may imply changes in the very psychological mechanisms that constitute the basis for our interpretations of the world. And this form of learning is not restricted to the deepest levels of personality; it is also related to our social role and social relationships. When individuals engage in critical questioning of conventional assumptions, justifications, structures and actions in their common workplace, they can experience confusion or hostility from their colleagues, and they risk being socially marginalized. They can be seen as subversive troublemakers that make life uncomfortable for the professionals around them. The deep learning from critical reflection implies actions causing conflicts and maybe changes at the social level.

An interesting area of reflection is critical reflection on organizational values. When individuals question and exchange knowledge and understanding about existing organizational values, and the management of the organization creates space for these processes and values these processes as resources for organizational development, then reflection may imply involvement of members of the organization in organizational learning. Reflection builds the bridge between individual and organizational learning and this implies that we may extend our categories of learning outcomes with this dimension.

Conclusions

- From our theoretical analysis, it is clear that *reflection supports learning in counteracting the shortcomings of experiential learning*. The learning outcome of experiential and natural learning may be tacit, personal and context-specific, and can be outdated and wrong and may include uncritically adopted beliefs through socialization. Experiential learning may involve a mere reproduction of existing practice. Reflection makes it possible to validate learning, to make it transparent to the individual, and to question existing practice and organizational values.
- Reflection supports learning in all three phases of learning: separation, initiation and return. Different theories point to different important elements of learning here.
- Reflection contributes to learning at a broad spectrum of learning outcomes: Expansion of personal capability, expansion of the individual's potential for action, expansion of sense of self and relatedness in relation to the social field, expansion of life perspective (changed frame of reference) and organizational learning.
- Through the lenses of reflection learning is *re-learning*. Learning involves reconstruction of knowledge performed by the individual learner. In the conceptualization of this we should refer to Malinen (2000). In reflection, first-order experiences are modified with the help of second-order experiences (Malinen, 2000, p. 85). First-order experiences are, in turn, memory experiences (ibid., p. 67). Second-order experiences are 'immediate', here-and-now experiences loaded with considerable intensity.

Reflection can be seen as an important mode of interaction between first- and second-order experiences. Reflection gives the learner a *temporal psychic distance* through which first-order experiences will come under scrutiny, and the relation between first- and second-order experiences too. In reflection, the split of experience and action gives the individual the possibility of making sense of his experiences.

The violating second-order experience is the cornerstone of learning – the individual gets *a choice*. He/she can defend the familiar way of seeing and doing, – or he/she can modify it. That is to learn. The choice also has a bearing on action. Reflection involves the individual's *choice* in the immediate situation: 'Am I going to modify my actions in order to solve the problem in a more precise or effective way?' Reflection this way involves learning in the sense of *modifying actions*.

Reflection can create a *motivation* for learning. In the process of returning to experience, the individual can assess the gap between first- and second-order experiences. The motivation lies in the optimal amount of discontinuity and the optimal amount of continuity to orient an adult to approach a familiar, but at the same time disturbing, phenomenon with fresh interest, but without arresting learning. *The second-order experience has to provide a learner with something genuinely new*, for implying motivation and learning, but at the same time not too new or too familiar, when compared with first-order experiences. The motivation lies in the personal significance of this combination of first- and second-order experiences. The motivation is crucial for the individual's willingness to explore the inadequacies of first-order experiences.

Motivation is also created through attending to feelings in reflection. The crash between first- and second-order experiences can produce negative feelings. Through attending to feelings, the negative feelings in the learning process can be elaborated and positive feelings can be underlined. Reflection can be *critical*. As mentioned above, one quality of first-order experiences is inadequacy or incompleteness. First-order experiences – the very basis for experiential learning – can be questioned and changed through critical reflection. Critical reflection this way promotes development in the individual's basic frame of reference. This may imply changes in the social field, too. If the critical reflection involves organizational values, organizational learning is a possible outcome.

References

Billett, S. (1996). Towards a Model of Workplace Learning: The Learning Curriculum. *Studies in Continuing Education*, 18(1), pp. 43–58.

Boud, D. et al. (1985). *Reflection: Turning experience into learning*. London: Kogan Page.

Cheetham, G., & Chivers, G. (2000). A new look at competence professional practice. *Journal of European Industrial Training*, 24(7), 374–383.

Dewey, J. (1980[1916]). Democracy and Education. In J. A. Boydston (ed.), *The Middle Works, 1899–1924*, Vol. 9. Carbondale and Edwardsville: Southern Illinois University Press.

Jarvis, P. (1996). *Adult and Continuing Education. Theory and Practice* (2nd edn.) London and New York: Routledge.

Kolb, D. A. (1984). *Experiential Learning: Experience as the Source of Learning and Development*. Englewood Cliffs, NJ: Prentice-Hall.

Lave, J. (1997). Apprenticeship – Learning as Social Practice. *Journal of Nordic Educational Research*, 3.

Malinen, A. (2000). *Towards the essence of adult experiential learning: A reading of the theories of Knowles, Mezirow, Revans and Schön*. University of Jyväskylä.

Merriam, S. B., & Clark, M. L. (1993). Learning from Life Experience: What Makes it Significant? *International Journal of Lifelong Education*, 12(2), 129–138.

Mezirow, J. (1981). A critical theory of adult learning and education. *Adult Education*, 32(1), 3–24.

Mezirow, J. (1990). How Critical Reflection Triggers Transformative Learning. In J. Mezirow *et al.* (eds), *Fostering Critical Reflection in Adulthood. A Guide to Transformative and Emancipatory Learning* (pp. 1–20). San Francisco,: Jossey-Bass.

Mezirow, J. (1991). *Transformative Dimensions of Adult Learning*. San Francisco,: Jossey-Bass.

Reynolds, M. (1998). Reflection and Critical Reflection in Management Learning. *Management Learning*, 29(2), 183–200.

Schön, D. A. (1983). *The Reflective Practitioner. How Professionals Think in Action*. New York: Basic Books.

Woerkom, M. (2003). *Critical Reflection at Work. Bridging individual and organizational learning*. PhD thesis, University of Twente, Print Partners Ipskamp, Enschede.

7
How to 'Bridge the Gap' – Experiences in Connecting the Educational and Work System

Lennart Svensson and Hanne Randle

There has been a great deal of talk about lifelong learning and competence development during the past few decades. But very little has happened for blue-collar employees or for those with a weaker position in the labour market. In fact, the amount of training paid for by employers has diminished during the last decade in Sweden (LO Report, 2001, 2002).

There are many reasons for the failure of lifelong learning, but some of these have to do with deep institutional obstacles in and between the educational and the work systems. The focus of the first section of this chapter is on obstacles and limitations on a system level – 'the gap' between the educational system and the work system.

Workplace learning may be seen as a way to 'bridge the gap' between the two systems. We make a brief presentation of a flexible method for organizing learning at work. Some preliminary results from different research projects are presented.

A central issue that is discussed is how local changes in workplace learning can have an effect on a systems level. The necessity of supporting mechanisms is put forward and different change strategies are described. The role of an R&D centre is analyzed in this context. A networking strategy to support learning between workplaces is discussed as an alternative to both a 'top down' strategy and a 'bottom up' strategy.

Obstacles to workplace learning – two different systems that do not interact

The strategy to support lifelong learning in Sweden has been *supply-based*, that is, anchored in the educational system. Different attempts have been made in 'pushing for' formal education. The ambition is to reach a greater number of people with formal training. Different reforms, programmes and projects have been initiated to support lifelong learning. What conclusions can be drawn from these attempts? We draw attention to the following positive aspects (Svensson, 2003):

- opportunities to continue studies later in life when one is more motivated or ready for (or forced into) a new occupation
- different alternatives (folk high schools, learning centres, net universities) which make learning more flexible – both for individuals and companies;
- the importance of different supporting systems – loans, subsidies, the right to leave for studies, job centers, learning centers, etc.
- the positive outcome of practical programmes for training at the workplace (qualified vocational training and apprentice programs), but these programmes are very limited in scope and directed at young people.

However, a closer look at these indicates several problems. The level of participation in higher education is very unequal – a mirror of the class system. There is a problem with integrating the different components in the educational system from an individual and a company perspective. The system seldom functions in practice, neither for the individual worker nor for the small firm. It is too much a top-down system, which is designed linearly and not adapted to real life and the dynamic of a rapidly changing society. The lack of a holistic perspective makes it difficult for an individual and for a small firm to take advantage of all the opportunities that are open. Most of all, it is not a system for lifelong learning in which work, living and learning are combined in a flexible and sustainable way.

We think that the vision of lifelong learning cannot be fulfilled with supply-based programmes that try occasionally to diffuse learning in 'small pieces'. Instead, learning must be a continuous activity in working life for all employees. There are huge differences between firms in respect of learning and training in different sectors of the labour market. Small firms that try to compete with low prices in highly competitive markets are less interested in formal training and lifelong learning, especially if there is a surplus of labour power (Randle & Svensson, 2002). But there are also many companies for which continuous training of their employees is a necessity. Increased competition necessitates quick changes in relation to markets and a high quality of products and services. These companies have to introduce a new more flexible, decentralized, integrated and customer-oriented organization, which presupposes a high level of competence among their employees. The growing problem of recruiting new personnel is putting additional pressure on the employers for more training and education.

If there is a need for more training, why is the demand so low? We will explain the failure of organizing lifelong learning by the gap between the educational and work system. This division between the two systems is well documented and analyzed in different reports – both by researchers and public authorities (SOU, 1994, p. 48; SOU, 1996, p. 64; SOU, 2000, p. 28; Ellström, 2002; Svensson & Åberg, 2001).

In Figure 7.1 we present different organizations and authorities represented as two different 'towers' – the 'educational tower' and the 'work

The gap at system level

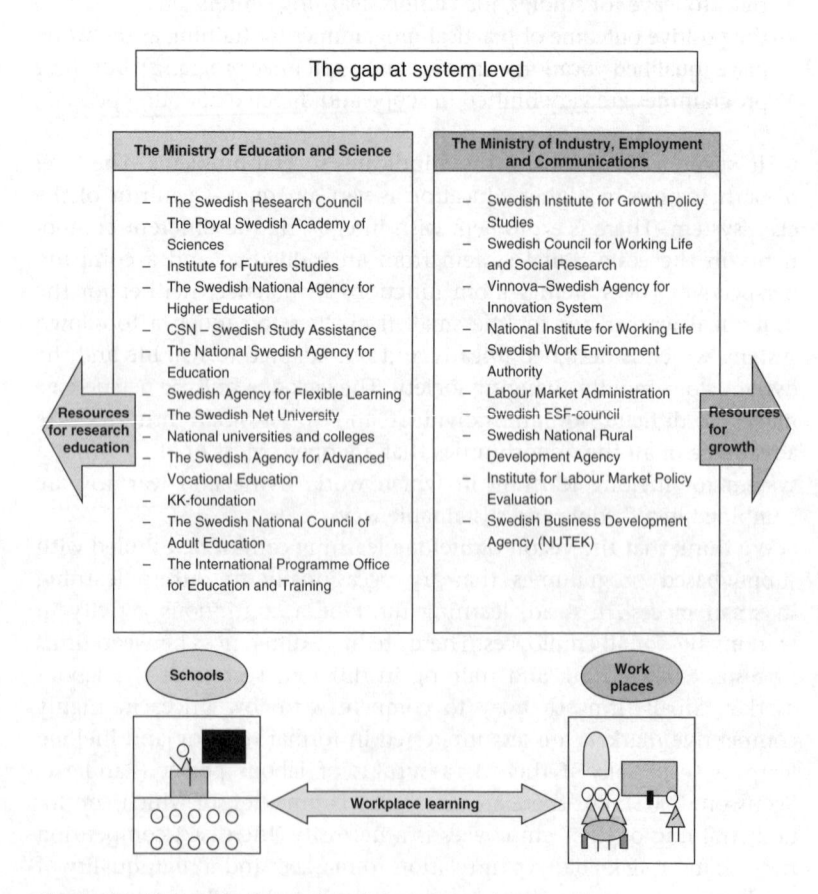

The Ministry of Education and Science	The Ministry of Industry, Employment and Communications
– The Swedish Research Council – The Royal Swedish Academy of Sciences – Institute for Futures Studies – The Swedish National Agency for Higher Education – CSN – Swedish Study Assistance – The National Swedish Agency for Education – Swedish Agency for Flexible Learning – The Swedish Net University – National universities and colleges – The Swedish Agency for Advanced Vocational Education – KK-foundation – The Swedish National Council of Adult Education – The International Programme Office for Education and Training	– Swedish Institute for Growth Policy Studies – Swedish Council for Working Life and Social Research – Vinnova–Swedish Agency for Innovation System – National Institute for Working Life – Swedish Work Environment Authority – Labour Market Administration – Swedish ESF-council – Swedish National Rural Development Agency – Institute for Labour Market Policy Evaluation – Swedish Business Development Agency (NUTEK)

⇐ Resources for research education

Resources for growth ⇒

Schools — Workplace learning — Work places

Figure 7.1: The gap between the educational and work system

tower' – as a 'gap' on a system level. The 'educational tower' represents a hierarchy – from the Department of Education down to the local schools. The 'work tower' represents in a similar way a hierarchy of its own – from the Department of Industry down to small local firms. These 'towers' represent two institutionalized systems – an educational system and a work system – each with its own logic, conflicting interests, diverse habits and practices, different time perspectives, disparate ways of assessing knowledge and having a dissimilar socio-spatial design. The two arrows in Figure 7.1 illustrate the divergent tendencies of the two systems. On the one hand, most of the teachers do not want to leave the secure classrooms and their routinized way of teaching and assessing knowledge. On the other hand, most firms are not interested in investing in formal education for their employees. They prefer learning that is useful 'here and now'. Many employers are afraid of developing a more general employability among their employees, because they will run the risk of losing them to their competitors.

The educational system works from a strong power position because of its traditions and its monopoly over the certification of knowledge. What is happening in a situation where the needs of individuals and companies are subordinated to an inflexible educational system? One important effect is the lack of integration between informal and formal learning, and also a split between individual and organizational learning. The lack of coordination between the economic and educational systems makes the outcome of different training programmes very limited – both for individuals and firms. The participants cannot practice what they have learnt. This lack of practical use can explain the low interest in education among many employers and workers. They have often adopted an instrumental attitude to learning. They want their investment in learning to have short payback periods. The individual worker and the companies are interested in a combination of practice and theory, a multidisciplinary approach, an equal communication structure, a flexible system, a problem-based pedagogy. Such learning will not be offered by the educational system.

In this situation the employers turn to private consulting agencies, which are open for a dialogue to make the training more flexible and accessible. A supply-based model to implement learning is replaced by a *demand-based* model. But the courses that are available on the market are often standardized, not tailor-made for the individual worker or the small firm. It is more profitable for the supplier to use a standard programme designed for bigger companies. These market deficiencies point to the limitations of a demand-based strategy for lifelong learning.

It will be the strongest consumers who determine the content and form of the learning programmes. The needs of the small firms and the employees with a weaker position on the labour market will be unheard by the market mechanisms. To compensate for these limitations in the demand model different national programmes have been initiated. Many of them focus on small companies and – such as Objective 3 in the European Social Fund. But the courses organized in these – and other similar – programmes are seldom part of the educational system. Participants will not get an accreditation for what they have learnt. The gap between the two systems is left intact.

We have presented a sociological analysis of the difficulties of lifelong learning, which focuses on conflicting institutional systems. The educational and work systems seem to be part of two different worlds that do not interact. The gap between the two systems will heavily restrict the outcome of both the supply-based and the demand-based strategy. Both have an 'either/or' perspective, that is, their focus is either on the work system or on the educational system. We think that the *interrelationship* between the two systems is of crucial importance if the 'gap' is to be 'bridged'. There has to be a 'merger' of some sort, which must be made on equal terms. But such an interaction will be difficult to organize because of the traditional separation and the power hierarchy between the two systems.

The complementarity of formal and informal learning

To establish an interaction between the work and educational system we have to acquire a deeper understanding of learning – both of formal learning (in the educational system) and informal learning (at work). In Figure 7.2 we have illustrated how a combination of formal and informal learning will lead to competence, which can be seen as an interrelationship between theoretical and practical knowledge.

As used here, the concept of formal learning refers to planned, goal-oriented learning that occurs within the boundaries of particular educational institutions (schools, colleges, universities, etc.). The concept of informal learning refers to learning that occurs in everyday life or at work. Everyday learning occurs spontaneously for the most part, but it can to some extent be organized – by work rotation, work exchange, field trips, benchmarking network meetings, supervisoral input, mentorship support, guidance etc. This learning is often referred to as non-formal.

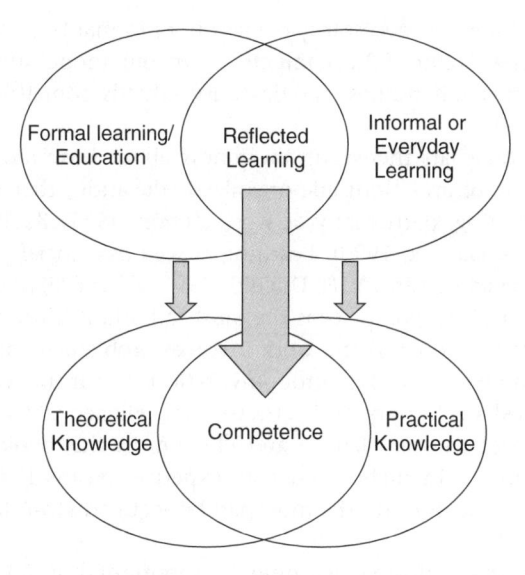

Figure 7.2: Competence as a result of reflective learning

In modern work life, neither formal education nor everyday learning alone is sufficient – both are needed and the two modes of learning should be viewed as complementary. Formal learning can be effective only if backed up by informal learning (Boud and Garrick, 1999). Conversely, informal learning could be made more effective if supported by formal learning. This is the case because informal learning presupposes conceptual tools and explicit knowledge about the task and the work process that cannot normally be acquired through experiential learning at work. Rather, the knowledge that is acquired through informal learning has typically a tacit character (Ellström, 1992). The experience-based learning also runs the risk of being adaptive, reproductive and being of a single-loop character (Svensson & Åberg, 2001).

It is precisely this combination of formal and informal learning that results in *reflective learning* (see Figure 7.2). The distinction between formal and informal learning is important in order to emphasize that learning is not to be equated with education. Education offers explicit, theoretical knowledge so-called propositional knowledge. This can go on without the participants learning anything that can be used in a practical way in everyday life or at work (Ellström, 1996, p. 87). *Competence* is not something that necessarily comes out of formal learning – that is, education (see Figure 7.2). Competence in our model also includes skills – in terms of handiness and dexterity – that is, something that has to be practised.

There is today an increasing awareness about how most learning occurs outside of and alongside organized education, that is, through everyday learning, particularly at work (Schön, 1987; Boud & Feletti, 2001; Boud & Garrick, 1999). Learning is seen as a social process and situated in practice (Brown & Duguid, 1991; Gherardi, 1999, Lave & Wenger, 1991). The workplace is the most important learning environment for many people. If the work involves problem solving and the organization gives room for autonomy, reflective learning can develop at work based on inquiry and reflection (cf. Elkjaer, 2001, 2003; the contribution of Laursen, Jensen and Ellström in this book). The way companies invest in niches and core expertise means that the task-oriented expertise must for the most part be acquired at work (Aronsson & Sjögren, 1995).

We agree that informal learning is important but not sufficient neither for the working life of today or tomorrow. It must be complemented with different forms of planned education. Modern, integrated production systems mean intellectualizing work, that is, increased demand for theoretical knowledge and intellectual skills – such as the ability to discover, identify and solve problems. The new production systems put greater demands on the integration of different types of knowledge, that is, the ability to discover correlations and understand the whole work system and the production flow. Expertise thus presupposes a combination of practical and theoretical knowledge (see Figure 7.2). The trade unions in Sweden stress the importance of formal learning as a way to increase the general employability of employees (LO Report, 2001, 2002). To produce general and theoretical knowledge is a legitimate objective, especially when the demands in working life are often of a short-term and instrumental character.

One may wonder why so many well-educated researches show such a poor interest in providing formal training for people with a low level of education. And why is the interest among the educational providers so low when it comes to experimentation and innovation with new forms of learning outside of the educational institutions? Innovative practices seem to take place on the outskirts of the system boundaries, where institutional control is weaker. A small learning centre together with some 'practitioners' have developed in recent years 'model' for workplace learning, which should give researchers in pedagogy and educational providers something to think about.

A flexible model for workplace learning

We now make a brief presentation of this model of workplace learning – derived from the so-called *Blästerugn Project*. This project has been described by those centrally responsible for educational systems and labour representatives as one of the most interesting and innovative projects in Sweden (SOU, 1998: 84). This 'model' for learning is quickly being diffused to different sectors and parts of the Swedish labour market. There is also a growing interest from outside of Sweden for this flexible way of organizing learning at work.

The model has been developed by a learning centre in a small municipality situated in an old industrial region in the middle of Sweden – Lindesberg. The aim of this project has been to make education *accessible* to small- and medium-sized companies and their employees by using a flexible means of organizing learning. The courses taught are at the upper secondary level of education – often in Swedish, English, mathematics, chemistry, production technology, etc.

The Blästerugn Project has the following important points of departure (Svensson & Åberg, 2001):

- A mini-learning centre is equipped with computers and equipment for distant communication (internet, video conferences, etc). A mini-learning centre can be designed in a flexible and cost effective way. Large investments are not necessary. To get started only one or a few computers are needed. Smaller companies can borrow equipment from the learning centre. The mini-learning centre is a meeting point for decentralized learning – study circles, e-learning, distance courses, and communication with the teachers.
- In a preparatory module, the participants are given an introduction – both technical and pedagogical. They also obtain an accreditation of their prior knowledge. An individual action plan is provided which tries to combine the individual goals with the content of the training programme.
- A supportive social structure for learning is organized. Facilitators or tutors – that is, interested employees – are trained to provide technical, social and pedagogical support to the learners. Study guides and interactive study materials are provided to motivate the participants and to stimulate reflective learning. The management and

union are involved to provide organizational and financial support to the learning process.

Some examples of workplace learning

In our research group (APeL, see below) we have evaluated workplace learning organized according to this model in different situations – in a hospital, in the explosives industry, in a training programme for bus drivers, in an engineering shop, in the food industry and in a carpentry shop. We summarize the preliminary results of these case studies below.

The effect of this model for learning is increased *accessibility* and flexibility. Accessibility is not only a matter of the equipment for communication being used, but also and more important is the opportunity for on-the-spot supervision, the setting up of the education in a flexible way, alternative forms for assessments, etc. Flexible learning should be independent of time and space and adapted to the preferences of the participants – in terms of pedagogy and means of learning. The participants can borrow a computer and work from home if they wish. They can work at their own speed and choose the level of complexity with which they are comfortable.

The relationships between the participants and the teachers are more equal compared to relationships in traditional formal training. At work, the learning can take place in a situation where the learner feels secure and can relate the content of the teaching to a situation about which he/she has a better knowledge than the teacher. The layout of a mini-learning centre is also different from the traditional teacher-centred classroom. It is based on teamwork and informal communication.

The formal part of the training is important. Although many of the employees have a negative experience of the school system, they often want to have an accreditation of their knowledge. The courses taught are usually part of different programmes in the upper secondary school. In this way the learners do acquire a more general level of employability. They will not be stuck in their companies for life, but can choose to work in another firm or continue with their studies outside work. By using courses from the educational system, they are also free of charge, which is an important supporting argument both for the employees and the employers.

The idea behind this model of workplace learning has been to pursue such learning during slack production periods, but this has been difficult to accomplish. Most learners and their supervisors did prefer a schedule, which would make it easier to plan the learning. In some firms the employees were paid for half of the time for their studies, but they had to invest their leisure time in respect of the other half.

The overall organization of the learning process was of crucial importance. The different ingredients of the model – accreditation, guidance, support from a tutor and a teacher, technical assistance, study materials, Internet communications, team learning – had to be combined into a 'system' for workplace learning.

The interest in taking part in education did increase rapidly when the training was carried out at the workplace. At the hospital, more than 150 employees (out of a total of 600) have been involved in different courses during the first year. From the interviews we can discern different explanations for this growing interest in learning. Some point to the practical advantages of not losing time for travelling to and from the school. The support from the team and the tutor are other explanations for the new interest in learning. Or it could be said that their latent interest in learning was released when it was available at the workplace in a new form.

In our research, we are trying to analyze to what degree informal and formal learning are combined in these examples. According to some research, workplace learning provides the learner with better possibilities to integrate informal and formal learning (Boud *et al.*, 1985; Boud & Garrick, 1999). When education is carried out at work, the learner can practise what is being taught. Being *competent* is to be able to accomplish something, to bring about results in a certain situation, which includes practical skills (Ellström, 1992). We learn by doing things – by moving forward through testing and experimenting (Dewey, 1989), but this presupposes autonomy for action and a time for reflection (Ellström, 1996). The theory can give an input to reflection by creating a necessary distance from the daily practice in which adaptive learning is dominant. In this way a developmental learning can be possible (Ellström, 1992). We learn together with others – through dialogue and collaboration. In workplace learning the team or the study group can be an important factor for learning and reflection (Boud *et al.*, 1985; Boud & Garrick, 1999). In a school, such cooperation between the students is often considered to be cheating.

What were the outcomes of the case studies in these respects? Did our result confirm the research presented above? In a learning programme for truck drivers, the use of experience-based learning has meant an increased interest among the learners in theoretical subjects. The use of mathematics was obvious when the learners in a real situation had to calculate how to load and secure their load according to new EU rules.

The use of trigonometry was made visible to some carpenters in a factory because of the new demands for quality in their production of equipment with complicated angles. In the training of nurses in a municipality, it was much easier to develop and assess their social competence in a real situation. In some cases it has meant that some of the learners had to leave the programme. Social care work cannot be learnt in an artificial theoretical context – such as the classroom. A competence has to be developed and assessed in a real context.

One objective of the model presented above was to integrate *individual* and *organizational learning*. To make the education useful, it has to be a part of the daily operations at the workplace. What an individual has learned must be practised. The ambition to accomplish this integration of individual and organizational learning was not fulfilled. There was no strategy to realize this ambition. The organizational hierarchy often put limits on the individual to experiment and to solve problems at work. Another obstacle was the lack of time for reflection and support in the downsized and heavily rationalized organizations. This deficit in the implementation of this model points to the necessity for a deeper involvement of management and supervisors in the planning and carrying out of the learning programmes.

In sum, the model investigated has many promising elements that can function as a bridge between the educational and work towers. By starting from the workplace, the idea of lifelong learning becomes more realistic – at least for some sectors of the labour market. For most people it is more natural to go work than to go to school. In this way, formal learning can be a natural and continuous part of our lives. We have seen many practical advantages in the model presented, but the most important question remains unsolved – how to make formal learning more problem-based and useful for the participants and the companies. In many of the courses, the traditional ways of teaching were still intact. If workplace learning is just a way to move the classroom into a new environment, not much has been gained. Opportunities to practise and reflect in the workplace together with the team and in a dialogue the management were seldom available.

Workplace learning will not in itself close the gap to the educational system. It depends on how it is organized. Much remains to be done in the future by means of bridging the systems together. The model presented here has to be developed further if workplace learning is to become a way of 'bridging the gap'.

The outcome of our research points to the possibilities with workplace learning when both management and the employees are involved in the organization of the learning process. It becomes more natural to use a problem-based pedagogy and the workplace will be a more relaxed atmosphere for learning for employees with a low level of formal education. At the workplace the relationship between the participants and the teachers will be more equal and reciprocal.

What strategy can be used?

Changes like that we have described above at a few workplaces will not be enough 'to bridge the gap'. Such a voluntaristic approach, primarily based on the involvement of the participants in different and isolated workplaces, will not be sufficient. These changes – even if they are successful in the short run – will not be diffused by themselves and will leave the structures of the two systems intact. The examples presented above seem to be a success in many ways, but the diffusion of such examples is complicated to organize and needs a long-term perspective.

The traditional bureaucratic way to implement changes is not an alternative. A centrally organized 'top-down' strategy has often been used in trying to make the educational system more effective. But this is not a solution for developing the 'inner life' of the educational system – only the formal aspect of it. Such a central strategy will result in a centralization and standardized solutions. It will also lead to strong resistance from the teachers and headmasters. The local adaptations will be made more difficult, as will local involvement. The dynamics in the change process will be lost. Workplace learning is not something that can be organized 'top-down' linearly and mechanistically. The demands for flexibility, local adaptability, and continuous development mean that a nationally steered programme for workplace learning is doomed to fail (Svensson & von Otter, 2000).

So, what are the alternatives if neither a change 'from below' nor 'from above' is the solution for innovative and sustainable change of the two systems? A *networking* strategy is an alternative in creating a sustainable change process (Björn et al., 2002). In a network, different workplaces can learn together and support each other in the change process. Different local initiatives can be coordinated and integrated, both on a horizontal and vertical level. A necessary 'critical mass' can be organized, which makes it easier for the participants to have an impact on a structural level in society (Gustavsen et al., 2001; Gustavsen et al., 1995). External professional support can be provided if different actors share the costs. Such external support is often a necessity in creating a developmental learning between the participants in a network. There is otherwise a major risk that the relationship in the network will be of a polite and uncritical kind (Svensson *et al.*, 2001).

Supportive structures are needed

Institutional changes to the educational and work systems will not come about by themselves. Such changes will need involved participants; pressures from different groups (both the learners and the companies), changes in attitudes (both among the teachers and students), legislative reforms, and experimentation with new methods for teaching, examination, accreditation, guidance, etc.

Such a complicated change process has to be supported in different ways. What kind of external support is needed to support innovation and diffusion of new models for workplace learning that combine informal and formal learning? Which organizations will offer developmental support and where should this responsibility be located? Learning centres are organized in many municipalities to promote adult learning by making the education more accessible and flexible but their resources for developmental work are very limited.

Developmental support must include different levels in order to be effective. The point of departure for cooperation and support is the *regional* level, but the local workplace will be the basis for experimentation and innovation. National and international connections are important in order to affect the framework factors as well as for financing, promulgation, expert support, etc. Creating 'vertical' learning processes between actors on the local, regional, national and international level is a necessity to change the structures – rules, regulations, and restrictions – of the two systems. This vertical learning will be a part of *developmental coalitions* to support innovation and a sustainable change process. Creating networks between networks (of learning organizations) as a part of an innovative system is a way of making development and diffusion a simultaneous process. In this way a necessary *critical mass* is organized (Gustavsen *et al.*, 2001).

We will not try to prescribe a solution to how the 'gap' between the two systems should be 'bridged', but something new is needed. We think that there have to be different actors to promote change and stimulate an interaction between the two systems on different levels – the local, regional, national and international levels. To illustrate this need for independent actors we will present how an R&D centre for workplace learning is functioning. The aim is not to examine, evaluate or give prominence to the operations in this centre. Instead, the objective is to discuss how developmental support for workplace learning can be organized to achieve breadth and breakthrough power.

The thoughts on how external support for workplace learning might be achieved have taken concrete shape at APeL (www.apel.nu),[1] a regional research and development centre. APeL is located in Lindesberg, a small municipality in a traditional industrial area of Sweden. We want to be close to the companies in the region and we prefer to be outside the university system to be able to act in a flexible and interactive way. Connections with different universities are well developed. APeL's operational idea, which is based on the discussion we have presented above, can be summarized as:

- To initiate and give support to local and innovative projects with a focus on workplace learning. One way to give this support is to organize 'horizontal' learning networks between workplaces, which develop new learning methods.
- To use *interactive* research to support reflection and analysis as a part of a joint learning among the participants and the research group (Svensson *et al.*, 2002).
- To scientifically evaluate, analyze and document interesting developmental projects and study programmes.
- To give support to local and regional collaboration between different actors in the area of education and work. One such project is being organized in a county. The idea is to bring all educational providers together for cooperation and strategic decision making.
- To contribute to information dissemination as well as knowledge and opinion building. We have organized or actively participated in about fifty seminars or conferences during the last three years.
- To take part in strategic discussions about lifelong learning. We have been involved in work groups, committees, decision-making bodies, funding organizations, etc. in trying to promote workplace learning as a part of a strategy to 'close the gap' between the two systems.

Some final reflections

How can lifelong learning be actualised and become more equally distributed? We have focused our analysis on a 'gap' between the educational and work systems. Our point is that workplace learning *can* provide the means to radically change conditions for the scope and content of adult education by combining informal and formal learning and in this way 'bridge the gap' between the educational and work system.

We have presented a model for organizing workplace learning. This model for workplace learning radically questions traditional education – regarding time, place, work form, pedagogy, means of communication, supervision, the teaching role, etc. If the workplace is transformed into a learning arena a problem-based and experience-based pedagogy can be applied. Informal and formal learning can be combined as well as individual and organizational learning. But much remains to be done if the visions implicit in this model are to be fulfilled.

But institutional changes will not come about by themselves. Local experimentation, political pressure, informal networking, professional support and interactive research will all be needed to implement a new policy of lifelong learning. We think that regionally based R&D centres can be one way to support changes of this complicated nature. It is too early to value our own efforts to 'bridge the gap' on these higher levels (see above), but a network has been created between participants from the two systems.[2]

We have focused on the workplace as an arena for learning, well aware of all the shortcomings and limitations of this perspective – in terms of inequalities, segmentation of the labour market, short-sighted instrumental attitudes, etc. But these obstacles and a more structural analysis have been dealt with elsewhere (see Svensson, 2003; Svensson et al., 2003; Svensson & Larsson, 2004). In this chapter – which is of a more tentative character – we have tried to be constructive and visionary.

There are of course other ways to 'bridge the gap'. Life-wide learning is not restricted to either the educational or work system. It is built on an individual motivation for development and learning. Every year, 1.8 million Swedes take part in study circles! At the same time we talk about the problems of motivating people for studies!

If we start from what is actually going on in a natural and spontaneous way in society, we will find the mechanisms for combining living, learning and working. But as the researchers have to explore these innovations together with the people involved, that is, by using interactive methods.

References

Aronsson, G., & Sjögren, A. (1995). *Samhällsomvandling och arbetsliv*. [Societal change and work life]. Stockholm: Arbetslivsinstitutet.

Björn, C., Ekman-Philips, M., & Svensson, L. (2002). *Att organisera för lärande*. [To Organize for Learning]. Lund: Studentlitteratur.

Boud, D., Keogh, R., & Walker, D. (1985). *Reflection: Turning experience into learning*. London: Kogan Page.

Boud, D., & Garrick, J. (eds). (1999). *Understanding Learning at Work*. London: Routledge.
Boud, D., & Felletti, G. (eds). (2001). *The Challenge of Problem-based Learning*. London: Kogan Page.
Brown, J., & Dugiud, P. (1991). Organizational Learning and Communities-of-Practice. Toward a Unified View of Working, Learning and Innovation. *Organizational Science*, 2(1), pp. 40–57.
Dewey, J. (1933[1989]). *The Later Works, 1925–1953, Volume 8. Essays and How We Think*. Carbondale: Southern Illinois University Press.
Elkjaer, B. (2001). The Learning Organization: An Undelivered Promise. *Management Learning*, 32(4), 437–52.
Elkjaer, B. (2003). Social Learning Theory: Learning as Participation in Social Processes. In M. Easterby-Smith & M. Lyles (eds), *Handbook on Organizational Learning and Knowledge Management*. London: Blackwell.
Ellström, P.-E. (1992). *Kompetens, utbildning och lärande i arbetslivet*. [Competence, Education and Workplace Learning]. Stockholm: Publica.
Ellström, P.-E. (1996). *Arbete och lärande. Förutsättningar och hinder för lärande i dagligt arbete*. [Work and Learning. Prerequisites and Obstacles to Learning in Daily Life]. Stockholm: Arbetslivsinstitutet.
Ellström, P.-E. (2002). *Workplace Learning, Reflection, and Time*. Linköping Centre for Studies of Humans, Technology, and Organizations: Linköping University.
Gherardi, S. (1999). Learning as Problem-driven or Learning in the Face of Mystery. *Organization Studies*, 20(1), pp. 101–24.
Gustavsen, B., Finne, H., & Oscarsson, B. (2001). *Creating Connectedness. The Role of Social Research in Innovative Policy*. Amsterdam: John Benjamins.
Gustavsen, B., Hofmaier, B., Ekman-Philips, M., & Wikman, A. (1995). *Utvecklingslinjer i arbetslivet och Arbetslivsfondens roll*. [Developmental Strategies in Working Life and the Role of the Fund for Working Life]. Stockholm: Arbetslivsinstitutet.
Lave, J., & Wenger, E. (1991). *Situated Learning: Legitimate Peripheral Participation*. Cambridge: Cambridge University Press.
LO (Trade Union Confederation, Report) (2001). *Kompetensutveckling*. [Competence development]. LO-facken i Göteborg.
LO (Trade Union Confederation, Report) (2002). *Utbildning – för tillväxten, jobben och rättvisan*. [Education – for Growth, Jobs and Justice]. Stockholm: LO.
Randle, H., & Svensson, L. (2002). *Lifelong learning – a fiction or reality*. EU-report, Learnpartner, University of Leeds.
Schön, D. (1987). *Educating the Reflecting Practitioner*. San Francisco: Jossey-Bass.
SOU (1994:48). *Kunskap för utveckling*. [Knowledge for Development]. Betänkande av utredning om kunskapsbildning i arbetslivet. Stockholm: Allmänna Förlaget.
SOU (1996:64). *Livslångt lärande i arbetslivet – steg på vägen mot kunskapssamhället*. [Lifelong learning in Working life – Steps on the Route towards the Knowledge Society]. Utbildningsdepartementet.
SOU (1998:84). *DUKOM, Flexibel utbildning på distans*. [Flexible Education on a Distance]. Utbildningsdepartementet.
SOU (2000:28). *Kunskapsbygget 2000 – det livslånga lärandet*. [Knowledge Building 2000 – Lifelong Learning]. Slutbetänkande från Kunskapslyftskommittén.
Svensson, L. (2003). Lifelong Learning – A Clash Between a Production and a Learning Logic. In C. Garsten & K. Jakobsson (eds), *Learning to be Employable*. London: Palgrave.

Svensson, L., & Åberg, C. (2001). *E-learning och arbetsplatslärande*. [E-learning and Workplace Learning]. Stockholm: Bilda Förlag.

Svensson, L., & Larsson, K. (2004). Workplace Learning – A Way to Organize Reflection? In D. Boud, P. Cressey & P. Docherty (eds), *Reflection and Learning at Work* (forthcoming).

Svensson, L., & von Otter, C. (2000). *Projektarbete – praktik med teori*. [Project Work – Practice with Theory]. Stockholm: Santérus förlag.

Svensson, L., Brulin, G., Ellström, P.-E., & Widegren, Ö. (2002). *Interaktiv forskning – för utveckling av teori och praktik*. [Interactive Research – For the Development of Theory and Practice]. Stockholm: Arbetslivsinstitutet.

Svensson, L., Jakobsson, E., & Åberg, C. (2001): *Utvecklingskraften i nätverk. Om lärande mellan företag*. [The Strength of Developmental Networks. About learning Between Enterprises]. Stockholm: Santérus förlag.

Svensson, L., Randle, H., & Åberg, C. (2003). *Organizing Learning Between Learning Organizations*. Paper presented to the 3rd International Conference on Researching Work and Learning, July 2003. Tampere.

Notes

1 APeL is short for Workplace Learning Based on Experience. During its first three years, operations have been carried out in project form with different sources of public funds. Twelve people work at APeL, four of whom are doctoral students. The total budget per year is 25 million Swedish krona. APeL is a part of the Swedish National Institute for Working Life.

2 This network is called 'The academy for flexible learning' (AFL – Akademin för flexibelt lärande). It is financed by the EU programme Objective 3.

8
The Workplace – a Landscape of Learning

Klaus Nielsen and Steinar Kvale

The following outline of a workplace landscape of learning is one way of charting some of the learning resources outside of the current educational system. Whereas learning in schools has been extensively researched, workplace learning has enjoyed less attention from educational researchers. The purpose of this chapter is to describe key learning resources at the workplace. Vocational students tend to prefer learning their profession in the workplace rather than at school. In the dual system of vocational training in the Scandinavian countries, students spend part of their four years of training in a workplace and part of it at school. In a Danish questionnaire survey, the majority expressed a preference to learning their profession in a workplace rather than at school (Nielsen, 2003a). Similarly, a Norwegian study found that more than 90% expressed how they preferred the workplace to the school (Mjelde, 2003).

These findings are rather remarkable in several respects: (1) teaching is not the primary purpose of the workplaces, yet the students prefer to learn their profession in the workplace; the learning that takes place is rather a side effect of participating in collective work tasks; (2) the work situations, which the students prefer as learning arenas, have often been criticized for exploiting the apprentices as cheap labour by assigning them routine tasks with no learning value; (3) training in the workplace is undertaken by masters and workers without any pedagogical education – still the students prefer learning the profession from them rather than from teachers in vocational schools.

The vocational students' strong motivation for learning in the workplace inspires one to take a closer look at the nature of workplaces as learning arenas. There are also other reasons today to examine the learning potentials of the workplace. Thus, in Scandinavian vocational training there has in recent years been a scholastic tendency to substitute workplace learning with school learning and school-based work practice. In contrast to this, with regard to increasing demands upon learning in a knowledge-based society and economy, the current educational policy of the European Union is to move beyond the formal learning of the school system and include non-formal learning in workplaces as well as formal learning in everyday life contexts. So far, the formal school learning has dominated our understanding of 'real' learning, whereas the EU Memorandum (2000) on lifelong and life-wide learning emphasizes the need for stronger implementation of the enormous learning resources outside of schools.

The workplace may mainly appear as a practical field of application for the basic theoretical knowledge that is acquired in school. Furthermore, educational research strongly emphasizes the attributes of individual learners, whereby less attention has been given to the nature of the manifold situations in which learning occurs. Educational, and in particular psychological, research on learning has also tended to postulate the existence of internal cognitive processes in order to explain learning; in contrast, we refrain from constructing inner mental representations to explain the multiple relations of the learners to the world. In addition, educational research has often assumed that learning depends upon teaching, and has focused on formal, intentional and reflective types of learning.

We wish instead to focus on non-formal types of workplace learning by applying the metaphor of a learning landscape.[1] This is a landscape in a general sense, not some national park where nature is ideally untouched by human hands, but a cultural landscape inhabited and shaped by human beings through hundreds or thousands of years. We move attention away from the individual habitants of the landscape and try to capture the very aspects that make the landscape habitable, and the paths, which the habitants follow through the landscape (it is worth noting that the etymological meaning of 'learning' contains spatial implications, that is, to gain experience by following a track – presumably for life) (Nielsen, 1997). Our attention has shifted from the attributes of individual participants to the aspects of the environment that make learning possible. This decentralization implies a movement from individuals who learn in isolation to communities of practice where learning occurs. Furthermore, introducing the landscape metaphor is an attempt to move beyond a rationalistic conception of learning by instead bringing out non-scholastic modes of learning that take place without formal instruction. These modes of learning have existed for thousands of years; humans learned to live and work before formal schools were introduced. The many subtle types of learning in the environment tend to disappear when perceived through the formal lenses of school learning. We assume that extensive descriptions of the resources in a learning landscape and the modes of inhabiting a landscape will reduce the need to resort to inner cognitive processes in order to understand learning. Our starting point is the living and changeable relations, which we as individuals enter into with other people, as well as tools, work procedures and routines in the various learning communities.

Before outlining features of the workplace, which make it a rich landscape of learning resources, we wish to exemplify our environmental approach by considering learning from another area, one which may be the most complex learning task in a person's life. A child learns its mother tongue by participating in an environment replete with learning resources. In the family, the child is surrounded by and participates in a linguistic community. The child learns through listening, imitating and by being corrected by parents and siblings. The child lives in a rich linguistic environment in which it can observe and listen to different language users, and simultaneously has the opportunity to practice, test, succeed or fail in the use of its linguistic competences in communication with others. There is a close interplay in the family in which the child's gradual linguistic progress attracts attention, is acknowledged or corrected, ranging from babbling to preliminary speech, which is only understandable to the parents, to when the child finally becomes a competent language user and can communicate outside the family. Regarding the linguistic landscape of learning in families, its efficiency is impressive.

Basically, in the family all children learn to use language at a functional level, that is, they master a language in such a way that their integration in society becomes possible. Although, human languages are a very complex learning object, a normal child's language learning proceeds without any intervention from professionally trained speech pedagogues or learning psychologists. Parents and siblings are able to support the linguistic competencies of the child to a workable level without courses on grammar and syntax or the latest theories from developmental psychology and linguistics. The complex cognitive task of learning a mother tongue is rather a side effect of how the child learns to become part of a family community.

The metaphor of a learning landscape takes its point of departure in the learning-based theory of Lave & Wenger (1991). Their socially based perspective sees learning as part of a process of becoming a member of a community of practice. To claim that learning is socially based also means that learning is an aspect of one's activities in the world. Learning is not primarily something we do beforehand here, in order to apply it later, over there. Learning is regarded as people's participation in an ongoing social practice and is a process of constructing an identity – becoming somebody in a community of practice. In this perspective, learning as socially situated focuses on learning in its everyday practice, and not as something that exclusively happens at certain times and in certain locations, nor primarily in formal school settings.

We now turn to workplace learning, which is generally a side effect of participation in production. We outline the learning resources in a learning landscape at complex and varied workplaces. First, we describe key structures in the landscape which new vocational students or apprentices encounter upon entering the workplace. Second, we describe their personal learning horizons by following the learners on their trajectories through the workplace's learning landscape.

The landscape of learning at work

By focusing on the landscape of learning, we attempt to anchor learning in specific life contexts. The focus is on collectively shared work activities rather than on individual learning processes. We focus on the descriptions of how people participate and learn in relation to a community of practice that they are about to become part of by seeking to develop a sense of belonging as well as identifying with this community. Furthermore, we wish to point out that learning is related to body, habits, and use of tools, which entails a type of knowledge that is difficult to formulate verbally.

Three main dimensions of the landscape of learning are outlined: learning in a community of practice, learning through participation in practice, and learning through assessment of practice. The focus on learning in communities of practice is primarily taken from situated learning theory (Lave & Wenger, 1991). This discussion has a stronger emphasis on the European apprentice-like types of learning in the workplace, and with a more explicit emphasis on learning through assuming responsibility in relation to the community. The types of learning and, in particular, the types of assessment, have been developed in connection with the authors' research project on apprenticeship and vocational training. Some key features of apprenticeship learning were discussed from a situated perspective in an earlier article (Nielsen & Kvale, 1997). The metaphor of a learning landscape was worked out on the basis of empirical research of learning in the Danish dual system of vocational training. A group of researchers studied a wide field of workplaces – ranging from bakers, blacksmiths, carpenters, to shop assistants, social workers, nurses and web designers. The main results of the studies, which encompassed interviews, field observations and a questionnaire, are reported in two Danish anthologies (Nielsen & Kvale, 1999, 2003).

In Figure 8.1, the community of practice and some of the learning and assessment resources, which new apprentices encounter at the workplace are described, based on the above-mentioned empirical data. This formalized presentation of a learning landscape might contribute to highlight the many resources of learning existing in local work situations. We now describe in more detail key aspects of the workplace landscape of learning.

Learning in a community of practice

Learning occurs as participation in a community of practice. The term 'community of practice' relates to the participation of subjects together with others, when participants share a common understanding of what they do and what it means to their lives and to the community. To learn in practice is of crucial importance if the workshop, shop, company, enterprise or department wants to survive. A school is organized and

---

Learning in a community of practice
- To learn in a community of practice
- To make visible and grant access to learning
- To learn by assuming responsibility for the community

Learning through participation in practice
- To learn through practice and performance
- The body as a learning subject
- To learn through observation, imitation and identification
- To learn about and with tools

Learning through assessment of practice
- Assessment through consequences
- Assessment through use
- Assessment through increased responsibility
- The assessment situation as visualization of a profession's quality standards

---

Figure 8.1: Learning resources in the learning landscape

divided in relation to given subjects of a discipline, whereas a workplace is organized in order to complete certain assignments in the production. The apprentices thus have to take part in several different work operations at the workplace. They have to empty the rubbish, clean, pick up mail, clean the dishes, and sweep the floor. Learning in the workplace entails becoming part of the culture of the workplace. The apprentice has to learn the rhythm, the jargon at the workplace, and show that he/she is capable of participating in the various inter-human relations in order to gain access to the more professional tasks.

For the community of practice it is essential that the workplace as whole functions – the learning processes of the apprentices are secondary. In a school community, in contrast, it is essential that the individual student learn the knowledge of the discipline as it is outlined in the school curriculum.

In a workplace, many different people from whom he/she can learn, support an apprentice's learning process. The apprentice is situated in a multi-generational environment and encounters a variety of different learning resources in the job situation. An important part of workplace learning is for the apprentice or student to find the person who masters the specific part of the learning process that the apprentice is to learn. In a school, the pupils are divided into classes in which everyone is at the same level and, thus, some of the learning potential that exists in a manifold multi-generational environment is discarded. In other words, the school and the workplace as communities of practice are organized differently.

To understand that learning happens in a landscape of learning leads to focusing on the organization of the learner's community of practice. To which learning resources does the apprentice or the student have access? And which barriers prevent access to learning resources? Do apprentices have the opportunity to observe the more experienced practitioners work, and maybe consult with them? Are they restricted to the same assignments in the majority of their trainee period, or is there variation in the assignments they are taught? Questions such as these are raised when focus is on the correlation between learning and the organization of the communities of practice.

Learning has often been comprehended as a hierarchical one-way process in keeping with an educational assumption that learning is a consequence of teaching. In descriptions from the activities of the workplace, learning is situated in a multi-dimensional network of social and material resources. In the workplace, learning takes place in a criss-cross of relations between the experienced and inexperienced employees. The following emphasizes some of the interrelations in which workplace learning takes place.

To learn from above. In principle, the master is an expert of the craft, whose skilful performances the apprentices need to approach. The master is a role model and responsible for the apprentices' training. However, from our studies we find that the master is often barely visible in the workplace; he is mostly in an office away from the working processes, although he makes regular, short inspections of the workplace. It is typically the workers who are responsible for the production and for the day-to-day training of the apprentices.

To learn from the person next to you (neighbour learning). Much learning takes place as neighbour learning, that is, the apprentice learns form a more experienced apprentice next to him/her. Nielsen (2003a) describes how more experienced baker apprentices actively introduce new apprentices to the work tasks. The new apprentices may struggle to understand the masters' and workers' demands and may be afraid to ask for help or clarification. In that context, the more experienced apprentices can serve as interpreters of the requirements for the new apprentices. The inexperienced apprentices can, as a spin-off for the experienced apprentices, take over some of the more tedious routine assignments, and the experienced apprentices can advance to more challenging assigments.

To learn from below. Learning can also occur from below, when the experienced workers learn from the inexperienced. Shop assistant apprentices who arrive directly from school may pass on the latest knowledge of merchandise to the shopkeeper (Aarkrog, 2003). Some apprentices proudly report how they have learnt about the latest computer programs at school, which they then teach to the master and workers at the workplace.

To learn from the outside. The apprentices form their own communities across or outside the traditional workplace communities. Tanggaard and Elmholdt (2003) describe how electrician apprentices create 'moonlight' communities with other apprentices as a supplement to the traditional training in the workplace. In these informal communities the apprentices compare competences, and it is here the apprentices learn the prestige that goes with the various work assignments. Tanggaard and Elmholdt conclude that the apprentices gain a sense of belonging to the trade by participating in these moonlight communities. In terms of understanding the progression of the individual's learning processes in multiple relations at the workplace, we need to focus on responsibility.

The concept of responsibility is brought to light in order to emphasize the relational and social dimensions of the learning process. By relating learning with responsibility, the learning process is seen as mutual interaction and as active dialogue between individual and environment. In other words, responsibility is seen as being responsible for what one does in relation to others. To have learned something means being capable of doing something responsibly. By emphasizing responsibility as a central element in the practical learning process, the learning process comes to involve being responsible, sharing responsibility and feeling responsible.

Being responsible. A substantial part of workplace learning is related to the fact that the apprentice is held responsible for a part of the production, which also means that he/she has to consider him or herself as part of a large unit. This is expressed in how the apprentice is not only responsible for own learning, but also faces a responsibility in relation to others within the company. Learning takes place as a movement from an 'I' perspective to a sense of 'we'.

Sharing responsibility. To participate responsibly also refers to a competence dimension, in which the individual as part of the learning process gradually improves in order to live up to and complete his/her assignments. The learning task is completed when the student or apprentice is properly capable of fulfilling the demands of the craft, which are required in order to fulfil an assignment, and the apprentice is capable of assuming the assigned responsibility.

Feeling responsible. Learning as participation involves an emotional aspect. There is a movement away from merely being present in several contexts to developing a sense of belonging to the community of practice of which the person gradually becomes a part.

Learning through participation in practice

Here, learning is used in a broad sense as a process in which the student changes his/her participation from just taking part to becoming a responsible participant in a community of practice. This emphasis on participation and responsibility differs from conceiving learning as primarily an acquisition process (see Elmholdt's (2003b) discussion of the 'acquisition' and 'participation' metaphors of learning). To understand learning as acquisition suggests that the outer social world is incorporated in an inner mental world, and only this process is seen as genuine learning. When the primary focus is on the individual's acquisition of the outer world, the common social world dissipates. We wish, as an alternative, to emphasize that learning first and foremost consists of taking part in and becoming a member of a given community or culture.

A socially situated concept of learning is not confined to the formal and intentional learning in schools, but also includes what is often defined as socialization, namely, the learning process in which children and young people play an active, involved and responsible part in the characteristic behaviour patterns, norms, and values in their surrounding society. This includes unintended learning and co-learning, which take place as part of activities such as work, and does not have learning as its primary goal.

If we look at the learning that takes place in practical situations, the learning may rarely be the result of direct teaching. Learning is incorporated in daily activities, whereby one hardly notices that learning takes place. At this point learning is indirect; it is a side effect when completing existing assignments.

An important element is that when learning happens through participation of practice, the individual apprentice is 'thrown into' practical assignments. The apprentices are first thrown into different assignments, after which they later on develop an understanding for the context and the meaning of the assignments. In traditional schools, students are seldom thrown into different assignments. They are usually taught the principles and theoretical background first, whereby they gain an understanding of what they need to do in order to complete the given assignments.

Another aspect of learning through participation of practice is that the apprentices themselves have to be active and search for learning occasions in order to utilize existing learning resources in the workplace (cf. Becker, 1972). In our study there are several examples of how apprentices make workers or masters aware of the fact that they need more demanding work assignments.

The learning processes in a workplace can be rather invisible. The carrying out of an assignment may appear as a daily routine, without being seen as learning. Imitation of other participants in a community of practice, and also identification with more experienced agents of the subject takes place unintentionally. Learning through bodily action and by use of tools is incorporated in the daily contact with the surroundings, and learning may take place without a deliberate plan for learning. It may, first, be when new apprentices or students enter the workplace that the person in question experiences that he/she has learned something.

In the manual tasks of a profession, the hand is the dominant part. The body is the learning subject. The hands and the rest of the body are rather absent in educational theory because learning is primarily understood as an intellectual activity. In schools, the body has simply been deported to the practical subjects such as woodwork, sports, home economics, and art, which are traditionally low-status subjects within the educational area. The pedagogical practice in many schools is often based on the deskbound and listening student, whereas in the workplace the active, moving body is learning; the apprentice moves from area to area for different assignments in his/her learning process. In our studies of vocational training, we discovered that some apprentices, when they return to school, find it almost painful to sit on a chair for so many hours, because they are used to moving around and using their body every day in the workplace. The physical routines in a workplace are resources, and among the participants it is unnecessary every day to negotiate everything over and over again. In many cases practitioners rely on bodily feelings and intuition instead of on calculated analyses of a given problem.

Imitations and routine work play a central role when addressing issues of learning in workplaces. Generally, today, educational researchers accentuate innovative learning and ignore how innovation is rooted in familiar routines and traditions. Performing odd jobs and routine assignments may be viewed as a way of gaining access to a workplace culture, in which the apprentices learn to accept a shared responsibility for the workplace and become accepted members of the work community. In addition, performing routine assignments provides the new apprentices with an opportunity to obtain a general understanding of the various work processes (Museaus, 2003). Needless to say, performing only routine assignments throughout the whole period of workplace training is of little value to the apprentices.

However, we do not regard imitation and innovation as opposites. In a comparative study of a shipyard and an IT company, Elmholdt (2003a) thus finds that both types of learning are important. In some workplaces the reproductive learning processes are prevalent, offering little room for innovation. In other workplaces innovation is high on the agenda, excluding routines that could secure important know-how being implemented in the workplace. Elmholdt describes how both imitative, reproductive and creative innovative learning processes are important when learning the different task of a shipyard and an IT company.

The relative value of imitative and creative learning depends on the context. For example, in schools innovative learning is appreciated in the students' Danish essays with regard to choice of words and style, while innovative spelling may be seen as a case of dyslexia, and a school psychologist may need to be consulted. Imitative learning does not necessarily lead to mechanical copying. Apprentice bakers report how they often compare various skilled experts' ways of performing certain work processes, such as making white bread, rye bread or Danish pastry, and then compound their own style of doing things as a central way of learning (Nielsen, 2003b).

In most workplaces, tools and equipment are dominant parts of the organization of the place. Screwdrivers, computers, hammers, briefcases, adjustable spanners, etc., hang on the wall, lay on the table or stand on the floor. On an immediate level of experience, these tools address us in the daily performance of working assignments: when a mechanic sees a loose screw in the body of a car, it immediately becomes evident which screwdriver to use. To a certain extent one could say that the tools are active participants in the landscape of learning, and the wordless communication between the apprentice and the tool often contains elements of learning. The organization of the workplace itself has a meaning for the learning process. The order in which the tools are placed at the workplace, for example, in a garage, enables the mechanic, with a single look, to find the appropriate tool with the right dimension needed in order to complete the task. The tools and their positions in the room mean that there are parts of the work process with which the apprentice does not have to be deliberately concerned. Within a school context, the pupil's memory is central to problem solving and the organization of the classroom rarely supports their problem solving and learning.

Learning through assessment of practice

The survival of a workplace depends on the quality of its products. So, ideally, anyone who participates in the process of production is responsible for the quality of the product. The apprentice's work is frequently checked to assess whether it fulfils the expected professional standards. If the quality is unsatisfactory and mistakes have been made, it may have consequences for the entire community of practice. In other words, in a community of practice the shared responsibility for the production also involves a responsibility for others' learning. Praise, recognition or 'positive feedback' make the apprentices grow through their own self-knowledge, whereas criticism, triviality or 'negative feedback' is experienced as hurtful. In both cases, emotional involvement plays an important role in the learning process.

The assessment aims of the individual apprentice's work pertain to its value for the work community. This means that actions are assessed in terms of their usefulness, providing the assessment with a crucial role in the process of learning. When the apprentice is responsible for making a product, it is through the product that his/her process of learning is assessed. Is the table straight? Are the tiles even? Does the bread rise? These types of evaluations are made instantly as an integrated part of the work process in which it is decided whether a carpenter's, a tilemaker's or gardener's skills are sufficiently consolidated, when considering what he/she has produced.

Professional assessments are part of the social structure in a workplace, because the apprentice often spends substantial parts of his/her training with a skilled worker. He/she functions both as a model to the apprentice and as the one who constantly keeps an eye on the quality of the apprentice's production. Several apprentices mention that they prefer the personal assessment at the workplace to the more impersonal and abstract assessments at school. In a safe workplace, the apprentices themselves can freely test their skills without criticism. In the course of their training period, the apprentices gradually become capable of assessing their own and other workers' professional skills, whereby the professional, independent assessment becomes dominant in their working lives.

Our actions have consequences for others in a community of practice. They acknowledge or invalidate the value of our acts. Older colleagues may assess the product with a brief comment, possibly just with a nod or a shake of the head. A significant type of assessment may take place with hardly any verbal comments on the task performed, by assigning the apprentice to tasks that demand greater responsibility. The recognition for a job well done is directly met by letting the apprentice participate in more complex and significant parts of the work process. In the apprentices' work descriptions, an assessment that leads to increased responsibility plays an important role. The different ways in which the apprentices participate in the work processes can be illustrated as a ladder of increasing responsibility (Wilbrandt, 2002). The apprentices move from the lower steps up in a continuous, and mostly tacit assessment process. Figure 8.2 illustrates the apprentices' increased responsibility on this ladder of tasks.

Figure 8.2 contains a slightly modified version of Wilbrandt's (2002) description of workplace evaluation as a ladder of tasks with increasing responsibility, starting from simple routine tasks, such as sweeping the floor, to more demanding tasks under the supervision of a skilled worker, to performing the tasks alone, and finally with full responsibility for the tasks and directing the work of the new apprentices and performing tasks 'outside'. The assigned tasks and the applied tools indicate which level of responsibility the apprentice has obtained in the workplace community. To evaluate means etymologically to ascertain

Tasks

Steps

Task	Step
Work independently on assignments 'outside' of the workshop and managing the work of other apprentices.	
Work alone (without skilled workers) on complex tasks; the result of the work is unknown.	6
Work alone (without skilled workers) on easy routine tasks; the apprentice knows the procedure and expected result.	5
Perform day-to-day tasks of the trade, as instructed by skilled workers.	4
Observe skilled workers work on complex work tasks, tasks, which display the skills of the craft.	3
Perform simple minor tasks (run cables and wires); the apprentices take care of activities, which require no particular skills belonging to the trade.	2
Perform simple apprenticeship task (e.g., sweeping floor, cleaning, stocktaking), which are not specific to the trade.	1

Figure 8.2: The apprentices' ladder of increasing responsibility

the value of something – to the apprentice the level of responsibility for tasks, which are of real value to the workplace, is the supreme evaluation of his progress towards becoming a master of his profession.

Learning barriers in the workplace landscape of learning

So far, the many learning resources in the workplace have been discussed. Some barriers to learning in the workplace also ought to be mentioned briefly (see Nielsen & Kvale, 2003; Wilbrandt, 2002). Thus, learning in a workplace is prevented if the apprentice is denied access to learning resources within the craft, be it due to lack of skilled practitioners or of access to work alongside experienced craftsmen and observe their work. Maybe the apprentices are assigned non-qualifying routine tasks with minimal learning throughout their apprenticeship. Furthermore, in several areas, companies are moving from craftsmanship production to more specialized and also automated types of production, which reduces the opportunities to learn the entire craft in a workplace. Piecework can in several workplaces be a barrier to learning because tempo rules the work, allowing little time to instruct new apprentices in the more qualified areas. Further, lack of feedback and of recognition of work, makes it difficult to acquire skills. Whether such barriers play a significant role will to a large extent depend upon the organization of the workplace. The tension between potential and limitations of learning through work is, however, important to keep in mind.

The personal learning horizon

We now turn from the more or less common features of the workplace landscape of learning to the individual paths, or 'trajectories' (see Dreier, 1999), which novices follow through the landscape of learning. This also means that participation in the landscape of learning must be seen in relation to the apprentices' personal learning horizons, of which we consider some common aspects. It is, particularly, aspects regarding identity that play a significant role in connection with learning processes (Nielsen, 1997).

Emphasizing the personal learning horizon, highlights how the temporal learning process obtains its significance from the future context in which it is imagined. That is, what motivates the learning process is not primarily underlying needs, drives, inhibitions or repressed conflicts, but rather ideas about a certain future within a certain craft. Thus, the learning has a temporal dimension to it, whereby a certain career as, for example, a blacksmith, baker or engineer, places a horizon on the learning process. In the actual tasks to be learned, the learning process is not the primary aim, but a specific professional identity is. Thereby, an extra dimension is introduced in the landscape of learning in which also the apprentices' visions for the future determine what is perceived respectively as learning resources or barriers.

Figure 8.3 presents resource aspects of the apprentices' personal learning horizon regarding trajectories of learning towards an identity as a craftsman. In line with our a relational approach to learning, the individual apprentices' learning will be presented as personal trajectories of learning in which identity is an active, specific project that takes shape from the individuals' participation in different communities of practice (Nielsen, 1997).

- Learning directed at establishing an identity in the community of practice
- Available positions in the community of practice
- Strong professional role models
- A general recognition of the profession in society

Figure 8.3: The personal learning horizon

Learning directed at development of identity

One consequence of considering learning as participation in communities of practice is that the learning process is directed at making the individual a part of these communities. Learning is not merely about acquiring specific individual skills or obtaining academic knowledge, but also encompasses the experience of context and values; the learning process involves full and complete participation in specific communities of practice in which the participants' existence and future is at stake. Therefore, it is necessary to include the learners' own perspective on what they are doing.

One reason why so many apprentices prefer to learn in the workplace rather than at school, can be seen in light of how they identify with the workplace where their future lies, and not at school. In other words, the apprentices orient themselves in the learning process towards what is valuable for their future. What is important for the apprentices is not necessarily the amount of skills and knowledge, but how knowledge relates to their future in terms of work.

Apprentices' personal learning horizons differ and their developments towards a professional identity follow rather diverse trajectories, where they actively seek to coordinate and combine their participation in the different communities of practice into a coherent self-understanding. This will be exemplified by presenting central features in the vocational apprentices' trajectories of learning in our study. One group of apprentices identify with their craft. Here strong identification models play a vital role to the apprentices' personal learning horizons. It may be close identification models, for example, uncles or cousins, who work within a trade, and who through their personal example make the trade attractive. Also, the media's exposure of certain professions plays a role. For example, television programmes about cooking automatically focus on chefs who appear as strong role models. Social or economic aspects of completing a professional education constitute other learning horizons. There are apprentices who wish to be part of a work community in the workplace for social reasons, or they may be directed towards a job where they have the opportunity of making good money. A further learning horizon can be found when some apprentices aim for further education, and thereby see the training in the craft as a step to further education, for example, blacksmith apprentices who want to use their education to study at Denmark's Technical University.

Our point of presenting these personal trajectories of learning is that they help determine what are considered significant resources of learning by the individual apprentice or student. For example, the apprentices with a craft-dominated learning horizon find that they learn more in the workplace. They want the knowledge that they bring from at school to be easily transferred to the work practice in which they will later participate. The apprentices whose personal learning horizon involves further education expect to a higher extent to be shown theoretical tools at the vocational school, which will make them understand the processes behind the work functions in practice. They participate in a different manner in both training and school tuition than do apprentices with a craft-dominated learning horizon. The different personal learning horizons help determine what the apprentices perceive as essential with regard to learning both in workplace and school communities of practice.

Conclusion

This chapter has outlined abundant resources of learning in the workplace. The plenitude of options for learning in the workplace makes it understandable why vocational students generally prefer to learn their profession in the workplace, rather than at school. Of key importance is the membership of a working community and the possibilities of identification with competent skilled workers and masters of the trade, to develop and identify with a trade. The strength of the workplace as a learning arena, suggests some caution with regard to current trends of making vocational training very academic.

This chapter has focused on learning resources in the workplace and has not addressed the better researched learning resources at school. With the increasing importance of theoretical types of knowledge in many professions today, the relation of learning at school and at work becomes a key issue. To promote training for the crafts and professions today, more specific analyses are needed of the types of knowledge that are best learned in school and in the workplace respectively, an issue which involves the optimum interaction between theoretical and practical training in a craft and a profession. We hope here, as a supplement to the many studies of learning in school, to have contributed with an outline of the potentials of workplace learning.

References

Aarkrog, V. (2003) Læring i detailhandlen. In K. Nielsen & S. Kvale (eds), *Praktikkens Læringslandskab*. København: Akademisk Forlag.
Becker, H. S. (1972). The School is a Lousy Place to Learn Anything in. *American Behavioral Scientist*, 16, 85–105.

Dreier, O. (1999). Psychotherapy in client's trajectories of participation in social practices. In C. Mattingly & L. Garro (eds), *Narratives and the Cultural Construction of Illness and Healing*. Berkeley: University of California Press.

Elmholdt, C. (2003a). Kreativ læring er ikke nok. In K. Nielsen & S. Kvale (eds), *Praktikkens Læringslandskab*. København: Akademisk Forlag

Elmholdt, C. (2003b). Metaphors for learning: Cognitive acquisition versus social participation. *Scandinavian Journal of Educational Research*, 47(2), pp. 115–31.

EU Memorandum om livslang læring. Bruxelles. 2000; at <http://us.uvm.dk.videre/voksenuddannelse.dk/livslanglaering/memorandum.pdf>.

Greene, M. (1978). *Landscapes of Learning*. New York: Teacher College Press.

Lave, J., & Wenger, E. (1991). *Situated Learning: Legitimate Peripheral Participation*. Cambridge: Cambridge University Press.

Mjelde, L. (2003). Hvad skal jeg med teori, når jeg skal være trykker. In K. Nielsen & S. Kvale (eds), *Praktikkens Læringslandskab*. København: Akademisk Forlag.

Museaus, P. (2003). Forefaldende arbejde – uddannelse eller udnyttelse. In K. Nielsen & S. Kvale (eds), *Praktikkens Læringslandskab*. København: Akademisk Forlag.

Nielsen, K. (1997). Musical Apprenticeship: Trajectories of Participation at the Academy of Music. *Journal of Nordic Educational Research*, 17, 160–169.

Nielsen, K. (2003a). Når eleverne selv skal sige det. Resultater fra en spørgeskemaundersøgelse. In K. Nielsen & S. Kvale (eds), *Praktikkens Læringslandskab*. København: Akademisk Forlag.

Nielsen, K. (2003b). Lærlingelære i bageriet. In K. Nielsen & S. Kvale (eds), *Praktikkens Læringslandskab*. København: Akademisk Forlag.

Nielsen, K., & Kvale, S. (1997). Current Issues of Apprenticeship. *Journal of Nordic Educational Research*, 17, 130–140.

Nielsen, K., & Kvale, S. (1999). *Mesterlære – læring som social praksis*. København: Hans Reitzels Forlag.

Nielsen, K., & Kvale, S. (eds) (2003). *Praktikkens læringslandskab – at lære gennem arbejde*. København: Akademisk Forlag.

Tanggaard, L., & Elmholdt, C. (2003). Det er ikke snyd at abe efter – Forsøg med ekspert-og sidemandsoplæring på en malerskole. In K. Nielsen & S. Kvale (eds), *Praktikkens Læringslandskab*. København: Akademisk Forlag.

Wilbrandt, J. (2002). *Vekseluddannelse i håndværksuddannelser. Lærlinges oplæring, faglighed og identitet mellem skole og virksomhed*. (UVM 7–355). Uddannelsesstyrelsens temahæfteserie, 2002, nr.14.

Note

1 The expression 'learning landscape' is borrowed from Maxine Greene's book *Landscapes of Learning* (1978). Inspired by Merleau-Ponty, she speaks of landscape in a temporal dimension, in the sense that people are founded in their personal histories. The extended use of the landscape metaphor in cultural contexts today can be seen as expressing a development from focusing on the individual and its cognitive processes to concentrating on man in a socially situated practice.

Part III
Learning and Knowing in Work Organizations

Part III

9
Configuring Places for Learning – Participatory Development of Learning Practices at Work

Thomas Binder, Erling Björgvinsson and Per-Anders Hillgren

Participatory approaches to the development of new practices at work have been widespread in Scandinavia, due largely to the tradition of collaboration and collective agreements on the labour market. Since the late 1980s, participation and change have increasingly been coupled to various notions of learning and learning organizations (for an overview, see Sandberg, 1992). Similarly, technological change became increasingly addressed as an issue of design rather than as a given precondition for changes in working life (Bjerknes *et al.*, 1987). In the so-called Scandinavian tradition of systems design, IT systems for a particular customer organization are developed through a process of participatory design (Greenbaum & Kyng, 1991). Existing work practices are studied in a mixture of ethnographically inspired fieldwork, interviews and dialogue sessions. New IT systems are developed in iterative design cycles involving representative users in drafting and evaluating system prototypes. And a final system is typically put in place with the involved users acting as strong proponents for the chosen design. This tradition of user-oriented design of IT systems has shed new light on the relation between participation, learning and change and in particular the literature on computer supported cooperative work has contributed to the study of how practices at work evolve around communication artefacts. Wenger studied the processing of insurance claims in bureaucratic organizations and found that different groups of employees could be seen as communities of practice continuously engaged with negotiating the ordering of the claims in a process constantly shifting between what he called participation and reification (Wenger, 1998).

Together with Lave, he developed the notion of learning as legitimate peripheral participation in these communities (Lave & Wenger, 1991) and in relation to systems design he suggests to see designers and potential users as communities of practice interacting and challenging each other in the design process (Binder, 1996). The situatedness of interaction between people and artefacts also beyond the design process was demonstrated for example in the work of Suchman (1987), and even if this was not always accounted for in the work of participatory designers (for a discussion of this, see, e.g., Binder, 2002) the collaborative design process provided an attractive format in which such interactions could be anticipated (Blomberg *et al.*, 1996). Orr has studied the collaboration among service technicians and he has found that communal storytelling in the form of what he calls war stories, plays an important role in developing and maintaining the competency of the technicians (Orr, 1996). Several authors have developed strategies for the study of technology in use (Luff *et al.*, 2000) and for the contextual inquiries relevant in design of computers in context (Beyer & Holtzblatt, 1998; Kensing, 2003). Finally, the role of artefacts in collaborative activities have been extensively discussed, both with reference to the sharing of design artefacts in the design process (Henderson, 1999; Star, 1995) and to the way artefacts coordinate everyday activities at work in general (Berg, 1999).

To address learning and change processes directly with participatory design approaches was not within the scope of the Scandinavian tradition, but fuelled with the growing interest in situated learning and to some extent also constructionist learning approaches, we have in later years seen several groups turning collaborative design processes into the nexus of interventionist approaches aiming at facilitating learning. Some groups have emphasized the construction of new learning artefacts that offer new modalities of interaction in school-like settings often with a strong base in a particular theoretical approach to learning (Resnick & Kafai, 1994).

Others have developed notions of computer-based collaborative learning from a starting point in cognitive science (Fischer, 2000). Among the groups most closely aligned to the Scandinavian tradition, Engeström has developed collaborative processes called change laboratories in which different professional communities collaboratively envision organizational change and the associated needs for organizational and individual learning based on joint explorations of existing practices (Engeström, 1999). What these groups share is the assumption that new learning practices have to be developed in close interaction with people from the relevant communities and that mediating artefacts must be constructed collaboratively to reify the possible transition from existing to emerging ways of knowing and learning.

With a background in the participatory design tradition and with insights gained within the field of collaborative design of IT systems, we have been interested in participatory approaches that probe for new learning opportunities at work. We have been particularly interested in enhancing and extending informal learning practices at work in ways that expand the space for peer-to-peer reflection and learning. As in other participatory projects, we see the process of participation in itself as a setting for mutual learning, and we have extended this perspective by framing the participatory process as prototypical for the kind of reflective learning practices that can be envisioned (Binder, 2002). We return to this issue of congruence between participatory engagement with change and the change anticipated as in the light of two concrete project examples we take up a discussion on how the local process of participation relates to larger discourses on learning and change.

In the following we report on two participatory projects that have both sought to explore ways through which people can get new opportunities to learn from one another. In both projects we have been particularly interested in video as a soft medium for exposing and documenting work practices. Like others, we have found that video documents provides a strong starting point for reflection (Buur *et al.*, 2000; Karasti, 2001; Lanzara, 1991), and unlike more formal descriptions, video is well suited for exposing work practices without codifying them into preconceived schemes of knowledge (Minneman, 1991). Towards the end of the chapter we discuss whatever similar strategies could be pursued using other media.

Machine setters on video

In a research project initiated by the European Association of Spring Makers, we were asked to develop support for informal on the job training of new machinists entering the spring industry. Very little formal knowledge exists outside of the workshop on how to set up machines for spring making. There are few formal training schemes and the work of the machinists is a typical example of a practice developed and maintained within the local community. Our point of entry was the suggestion to video recording machine setters as they worked. From these recordings we wanted to edit small video sequences that could capture important aspects of the setting operation without abstracting work practices into formalized rules or instructions. As we established collaboration with a group of setters we found ourselves involved in a collaborative inquiry into what knowing means in machine setting. We made video recordings suggested by the setters and we returned to the factory with edited videos.

Discussions emerged among the setters as the videos were closely examined. The different setters had individual preferences for what type of iterative adjustments to make during the set up, and they also differed in terms of the extent to which they employed one or many strategies towards particular set-up problems. These differences were not seen as problematic by the setters and the variety of possible approaches was widely acknowledged. The lack of canonical procedures did however shed new light on what others have called the tacit knowledge of machine setting (Böhle & Helmuth, 1992). The professionalism of the setters seemed not to reside with the capacity to perform a certain chain of uniform steps leading towards the goal. The competency of the setters was better captured as the skilled engagement and conversation with the setting situation in cycles of knowing-in-action and reflection-in-action, as proposed by Schön for other groups of more conventional professionals (Schön, 1987) (for a more elaborate treatment of this, see Binder, 1995). Despite the absence of an explicit canon of best practice the fact that we were entering the shop with a project on workplace learning initiated a vivid discussion and negotiation on how to expose the practices of machine setting. The continued work with recording and editing video functioned as the centre of this process. The setters engaged actively in planning which recordings to make and how to edit the tapes. As a result, they articulated stories of practice that in their view were compatible to the notion of learning from best practice that we brought into the collaboration. The videos became reifications of the ongoing discussion among the setters. The presence of our research team was both an opportunity and a challenge to the community of practice. On the one hand, our presence created an opportunity for articulating the practice of the setters. On the other hand, our project with its explicit emphasis on 'best practice' and 'informal on the job training' confronted the setters with discourses of learning outside the workshop (Wenger, 1998).

When we eventually had a finished video material on spring making, both our collaborators among the machine setters and we were enthusiastic. We had produced an artefact, which in a very direct fashion showed the complexity of machine setting. At the same time it created an view for outsiders into procedures and problem solving strategies that were not subsumed by an external epistemology of abstracted knowledge. The video materials became an important contribution to the industry's understanding of its knowledge base, and it spurred a considerable interest in how work practices could be nurtured at the company level. In a wider context, we used the project to advance two sets of arguments. Based on an analysis of the video materials collected, we argued that machine setters can be understood as reflective practitioners engaging similar strategies of knowing and acting as others have described for groups of professionals such as medical doctors, psychotherapists and architects (Passarge & Binder, 1996). Second, we analyzed the way in which the setters collaborated to produce the material and argued that the industrial workplace in general does not provide adequate room for reflection and dialogue on work practice, and that introducing video as a reflective medium in collaborative processes among industrial workers offers an opportunity to open up the realm of reflection (Binder *et al.*, 1998).

What we missed in our first interpretation of what had been accomplished was to critically examine how our joint work with the machine setters was translated into a more permanent change in the work practice on the shop floor. A small vignette (based on Meier, 1998) from a follow-up study in the same company where the video had been produced, shows that this is not trivial:

Two machine setters are together in front of a complicated machine. Close to them a computer is available with an interactive video production documenting 'best practice' as it has over the previous year been video recorded in the same machine shop. One of the machine setters has been part of the team that has gone through many discussions and many video recordings to find precisely what aspects of spring making are relevant to have documented on video to help 'newcomers' learn the complicated trade. The other machine setter is a skilled machinist with more than 20 years of experience from other machine shops. He has only been in this machine shop for a few weeks. The conversation does not run smoothly. The 'old timer' activates the interactive video and joins in with the video as he points out what the team has collaboratively found to be the best way to do the set up. He takes one thing at the time and he is cautious to emphasize the wording of procedures and tools, which he knows is the result of long and engaged discussions between his colleagues. The 'newcomer' is obviously uneasy with the situation. For his first week he has been given a machine not running ordinary production to 'get acquainted with spring making' and one gets a strong feeling that he considers himself put on display as a novice in the shop.

In the conversation with the 'old timer', he matches every explanation he gets with a story from his own repertoire of experiences. When the 'old timer' tells how to grind the tools forming the spring in order to get the right tension in the thread, the 'newcomer' answers by telling how he used to grind his tools 'when he once was in Egypt'. As they go on like this for a while, both become more and more openly frustrated. In the end 'the old timer' does the job and a few weeks later the 'newcomer' leaves the company.

The videos produced had the imprint of the collaborative process in which they were produced. As a finished artefact for learning, they did, however, change status, because they were no longer open for continued debate. The diversity of practices captured in the videos became implicitly for the newcomer an authoritative catalogue of legitimized approaches, which did not make room for the other experiences 'from when I was in Egypt'. Adding to this, the focus on learning turned out to be difficult to accommodate within the existing work practice. Where we may have expected to smoothen the entry for newcomers, the exposure of initial training seemed to obstruct what Lave and Wenger call 'legitimate peripheral participation' (Lave & Wenger, 1991). The conventional industrial workplace has obviously only few accepted places for learning, but trying to engineer new learning sites may as in this case single out learning as a new type of work, which keeps the newcomer distant from the practice in which he was meant to be a participant.

Self-produced video and everyday learning among intensive care nurses

More recently we had the opportunity to work with self-organized learning in collaboration with nurses at an intensive care unit. We came into the project with a focus on practice-based learning in line with Ingela Josefsson's notion of apprenticeship within in healthcare (Josefsson, 1995, 1998). Among the nurses there are well-established traditions for collaboration and mutual assistance and there is also a well-developed oral tradition for learning. The oral tradition is akin to the manner in which technicians share oral stories of difficult repair cases to develop their community, as observed by Orr (1996), and how nurses share paradigm cases of difficult patient cases that had engaged them both clinically and emotionally, as observed by Benner (1984). What was crucial to us from the start was to look for ways in which new learning situations could remain embedded in the day-to-day practice and furthermore to ensure that such new practices could gradually grow out of the participatory process we were staging together with the nurses (with inspiration from, i.e., Hartswood *et al.*, 2000).

Together with the staff, we developed a learning support where the staff made short instructional videos to each other on certain tasks. The videos are made available with barcode cards that are placed out in the workplace. The staff pick the desired card and with a handheld computer they scan the card that starts the movie.

In the first phase of the project we focused mostly on how well the videos and handheld computers could support the staff in the daily work and how the production could be done as smoothly as possible. Later, we realized that the production itself had value and was highly appreciated by the staff. It became clear that the learning process actually starts when the staff does the recordings. When making the video the cameraman and whomever is featuring in the movie, start reflecting and try to articulate how the content should be shaped and how the task is best carried out. The reflection and the articulation continue when colleagues review the movie. The whole process of making the videos have made the nurses work more visible, thus allowing for constructive reflection contributing to the improvement of their everyday practice. Rather than a pre-configured set of learning materials used at specific situations, the project turned out to be more of a 'never ending' process of learning engaging many different people and places throughout the unit. Below we follow a story exemplifying this, spanning more than one year:

A nurse's aide has developed a new procedure on how a stomach probe is taped to a patient's face and decides to make a movie about that procedure. A couple of weeks later the nurse's aide heard that parts of her film had been questioned at a film presentation. A spontaneous viewing of her film was arranged in an empty patient room. Two colleagues asked why a certain tape should be used. She explained that the tape needs to be narrow so it is easier avoiding putting it on the lip. They took her point and encouraged her to emphasize this in the movie. After finishing the negotiating of the content of the movie, they directly filmed a new version of it. In the movie she ardently points out the importance of making the strip of adhesive tape narrow. When colleagues later review the video during a film session, the senior physician and the nurse in charge of the professional development observed contradictions in the movie. They realize that while the nurse's aide on the movie was talking about the narrow tape of the stomach probe, the patient's tubes were at the same time taped with a tape that was too broad. It became clear that avoiding putting it on the lip should be regarded as a general problem and using a narrow strip of tape should therefore be underscored also when other probes and tubes are taped to the face. They suggested making a new video where the taping of other tubes and probes is also done with a narrow strip of tape.

In this instance, the video has helped make related problems visible as well as transferring experience from one case to others. The diverse competences and specialities of those involved in the reviewing session gives different perspectives on the videos. Jointly reviewing the videos gives insight into each other's skills and procedures. When watching the videos at reviewing sessions, the staff is not engaged in carrying out the task. Being disconnected from the task creates an analytical distance to the routine of performing it, but at the same time the videos help staff to revive their experiences of performing the work.

As a result of the review session, a different nurse responsible for the procedure of taping the ventilator to the patient's face had the opportunity to make a movie about this, emphasizing using a narrow tape and the articulation of best practice continuous. But the new tape movie reveals other problems:

A nurse sees the new movie and realizes that she cuts the tape in a much simpler way than how presented on the movie. She arranges a spontaneous reviewing of the video. Three experienced staff members join her, among them a nurses aide responsible for hygiene at the unit and a nurse responsible for deviations. Two of them are enthusiastic about the movie and procedure but the 'hygiene' nurse sees problems with it. As a part of the procedure in the movie, wasted paper from glued labels with appropriate properties is used when they cut the tape. The 'hygiene' nurse tells the story of carefulness and explains how small parts of glue on the tape come in contact with the patients skin and that the glue could cause allergic reactions. The 'hygiene' nurse says that she prefers finding another kind of paper, which is tested to be safe. They decide to follow her.

In the story, many staff members have participated in different ways at different locations and different times in a collaborative learning process and in an always ongoing articulation of best practice circling around the production of movies. The production and the watching of videos is a typical collaborative process. During the production, it can be argued that the movies function similar to what Kathryn Henderson calls conscription devices. Conscription devices serve simultaneously as inscription devices for capturing information and as boundary objects in the way that they are both plastic enough to adapt to local needs, yet robust enough to maintain a common identity across sites. The focus is, however, more on process, than in the case of boundary objects (Henderson, 1999). Similarly, the process at the ICU allows for different stakeholders with different agendas to produce a movie towards a common goal and focus their communications in reference to the movie. Even if it is a single person acting, it is not a single person's story. Instead, different staff members' views of what is relevant can be a part of a movie. The articulation continues out in the corridors and sometimes finds its way back again into the movie.

Watching a colleague on video

As mentioned above, the project presented an opportunity to discuss how the new IT artefacts could become part of nurses' work practice and how their use is intertwined with established and conventional views of knowing, teaching and learning. These conventional views of knowing, teaching and learning are not something that a project can discard. Both on the organizational level and the individual level, 'old' and 'new' ways coexist. Earlier views and experiences of knowing, teaching and learning are not simply thrown out.

What we have seen is that often two staff members working together on a task use the video. Using the video means that a new artefact is introduced into their collaborative setting and new ways of coordinating the activity are needed. As in the production of the videos, the configuration and articulation of what it can mean to know and learn with the artefact is not something that can be determined once and for all. It is a process that is open for negotiation:

K is about to connect a humidifier to a ventilator. She has worked at the ICU for three years. Having missed the course on active humidifying, she looks for assistance. A, an experienced nurse working in the administration, comes to her help. She fetches the humidifier and places this on a small mobile table a few steps away from the ventilator that is next to the patient and in preparation watches the video. On the left-hand side of the patient, K finishes testing an extra ventilator to which the patient has to be temporarily switched. K asks A if they should prepare anything else before switching over. Triggered by K's question, A casually decides to postpone switching the patient to the extra ventilator as well as starting with connecting the humidifier valve to the ventilator. Instead, she suggests they start with connecting the humidifier chamber. Standing next to each other by the table, A jumps into the video: past the introduction and the connection of the valve. A hands the chamber over to K and having seen how it is done, she connects the chamber. A starts the video and confirms that K did it correctly. A and K continue connecting the tubes and the heating cables, where A is in charge of the handheld computer communicating part of the time, to K the content of the video.

When K asked for help she started a process where places of action are constructed, where responsibilities are negotiated and commitments made. In this process she actively sought assistance in the role of a full member in her community of practice. The assistance is not forced on her and she does not perceive the place of action as a learning setting, but rather a way of solving the problem with which she is confronted. She is in charge of and responsible for the patient and takes an active role – testing the extra ventilator on her own. When she asks if they should prepare anything, she invites A to join her in deciding how to proceed.

A accepts K's role of being in charge of the patient. However, when they start mounting the humidifier, A sees the place of action as one of learning where, as she explained, she feels responsible to walk K through the task. A has therefore watched the video and is better prepared for the commitment. Having watched the video in advance, A has an overview of the task and the content of the video. When they start watching the video, A takes charge and skips parts of the video that she deems irrelevant for K. She assigns herself the role of the tutor, with main access to and control of the video. K's role is to get hands-on experience and A steps in only when K gets stuck. She communicates what is going on in the video while K is doing the mounting and she is checking and confirming what K does is correct. A perceives herself as K's primary source. The video is foremost to aid A in the role of the tutor. K commits to the role of being the one that follows the instructions partly from the video and partly from A. As A and K get deeper into the work the tutor–student relationship ceases:

A restarts the video and jumps to the part 'on filling the chamber'. She is unsure about the volume of water, but K states that it is self-regulating. K hands to A the power cable that goes behind the respirator and connects it to the power outlet. They proceed to configure the ventilator to run on active humidifying, but some of the ventilators have not been upgraded and they are unsure if their ventilator is upgraded. To save time, they decide that A should go and ask if their colleagues know. Meanwhile, K proceeds and connects and writes on the humidifier filter and then, assisted by two nurses' aides, switches the patient over to the extra ventilator. A returns, explaining that the ventilator is not upgraded for active humidifying. They proceed and finish the task.

Although A for a period takes charge, it is clear that K is a competent nurse that not only actively but also critically partakes in the mounting. Her prior experience is not excluded as in the case of the machine setter. When they fill the chamber, K shows that she has some prior knowledge, stating that she believes the chamber to be self-regulating, while A is unsure. A has no problem returning to a more collegial relationship, taking the role of the assistant when connecting the humidifier to the power outlet or when they do the ventilator function control. While A is getting information about the ventilator, K goes on – connecting the filter and switching the patient to the extra ventilator. She is still responsible to get the job done.

Similarly to the machine setters, the learning aid used is a video of best practice and the place of learning has been moved out to where the job gets done. But as in the case with A and K, the videos at the ICU have been used informally and not as part of an explicit learning setting. Further, although the videos show best practice and have a certain authority, they are just considered to be examples of how the job can be done and only as one part in the puzzle of carrying out the task. A, triggered by K's question as to if they should prepare anything before switching him over, decides to postpone the move. A does not hesitate postponing the move, even though she knows that it means that the chronology in the video will not correspond to how they carry out the task. In the video, the first component that is connected is the valve that goes to the slot on the ventilator to which the tube of K's patient is still connected. The video does not and cannot possibly account for all problems encountered. This does not render it obsolete because the video just shows an example of how to connect the humidifier and being an experienced nurse A knows that tasks can be competently done in many different ways. The video shows just one of many. And anyway, A creates a new path through the video by jumping back and forth on the timeline. For what the video does not account, and for anything they cannot solve on their own, they seek the answer to by looking for other colleagues at the unit.

The roles to which A and K commit (although drawing upon prior experience of learning) are not stable preconceived schemes either. The place is never explicitly defined as a learning setting or a work setting. Rather, it moves back and forth between being an informal learning setting as perceived by A, to being two colleagues solving a problem as perceived by K. The tutor role never gets to define fully the place of action; K's prior experience is not excluded and her role as the one in charge is not questioned. Although drawing upon known roles, A and K never rigidly commit to them. This leaves the place of action constructed and open for negotiation as they proceed.

Coming full circle

When writing about the early machine setter project, we suggested seeing collaborative design processes aiming at supporting workplace learning, as prototypical learning processes anticipating possible future appropriations of the designed artefacts. What we meant then was that the joint inquiry in which we engaged with the machine setters, had as much to do with exploring and envisioning new practices of knowing and learning for the machine setters involved as it was about constructing new learning aids for the 'newcomer'. We still see it in that way, but in retrospect we must realize that it is not until our encounters with the nurses in intensive care, that we have fully understood the consequences of this position.

Even if the two projects have many similarities in their approach to participation, in the decade that passed from the spring makers project to the nurse project, we have been taught several lessons about both learning and change. What we can see today is on the one hand that the congruence between the prototypical process of learning within the project and the learning processes that may later be invoked in everyday practices goes so far that it is fair to say that it is the process of continuously exposing, articulating and reflecting upon practices of knowing and learning that may as in the intensive care project be made permanent. The reification of 'best practices' into a canonical representation however soft this may is first and foremost a canon that almost inevitably will exclude 'the learner'. In this respect, it was striking how clearly the nurses rejected the idea that videos could provide authoritative explanations to nursing problems.

On the other hand, to abstain from creating a new canon means also that the evolving practices of peer-to-peer learning cannot be safeguarded from learning templates and learning discourses from 'outside'. We saw that the nurses position themselves towards one another in traditional tutor–student relationships well beyond what the actual tasks at hand could entail. The reason why this in our view does not seem to exhaust the potential of the learning environment is that the volatility of the process is matched by a volatility in the settings the nurses create for learning. In the interactions between A and K, new places of action are continuously constructed and reconstructed allowing both of them to re-position and re-interpret their internal relations. This would not have been possible if for example the learning materials were only available at a particular location or if access to production of new learning materials were monopolized by a smaller group of nurses.

One can ask if the outcome is here so modest that it could just as well have grown out of the everyday practice without external intervention. Our answer is that the kind of changes, in practice, that we have seen in the intensive care project is not in any way the exclusive outcome of such processes as we describe. The nurses, like other communities of practice, do continuously develop their practice along similar lines. But just as the intervention from outsiders may induce new learning agendas, it may also create the thrust and challenge needed for the practice to take a leap into new ways of knowing. The nurses found that they became able to raise issues of nursing and treatment in dialogue with, for example, medical doctors, more confidently and with larger impact as they engaged in the project described. Video as a medium here played an important role as it allowed for a more fine-grained oscillation between what Wenger calls 'participation and reification'. We will not exclude the relevance of other media in projects aimed at supporting informal learning at work, but as a distinct step away from associating knowing to formal descriptions video have many advantages which are still not fully acknowledged.

References

Benner, P. (1984). *From Novice to Expert: Excellence and Power in Clinical Nursing Practice*. Menlo Park, CA: Addison-Wesley.

Berg, M. (1999). Accumulating and Coordinating: Occasions for Information Technologies in Medical Work. *Computer Supported Cooperative Work*, 8(4), 373–401.

Beyer, H., & Holtzblatt, K. (1998). *Contextual Design: Defining Customer-Centered Systems*. San Francisco: Morgan Kauffman.

Binder, T. (1995). Designing for workplace learning, *AI & Society*, 9(3), 218–43.

Binder, T. (1996). Participation and reification in design of artifacts: An interview with Etienne Wenger. In T. Binder, M. Fischer & J. Nilsson (eds), *Learning with artifacts*, special issue of *AI & Society*, 10(1), 101–106.

Binder, T. (2002). Intent, Form and Materiality in the Design of Interaction Technology. In C. Floyd *et al.* (eds), *Social Thinking Software Practice*. Cambridge, MA: MIT Press.

Binder, T., Fischer, M., & Rasmussen, L. (1998). *What does computerization change in the industrial work place*. Paper presented at the first Whole-workshop in Leuven, 15–17 June 1998.

Bjerknes G., Ehn, P., & Kyng, M. (eds). (1987). *Computers and democracy: a Scandinavian challenge*. Aldershot: Avebury.
Blomberg, J., Suchman L., & Trigg, R. (1996). Reflections on a work-oriented design project. *Human-Computer Interaction*, 11, 237–65.
Böhle, F. & Helmuth, R. (1992). *Technik und erfarung, Arbeit in hochautomatisierten Systemen*. New York: Campus Verlag.
Buur, J., Binder, T., & Brandt, E. (2000). Taking Video beyond 'Hard Data' in User Centered Design. *Proceedings of the Participatory Design Conference 2000*, New York.
Engeström, Y. (1999). Expansive Visibilization of Work: An Activity-Theoretical Perspective, *Computer Supported Cooperative Work*, 8(1–2), 63–93.
Fischer, G. (2000). Lifelong Learning – More Than Training, Special Issue on Intelligent Systems/Tools. In Riichiro Mizoguchi & Piet A. M. Kommers (eds), *Training and Life-Long Learning* (eds), *Journal of Interactive Learning Research*, 11(3/4), 265–94.
Greenbaum J., & Kyng, M. (eds). (1991). *Design at work: Cooperative design of computer systems*. Hillsdale, NJ: Lawrence Erlbaum.
Hartswood, M., et al. (2000). Being there and doing IT in the workplace: A case study of a co-development approach in healthcare. *Proceedings of the Participatory Design Conference 2000*, New York, pp. 96–105.
Henderson, K. (1999). *On line and on paper: Visual Representations, Visual Culture and Computer Graphics in Design Engineering*. Cambridge, MA: MIT Press.
Josefsson, I. (1995). A confrontation between Different Traditions of Knowledge. In B. Göranzon (ed.), *Skill, Technology and Enlightment – on Practical Philosophy*. New York: Springer-Verlag.
Josefsson, I. (1988). The nurse as Engineer – the Theory of knowledge in Research in the Care Sector. In B. Göranzon & I. Josefson (eds), *Knowledge, Skill and Artificial Intelligence*. Berlin/Heidelberg: Springer-Verlag.
Karasti, H. (2001). Bridging Work Practice and System Design: Integrating Systemic Analysis, Appreciative Intervention and Practitioner Participation. *Computer Supported Cooperative Work*, 10(2), 211–46.
Kensing, F. (2003). *Methods and Practices in Participatory Design*. Copenhagen: ITU Press.
Lanzara, G. F. (1991). Shifting Stories: Learning from a reflective Experiment in a Design Process. In D. A. Schön (ed.), *The Reflective Turn: Case Studies in an Educational Practice* (pp. 285–320). New York: Teachers College Press.
Lave, J., & Wenger, E. (1991). *Situated Learning: Legitimate Peripheral Participation*. Cambridge: Cambridge University Press.
Luff, P., Hindmarsh, J., & Heath, C. (2000). *Workplace studies, recovering work practice and informing systems design*. Cambridge: Cambridge University Press.
Meier, F. (1998). *Læring er indviklet i praksis! – et speciale om læringsbegreber, uformelle læreprocesser og fjedervikling*. [Learning is complex in Practice]. Roskilde: Tek-Sam Forlaget. Rapportserien, 1998, nr. 63.
Minneman, S. L. (1991). *The social Construction of a Technical Reality: Empirical Studies of Group Engineering design Practice*. Doctoral dissertation, Stanford, Department of Mechanical Engineering.
Orr, J. E. (1996). *Talking about machines. An ethnography of a modern job*. Ithaca: ILR Press.
Passarge, L., & Binder, T. (1996). Supporting Reflection and Dialogue in a Community of Machine Setters. *AI & Society*, 10(1), pp. 79–88.

Resnick, M., & Kafai, Y. (1994). *Constructionism in Practice: Rethinking the Roles of Technology in Learning*. Research report. Cambridge, MA: MIT Media Lab.
Sandberg, Å. (1992). *Technological change and co-determination in Sweden*. Philadelphia, PA: Temple University Press.
Schön, D. A. (1987). *Educating the Reflective Practitioner – Toward a New Design for Teaching and Learning in the Professions*. New York: Basic Books.
Star, S. L. (1995). The Politics of Formal Representations: Wizards, Gurus and Organizational Complexity. In S. L. Star (ed.), *Ecologies of Knowledge*. Albany: State University of New York Press.
Suchman, L. A. (1987). *Plans and situated actions: the problem of human-machine communication*. Cambridge: Cambridge University Press.
Wenger, E. (1998). *Communities of Practice – Learning, Meaning, and Identity*. Cambridge: Cambridge University Press.

10
Learning in and for Work, and the Joint Construction of Mediational Artefacts: An Activity Theoretical View
Reijo Miettinen and Jaakko Virkkunen

During the past two decades, learning in and for work has been conceptualized in terms of 'organizational learning' (Argyris & Schön, 1978), 'knowledge management' (Nonaka & Takeuchi, 1995) and participation in 'communities of practice' (Lave & Wenger, 1991). All of these conceptions suggest that learning is a collective phenomenon, implying that cultural knowledge is somehow locally preserved, shared and transmitted to newcomers. Different explanations have been proposed for how learning results are actually preserved and further transmitted. In this chapter, we discuss three of the main theoretical explanations: the deposit of mental schemes in the mind, embodied skills, and the objectification of knowledge into artefacts.

We argue that the idea of joint creation and use of mediating artefacts has several merits when compared with the two other explanations within the analysis of learning in and for work. We elaborate on this position by analyzing the creation and implementation of a new set of tools that have been used in the work of labour-protection inspectors in Finland (Virkkunen, 1995). This case example helps us demonstrate the ways in which the construction of a new set of jointly used instruments has radically changed the way the labour protection district carries out its work, and how these new instrumentalities both demanded and enhanced inspectors' collective and individual learning.

How the results of learning are preserved, accumulated, and transmitted

Probably the most widely held theory regards learning at work as a process of developing a deposit of individual experiences of situations and inductive generalizations in the form of 'if-then' propositions in the actor's mind (Argyris, 1993; Kolb, 1984; Schön, 1983). This view has been extensively discussed. At present, epistemologists agree that perception is theory-laden, that is, it is penetrated by culturally developed models and presuppositions (Kuhn, 1970; Wartofsky, 1979). Two eminent philosophers of the mind have recently even suggested that consciousness cannot exist without external tools (Dennet, 2000; Clark, 2002). The metaphor of individual deposits of experience thus includes a serious philosophical problem. Furthermore, it lacks an explanation for the way in which expertise is shared, developed, and transmitted.

The second alternative for explaining the transmission of results of learning is based on the concepts *habitus* (Bordieu, 1977), *habit* (Joas, 1996) and *routine* (Nelson & Winter, 1982). Bourdieu's theory of habitus is based on the phenomenological ontology developed by Heidegger (1962) and Maurice Merleau-Ponty (1958). These philosophers reject the rationalistic idea of individual's internal representations or plans as the basis of their actions. Instead, they maintain that understanding exists in forms of embodied knowledge, skills and dispositions that are 'remembered' and transmitted within the form of bodily schemes. This type of knowledge is, by nature, pre-reflective and tacit. Bourdieu's concept of habitus and practical reason bears a strong resemblance to ethnomethodology (Bohman, 1999, p. 130) and also has much in common with the pragmatist concept of habit (Aboufalia, 1999; Joas, 1996).

There are two ways in which the phenomenological concept of habit and skill can be criticized. First, many psychologists and philosophers regard artefacts as a seminal condition for cultural learning (Vygotsky, 1986; Tomasello, 1999; Wartofsky, 1979). From this point of view, the idea of a body scheme as memory or deposit of cultural learning detached from artefacts is artificial. The things that are coded in the brain, as well as in the nervous system and the body, are social forms of using tools and instruments for human purposes. The human form of sociality is objectified within the tools themselves.[1]

Second, many philosophers and sociologists agree on the central limitation regarding the concept of embodied knowledge as also exemplified with the concept of habitus. This concept does not satisfactorily deal with transformative agency, that is, it does not deal with the ways in which subjects are able to articulate and elaborate alternatives to prevailing habits (Bohman, 1999; Burkitt, 1999; Butler, 1999; Emirbayer & Miche, 1998). Nick Crossley nicely summarizes these concerns (2001, p. 116): 'There is something more to agency than the concept of habit can fully capture; a creative and generative dynamic which makes and modifies habits'. The phenomenology-based theories of practice – in empathetically rejecting the idea of individual's internal representations – tend to ignore the problem of reflection and representation altogether.

Evolutionary economists (Nelson & Winter, 1982) and several organization theorists have suggested that the outcomes of learning are preserved by transforming organizational routines. Levitt and March (1988), for instance, maintain that, contrary to rationalistic theories, action is based on historically formed routines that are incrementally developed. These routines are transmitted to new individuals through the process of socialization. Lave and Wenger (1991) and Wenger (1998) also view learning as a process in which newcomers internalise the existing practices of a community of practice. While these explanations have the merit of making culture and artifacts a part of knowing and learning, they also do not pay proper attention to conscious attempts to change and transform the prevailing practices.

Joint creation of artefacts as a key to collective learning at work

According to activity theory and historical epistemology, the embodiment of forms of human activity within artefacts is the primary means of learning and transmitting human achievement. 'All forms of activity (active faculties) are passed on only in the form of objects created by man for man' (Ilyenkov, 1977, p. 277). This insight goes back to Hegel, who suggested that the 'spirit' develops through its objectifications into material forms, such as artefacts. Marx expressed his admiration of Hegel's phenomenology, because it grasps the nature of man 'as result of his own labour' (Marx, 1964, p. 177). The transformation of nature, the creation and use of cultural artefacts, and the development of man and his powers belong to one-and-the-same process. Marx suggested that the 'history of industry and the established objective existence of industry are the open book of man's essential powers' (ibid., p. 142). This idea seems all the more sensible in the present-day context of computers, electron microscopes, mobile phones and the Internet.

Numerous cultural psychologists, social scientists and philosophers have analyzed the significance of artefacts. Ian Burkitt calls cultural artefacts a 'prosthetic extension of the body' and regards them as the basic units of cultural development–instead of the 'memes' suggested by Richard Dawkins (Burkitt, 1999). Mervin Donald, in his theory regarding the emergence of human consciousness, demonstrates that human consciousness cannot be the result of biological evolution. Instead, the key to human consciousness is the external memory, which is composed of the world of material culture that has been created by human history and objectified in tools, buildings, laws and sign systems (Donald, 2001).

One premier philosopher of technology and science, Bruno Latour, has analyzed the ways in which man (humanity) 'delegates' tasks and norms to artefacts (Latour, 1992). As a result, technical artefacts have a script, an affordance, a function or programme of action and goals (Latour, 1994). Human agency is here distributed between men and artefacts. This has been demonstrated in empirical research conducted by Edwin Hutchins (1995) and other students of distributed cognition (Goodwin, 1994). Philosophers John Dewey and Veadislav Lektorsky both analyze the intentional and subjective nature of artefacts:

'A tool is also a mode of language. For it says something, to those who understand it, about the operations of use and their consequences,' Dewey states, adding: 'In the present cultural setting, these objects are so intimately bound up with intentions, occupations and purposes that they have an eloquent voice' (Dewey, 1991, p. 52).

'The instrumental man-made objects function as objective forms of expression of cognitive norms, standards and object-hypotheses existing outside the individual' (Lektorsky, 1980, p. 137).

The philosopher Marx Wartofsky suggests (1979, p. 201):

'The critical character of the human artefact is that its production, its use, and the attainment of the skill of these, can be transmitted, and thus preserved within the social group, and through time, from one generation to the next'.

Wartofsky also analyzes the functions of artefacts in activity, and concludes that tools are primary artefacts. According to Wartofsky representational artefacts, such as pictures or models of forms of action, are secondary artefacts 'created for the purpose of preserving and transmitting skills, in the production and use of primary artefacts' (ibid.). A third type of artefact, the tertiary artefact, makes it possible outside of the daily practice to create and depict imaginary worlds and practices that do not yet exist.

The creation of representational artefacts includes the use of abstraction and generalization. Important features of specific practices are made objects of shared attention and reflection. Part of the generalizations gained in human practice become preserved in the form of the actual tools and in the ways and methods of using them in productive work, as the theories based on embodied knowledge propose. The objectification of generalizations into secondary artefacts such as instructions, drawings and models is a historically more recent from of learning and knowledge creation, which makes learning much more effective, and opens up new possibilities for experimentation and design. One can both compose and play music without using notes, but understanding the skill of notation enormously enriches the possibilities for transferring, composing and learning music.

The theoretical literature we have briefly reviewed above suggests to us a view of learning at work as the development and use of mediating artefacts to solve vital problems and challenges of the work activity. This view, inspired by Lev Vygotsky (1986), depicts learning as a process of remediation or *retooling*. Cultural artefacts and the generalizations embodied in them cannot be derived from an individual, or by sheer organizational experience. They rather evolve as a long series of incremental improvements, combinations and transformations of pre-existing cultural artefacts. Often, the relevant tools for an activity are systematically developed, or can be found in the domains of culture that exist outside a singular organization or community.

In the following sections we analyze the use of artefacts in the transformation of the activity of the aforementioned labour-protection inspectors, and the creation of a new collective tool-kit that makes a new type of labour-safety inspection possible. We analyze how the new set of instruments influenced the conception of the overall object and purpose of the inspection activity, as well as the social forms of collaboration. Then, we analyze the creation and use of the new tool-kit, and how it changed the nature of learning in the labour-protection district.

The developmental contradictions of the labour-protection inspectors' work in the 1980s

In Finland, there exists state legislation and norms concerning working conditions and the safety of employees at work. The enforcement of this labour-protection legislation is the responsibility of eleven district authorities. The Ministry of Health and Social Welfare (formerly the National Board of Labour Protection) supervises this safety enforcement work. It also issues instructions and guidelines concerning working conditions, machinery and equipment.

The main form of activity within the labour-protection districts has traditionally been the inspection of working premises, which is carried out by labour-protection inspectors. The purpose of their work is to ensure that labour-protection regulations are being observed, and to give advise about the improvement of working conditions and work place safety. These inspectors typically have college- or university-level technical training, and/or a background as labour-protection managers or labour-protection delegates within the industry.

During the 1970s, the scope of workplaces to be inspected was radically broadened by new legislation. In order to manage this increased workload with a staff that did not increase proportionally, the newly established National Board of Labour Protection issued detailed instructions for the inspectors, and tried to standardize inspection procedures. The Board also developed a system of strategic planning to determine priorities and launched campaigns and projects to make sure the inspectors' work focused on important areas.

In the 1980s, the optimism of the reform work that took place during the 1970s was, however, lost. There was growing awareness and discussion that suggested that by making traditional kind of surveys in work premises inspectors could not get an accurate diagnostic picture of the safety situation, nor could they have an impact on the root causes of safety defects and hazards. The inspectors were frustrated by the lack of progress being made in safety at work, and they complained that the same defects appeared repeatedly, despite the instructions they had previously given.

In 1989, the National Board of Labour Protection initiated a project to develop the inspection practices. The second author of this article acted as a researcher-consultant in this process (Virkkunen, 1995). The following description of the change process has been based on the data collected and created during this project.

At the beginning of the project a task force of inspectors was established. It was their goal to analyze the historical development of labour inspectors' work, in order to recognize the historical roots of the present-day practices and to identify contradictions within inspectors' current activity. The ensuing analysis showed that despite the increased number of workplaces to be inspected and the rapid technological development that had taken place in production, the method and organization of inspectors' on-the-job activity had remained largely the same. Each inspector was in charge of set of workplaces representing certain industry or being located in a specific geographical area. This set might comprise hundreds of workplaces. In addition, inspectors encountered novel technologies and new types of hazards at the workplaces. Nevertheless, the inspectors felt that they should inspect their 'own' workplaces once each year, as in the earlier days, although this was really no longer possible because of the increased amount of workplaces to be inspected.

In its analysis, the task force identified two main problems calling for developmental measures. First, an inspector working alone had an over-extensive and increasingly heterogeneous set of workplaces to inspect. In addition, the inspectors' tools for analyzing the situation in the workplaces were partly inadequate in view of the rapidly changing safety problems. Second, because of the prevailing fixed division of labour among the inspectors, it was difficult to concentrate the inspections to important problem areas.

The analysis and possibilities with regard to developing the inspectors' activities were discussed in the common seminar of both management and representatives of the inspectors. A recurrent theme in the seminar was the necessity of concentrating the district's work efforts on the most severe problems. In this seminar, a model for a new form of inspection work was outlined. It comprised new instruments that would enable the labour-protection districts and the inspectors to identify important general safety problems, analyze their causes, and plan interventions to change the situation.

Creating new instruments for inspection work within the Uusimaa Labour Protection District

In 1990, a project was established in the Uusimaa Labour Protection District to develop the new instrument for the planning of inspection activities outlined in the seminar to solve the central problems the task force had identified in its analysis. A new set of tools called the 'System for Depicting the Field of Activity' (SDFA) was developed and tested. This system was based on a hierarchic three-tiered depiction of indices of safety problems within the district's jurisdiction area, allowing people to 'zoom in' on important areas of interest and intervention.

First, the project generated a general statistical description of the labour hazards, accidents, and occupational diseases as they existed in different branches of industry and different trades in the district's area. This first level of analysis made it possible to identify and delineate a set of important problem areas for a more detailed study. The second level of description focused on analyzing the occurrence, type and causes of the labour-safety hazards in these areas. The idea of the project group was that the third level of the SDFA would consist of a plan of intervention to remove the identified labour-safety problems.

According to the first level analysis, labour safety was weakest in construction industry. In 1991, the labour district initiated a project team to develop a way to analyze the factors affecting labour safety in construction industry. The task of the team was characterized in its report (19 September 1992) as follows:

'First, maps describing the construction activity in Uusimaa are formed. Then the risk indices describing the working conditions are inserted in them in a suitable way. Once the possible aggregations of the indices have been found, the reasons for the problems will be clarified'.

The team developed a database for recording data about labour safety in different forms of construction and in different trades within construction industry to be used as a second-level tool of the SDFA.

During this project, the second level of the SDFA was gradually constructed as a set of new instruments and social forms of collaboration. The new system was composed of four artefacts: (1) A conceptual map of the structure of an industrial field, with a corresponding database; (2) the hypothesis-driven checklist for the inspection of individual workplaces in the industry; (3) a new 'script' for inspection discussions; (4) the project report about the results of the studied field of industry.

The way in which these artefacts were interconnected was essential for the new form of inspection activity. Statistical data and knowledge from research on occupational diseases, accidents and well-being of workers in the industry were combined to the observations concerning defects in working conditions the inspectors had made in their inspections were recorded in the same database. This, therefore, served as a means of combining knowledge from different sources, and also served as a collective memory to which all of the inspectors had access.

The development and use of these new tools concretized and elaborated upon the vague idea of the new form of activity that was produced in the seminar. As the tools were taken in use, the inspectors' relationship to and interaction with the work places in the district's area became remediated and the object and motive of their work changed qualitatively. Instead of inspecting individual workplaces, they now analyzed the causes of lack of safety at work in different industries and created measures to improve labour safety. In this sense, the new set of tools formed an instrumentality, a complementary set of jointly used instruments that combine to produce a new object and motive for the work, as well as a new mentality within the inspectors' community. By defining a common

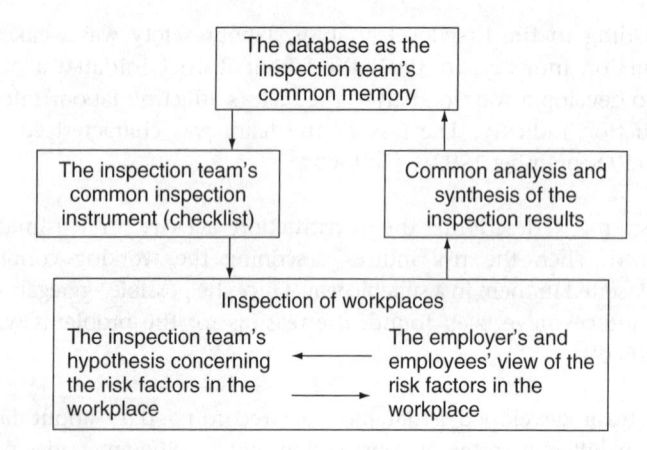

```
                    ┌──────────────────────┐
                    │ The database as the  │
                    │ inspection team's    │
                    │ common memory        │
                    └──────────────────────┘
                       ↑              ↑
    ┌──────────────────────┐   ┌──────────────────────┐
    │ The inspection team's│   │ Common analysis and  │
    │ common inspection    │   │ synthesis of the     │
    │ instrument (checklist)│  │ inspection results   │
    └──────────────────────┘   └──────────────────────┘
              │                          ↑
              ↓                          │
    ┌─────────────────────────────────────────────┐
    │         Inspection of workplaces            │
    │ The inspection team's   The employer's and  │
    │ hypothesis concerning ← employees' view of the│
    │ the risk factors in the  risk factors in the│
    │ workplace             →  workplace          │
    └─────────────────────────────────────────────┘
```

Figure 10.1: The new instrumentality as a set of tools, actions and forms of collaboration

object of attention and providing collectively used tools, the SDFA made the team a collective subject of both learning and productive work. The interdependencies between the new tools and actions are presented in Figure 10.1.

In the following, an account is presented of how each of the artefacts were constructed and used during the experimental project focusing on the construction industry.

The database as common memory and organizer of inquiries

After finalizing the conceptual map of the construction industry, the team began to collect data of construction firms and trades in the district's area. It analyzed also all of the available research results on labour safety in construction and recorded their findings in the database. The developing database aroused interest in the industry and a new type of network of cooperation began to develop between the district and the Confederation of Finnish Construction Industries as well as some large construction firms. These contacts also gave the group access to information that was not readily available in public statistics.

At first, the team collected their information manually, but it soon became evident that the amount of data was too overwhelming to be processed in that way. Consequently, one of the team members developed an electronic database using the database features of the MS Excel spreadsheet program. All of the collected information was then accessible to the members, and it became easy to update the database. When the first gathering of information had been accomplished, the team thoroughly analyzed the results along with the help of other inspectors working within the construction branch. Then, they set new inspection tasks, as well as tasks for further analysis.

The extended hypothesis-driven checklist for inspections as a means of intellectualization of inspection work

Next, the team prepared a new instrument – a type of checklist for the inspections, within which the most important safety risks found in the data analysis were included. The use of the list became a means to verify and further develop the results of the data analysis.

The deputy director of the Uusimaa Labour Protection District explained in an interview that the common preparation of a shared inspection instrument was very important. According to him each inspector had to interpret what the data collected in the common database meant in terms of the inspection work, and then relate it to his or her own experiences and conceptions concerning the causes of the hazards. The inspectors also began to systematically compare their observations. The collaborative analysis of the causes of hazards and the testing of hypotheses led the inspectors to assess and sharpen their views of the hazards' causes. Individual inspections got a new meaning as they were now connected to the use and development of the common database.

An altered script for inspection discussions as a means of stimulating a multi-voiced dialogue

The inspectors also changed the way they conducted their discussions during an inspection. Instead of only focusing on areas they individually regarded as important, they negotiated with the stakeholders of the workplace concerning the specific important problems that needed to be attended to. One-third of the discussion items were to be derived from the collected data, one-third from the inspector's experience, and one-third to be established at the workplace during the inspection. The inspectors who participated in the development of the new way of working reported that this new form of discussion gave them information about matters they did not even know existed. The inspectors' new approach turned the entire discussion into a dialogue, and led the inspectors also to recognize differences of opinion between the different actors in a given workplace.

The project report as means of synthesizing and drawing conclusions

After having inspected the selected workplaces and collected data, the inspectors summarized and analyzed their findings and discussed them with their colleagues. In the discussions, inspectors made further generalizations regarding their findings, and decided upon further targets by their inspection work. For example, it was found that occupational risks were often connected with the poor quality of construction machines used. These machines were often rented from equipment rental companies, who did not make sure that the machines they delivered were flawless. The district took action to encourage these firms to improve their quality control systems. It was also discovered that the commonly used subcontracting contracts were outdated and did not take into account new labour practices. This led the inspection team to take the initiative to change legislation and the control practices within the subcontracting trade. These examples demonstrate how the object of the inspectors' work had changed. Instead of working only with individual workplace site-specific safety defects, they now addressed the causes of safety defects and hazards on an industry-wide level in cooperation with other actors.

When using the database, the inspectors noticed that the number of accidents was not a good indicator of labour safety because of its random variation. To overcome this problem, the labour-protection district let a research organization construct an assessment instrument that would provide a quantitative estimate of the state of the risk factors in work conditions that they had deemed important. The inspectors next began to collect standardized assessment data on working conditions within construction sites using this instrument. Through analyzing this data, they could now demonstrate to the top managers the relative position of their firm as regards the quality of its working conditions. This knowledge proved to be an effective incentive for the managers to correct the situation within their firm.

> 'In practice it has sufficed for us to know what the problems are and to publish the analyses in public lectures and inspections, as opposed to demands.... We have simply demonstrated with this assessment that the working conditions within their firm are not on a satisfactory level, and they have themselves begun to repair the faults in their planning and subcontracting practices' (Follow-up interview 2 September 2003).

Many construction firms subsequently adopted the assessment tool and began using it independently in their own safety work. One firm even went so far as to develop a new ICT-based tool to be used for easily conducting and recording such assessments using a standard mobile telephone.

The reports of the project groups developed later into a set of systematic up to date analyses of the labour-safety situation in the various industries in the Uusimaa district. The district management used these analyses as a tool in its negotiations about objectives and resources with the ministry.

The instrumentality described above in effect *changed* the form of learning in and for work within the district radically. First, the SDFA provided an effective means for speaking about the inspections and planning the inspection activity. It made possible for the management and the inspectors in the Uusimaa Labour Protection District to identify and describe objects of work for the inspection teams. After the first pilot team, similar inspection teams were established to analyze other areas and to plan and execute labour-safety interventions on them. Second, then new instruments informed both the design and use of the checklists and later the standardized assessment method used in the inspections. Third, it extensively broadened the scope of variation in workplace conditions, as well as safety solutions the inspectors used in identifying and defining important factors affecting labour safety and good solutions to the recurrent safety problems. Fourth, the database and the use of the computer sped the processing of data dramatically, and made new types of comparisons possible. This contributed to the further analysis of causes of safety problems and identifying effective safety measures in the specific branch of industry. Fifth, the sharing of new assessment tool and the data radically extended the community of actors involved in the same collective learning process by providing comparable data and a way to compare and exchange experiences between construction firms.

Conclusions

We suggested that learning in and for work fruitfully can be analyzed as the processes of joint creation of mediating artefacts or 'collaborative retooling'. This view is also instrumental in analyzing the relationships between the transformation of the system of joint activity and the learning of individual practitioners who take part in it. The analysis of the construction of a new set of tools within the labour protection district is a good illustration of this. The creation and implementation of the SDFA instrumentality changed the activity of all stakeholders profoundly supplying a powerful new system of inquiry and learning for the safety inspectors.

According to activity theory human activities have a systemic nature. When a new set of instruments is introduced, the community of collaborating actors, the division of labour and the forms of collaboration also change. What is even more significant is that, the *new instrumentality* also creates a new object and purpose for the activity. In the Uusimaa Labour Protection District, the object of work evolved from inspecting the specific working conditions and labour-safety problems of individual workplaces into analyzing the reasons for major hazards in particular industrial sector. Accordingly, the measures that were taken from the correction the recommendations to correct separate local safety defects in individual workplaces grew into industry-wide preventive measures. Both the creation of the quality management system for the machine-rental firms, and the initiative to reform the form of subcontracting contracts required collaboration both with other public authorities and firms, and ended up influencing the entire construction industry.

The transformation process described above can be characterized in terms of Jean Bartunek's and Michael Moch's (1987) conception of third-order change as well as in terms of Chris Argyris' theory of double-loop learning (1993). Both theories envision higher-order learning and change as taking place primarily within the sphere of values and ideas. In the 'third-order change' or 'double-loop learning' that took place within the Uusimaa Labour Protection District, the subsequent changes in values were an integral part of the general qualitative transformation of the inspectors' work, in which the creation of new practical tools played a decisive role.

The new instrumentality and knowledge produced also began to change the relationship of the inspectors and the representatives of the workplaces into one that was more dialogical and analytical. Instead of focusing only on safety norms and recommendations, the inspectors now also used the collectively developed hypothesis of important safety factors in their inspections. The inspectors were supposed to supply the information from their inspections to the database for further analysis. The new script for the inspection discussion designated the inspectors to systematically encourage dialogue between the different parties of the workplace concerning the primary health hazards and risks. Both the construction of the database and the measures taken to eliminate the sources of the hazards broadened the collaboration between the inspectors and the other actors in the field. The new tool and the knowledge produced with it changed also the district's way of interacting with the management of firms.

The use of shared tools also increased the possibilities of individual inspectors to learn. The collective formulation of hypotheses made it possible for the inspectors to learn more from their inspections of separate workplaces, and to systematically compare their findings with those of others. This analysis of a field enabled a new level of understanding – the analysis of the major hazards in the field, and the causes of such hazards. This new level was the beginning of a cumulative account, if not theory, about the development of labour safety in Finnish working life.

This case emphasizes the 'informative' and epistemic potential of computer-based tools. The database made it possible to collect, compare and generalize observations that were gleaned from different sources of information, and from scores of separate working places. As a whole, the process of depicting and analyzing an area resembles the kind of learning typical to research work, although the inspections that brought the information to the analysis were ordinary inspections in the legal sense and led to corrections in individual work places: data was collected, a hypothesis was made, more data was gathered and, finally, an analysis led to a report with conclusions and suggestions for measures to be taken. This can be characterized as *learning by collective investigation*. However, there was no ready-made vision or plan at the beginning of the project as to what an analysis of the field should include. The idea was developed through the design and testing of the artefacts, and the actions that were related to them. The achievements of projects and analyses of fields were objectified in the tools, structure and content of the database used, as well as in the checklist for inspections and the content of reports. The artefacts, therefore, became 'carriers' of learning and transmitters of the new, rapidly evolving culture of labour protection inspection.

References

Aboufalia, M. A. (1999). A (neo) American in Paris: Bordieu, and Pragmatism. In R. Shusterman (ed.), *Bordieu. A Critical Reader* (pp. 153–74). Oxford: Blackwell.

Argyris, C. (1993). *Knowledge for Action: A Guide to Overcoming Barriers to Organizational Change*. San Francisco: Jossey-Bass.

Argyris, C., & Schön, D. A. (1978). *Organizational learning. A theory of action perspective*. Reading, MA: Addison-Wesley.

Bartunek, J., & Moch, M. K. (1987). First-Order, Second-Order, and Third-Order and Organization Development Interventions: Cognitive Approach. *Journal of Applied Behavioural Science*, 23(4), 483–500.

Bohman, D. (1999). Practical reason and cultural constraint. Agency in Bordieu's theory of practice. In R. Shusterman (ed.), *Bordieu. A Critical Reader* (pp. 129–52). Oxford: Blackwell.

Bourdieu, P. (1977). *Outline of a Theory of Practice*. Cambridge: Cambridge University Press.

Burkitt, I. (1999). *Bodies of Thought. Embodiment, Identity & Modernity*. London: Sage.

Butler, J. (1999). Peformativity's Social Magic. In R. Shusterman (ed.), *Bordieu. A Critical Reader* (pp. 113–28). Oxford: Blackwell.

Clark, A. (2002). Minds, Brains and Tools. In H. Clapin (ed.), *Philosophy of Mental Representations* (pp. 66–93). Oxford: Clarendon Press.

Crossley, N. (2001). *The Social Body. Habit, Identity and Desire.* London: Sage.

Dennet, D. (2000). Making Tools for Thinking. In D. Sperber (ed.), *Metapresentations: A Multidisciolary Perspective* (pp. 17–29). Oxford: Oxford University Press.

Dewey, J. (1991[1938]). Logic. The Theory of Enquiry. In J. A. Boydston (ed.), *The Later Works*, Vol. 12. Carbondale and Edwardsville: Southern Illinois University Press.

Donald, M. (2001). *The Mind so Rare. The Evolution of Human Consciousness.* New York: W.W. Norton.

Emirbayer, M., & Mische, A. (1998). What Is Agency? *American Journal of Sociology*, 103(4), 962–1023.

Goodwin, C. (1994). Seeing in Depth: Space, Technology and Interaction in a Scientific Research Vessel. *Social Studies of Science*, 25, 237–74.

Heidegger, M. (1962). *Being and Time.* New York: Harper & Row.

Hutchins, E. (1995). *Cognition in the Wild.* Cambridge, MA: MIT Press.

Ilyenkov, E. V. (1977). *Dialectical Logic. Essays on Its History and Theory.* Moscow: Progress Publishers.

Joas, H. (1996). *The Creativity of Action.* Chicago: University of Chicago Press.

Kolb, D. (1984). *Experiential Learning. Experience as the Source of Learning and Development.* Englewood Cliffs, NJ: Prentice-Hall.

Kuhn, T. (1970). *The Structure of Scientific Revolutions.* Chicago: University of Chicago Press.

Lakoff, G., & Johnson, M. (1999). *Philosophy of Flesh.* New York: Basic Books.

Latour, B. (1992). Where Are the Missing Masses? The Sociology of a Few Mundane Artefacts. In W. Bijker & J. Law (eds), *Shaping Technology/Building Society. Studies in Sociotechnical Change* (pp. 225–64). Cambridge, MA: MIT Press.

Latour, B (1994). On Technical Mediation. Philosophy, Sociology, Genealogy. *Common Knowledge*, 3, 29–64.

Lave, J., & Wenger, E. (1991). *Situated Learning: Legitimate Peripheral Participation.* Cambridge: Cambridge University Press.

Lektorsky, V. A. (1980). *Subject Object Cognition.* Moscow: Progress Publishers.

Levitt, B., & March, J. G. (1988). Organizational Learning. *Annual Review of Sociology*, (14), 319–340.

Marx, K. (1964). *The Economic & Philosophical Manuscripts of 1844.* New York: International Publishers.

Merleau-Ponty, M. (1958). *Phenomenology of Perception.* London and New York: Routledge.

Nelson, R., & Winter, S. (1982). *An Evolutionary Theory of Economic Change.* Cambridge, MA: Belknap Press.

Nonaka, I., & Takeuchi, H. (1995). *The Knowledge-Creating Company.* New York. Oxford University Press.

Schön, D. (1983). *The Reflective Practitioner. How Professional Think In Action.* London: Temple Smith.

Tomasello, M. (1999). *The Cultural Origins of Human Cognition.* Cambridge, MA: Harvard University Press.

Virkkunen, J. (1995). Työpaikkatarkastuksen ristiriidat ja niiden ylittämisen mahdollisuudet. [The Contradictions of the Labour Inspection Work and the Prospects of Overcoming Them]. Työministeriö. *Työpoliittinen tutkimus nr.* 123. Helsinki: Hakapaino.
Vygotsky, L. S. (1986). *Thought and Language.* Cambridge, MA: MIT Press.
Wartofsky, M. (1979). *Models: Representation and Scientific Understanding.* Dordrecht: Reidel.
Wenger, E. (1998). *Communities of Practice. Learning, Meaning, and Identity.* Cambridge: Cambridge University Press.

Note

1 It seems to us that this tension between biological and cultural epistemology is a major issue in contemporary theorizing on human activity. Joas (1996) refers to the affinity of his conception with Piaget's biological epistemology. The theory of embodied knowledge by Lakoff and Johnson (1999) searches the foundations of knowledge from the species-specific structure of the human body and sensory organs.

11
The Learning Processes in the Work Organization: From Theory to Design

Annikki Järvinen and Esa Poikela

Learning at work takes a key position when a policy for know-how is being made, and it must not be confused with traditional personnel training. The latter usually refers to the acquisition of the latest knowledge for employees by organizing various training sessions. The view of learning is normally that of traditional school learning: new knowledge is transferred to the students. Learning at work, however, should be seen as a regular part of work processes; employees have the opportunity to learn at work by questioning established practices, experimenting with new methods and also by acquiring if necessary the latest knowing.

Traditionally learning has been analyzed as a phenomenon occurring on the individual, group or organization levels, but recent research has shown that these levels are in fact tightly interlinked systems (see, e.g., Senge, 1990). Organizing learning processes at work is an inseparable part of the planning and development of work processes, and learning, planning and development cannot be studied as independent phenomena. This chapter examines learning at work from the viewpoint of the employee, in the work teams and the whole organization and it presents the process model of learning at work that combines these three viewpoints.

First, an account is given of the collaboration in development work between professional practitioners in a company of the construction sector and university researchers. The goals of this collaboration were to identify the core and sub-processes that produce the organization's learning and know-how by applying the process model of learning at work developed by Järvinen and Poikela (2001) as sensitizing lenses. Second, the chapter presents how the process model had earlier been constructed by combining the theories of experiential learning (Kolb, 1984), organizational knowledge creation (Nonaka, 1994) and organizational learning

(Crossan et al., 1999). This model is used as a design tool in YIT (innovative-building approach; Järvinen and Poikela, 2001). Finally, it is presented as an example, how professional practitioners in YIT used this model for designing initiative activities as learning processes.

The case organization

Our partner in the research is YIT Construction Ltd, which is the largest construction company in Finland, consisting of several production divisions and subsidiaries around the country and abroad. YIT Construction's business fields are building and property development along with property services. It serves as a main contractor, subcontractor and total supplier (design, building and property management) in different-sized construction projects. The company has an extensive service chain in Finland as well as in Estonia, Latvia, Lithuania and Russia, and activities range from land development through design and construction to property management and renovations. YIT Construction's net sales in 2002 amounted to euro 1,111.8 million. The number of employees at the end of 2002 was 4,843. In order to meet clients' needs and requirements, the building systems of the future will employ information and automation technology and tap into the opportunities opened by information networks. Large outlays are being made in the continuous development of the personnel, quality, the environment, health and safety.

YIT Construction has carried through a wide-ranging renewal of its strategy, in the final stage of which a learning management project was added. The new development manager wants to include a holistic analysis of the management of learning at work in the company's strategic planning. In spring 2002, he invited the authors (from the University of Tampere) to join the planning work, because he was familiar with our process model of learning at work and considered it to be applicable in YIT. The goal of the project is to create a learning and know-how management strategy for developing YIT's work processes and to launch a pilot project for the practical realization of the strategy. To get the work under way, a steering group was established, and whose task was to draw up a development programme. The task presupposed personal commitment, study and the acquisition of knowledge in order to clarify the bases for the management of learning and know-how.

The first task consisted of planning the organization of the development work. A typical problem arising in connection with far-reaching processes of change is how all the factors that affect the carrying out of the change can be made to function and how the process itself is to be organized. Development activity has special features that are very difficult for the *formal organization* to handle, concentrated as it is on maintaining and controlling routines. Development activity has to be creative and at the same time systematic. Alongside the formal organization an *informal organization* based on spontaneous human relations exists and this forms unofficial networks, interpretations and norms about ways of safeguarding employees' interests. The informal organization, too, is ill suited to serve as a basis for development work.

The solution lies between them and combines elements of both: the development organization which provides the possibility to think, talk, make decisions and act in a way which is qualitatively different from what happens normally in a work organization. It presupposes the birth of a culture, which differs qualitatively from the normal work situation (Bushe & Shani, 1991, pp. 9–11). In other words, the production process and a qualitative change process require their own functional structure. The development organization of YIT was formed of a steering group, project groups and working groups. The steering group consisted of a development manager and two other managers and two researchers in the field of learning at work, ourselves that is. A series of workshops for the steering group was begun during spring 2002 and it completed its work in spring 2003.

An important decision in the project concerned the working method, which had to facilitate the creation of a shared conceptual language and shared understanding of the activities to be developed. A deepening dialogue between the professional practitioners and the researchers was used to close the gap between the former's operational and the latter's theoretical language. The method can be compared to the model developed by Mahoney and Sanchez, which they named 'Managers' and Researchers' Interactive Double-Loop Learning' (Sanchez & Heene, 1997). Drawing on Argyris and Schön's research into organizational learning, they presented a model of purposeful double-loop learning for reconnecting the generalized strategy building of researchers with the contextually rich strategy theory building of managers.

YIT Construction's experts stated that work processes in their company required continuous learning and the ability to cooperate in solving everyday problems. An employee's level of know-how is not just a personal matter; a professional skill produced through working is something that has to be shared between employees. Especially in situations where an experienced employee who has mastered certain work processes leaves working life, the transference of his or her knowledge and skills can be problematic. The problem is actually bigger: an employee's know-how should be accessible to workgroups during her or his active working period.

Training in itself does not guarantee professional know-how in YIT Construction. Expertise evolves at work through changing work duties and long experience. Know-how that evolves at work is largely tacit knowledge, which is not easy to dress in verbal form. This kind of knowledge is the fruit of learning at work, but so far it has been treated as though it is almost entirely the individual's private concern. It is often the case that a brief period of familiarization or a short training course has made a contribution to the development of an employee's know-how, but supervision of learning at work has been rare. The question is how to begin exploiting the learning resources that people have; success requires the conscious guidance and management of learning at work and the production of know-how.

In the first joint workshop the YIT Construction representatives summarized the problems relating to the production, sharing and evaluation of know-how in the company as follows:

- A large number of employees will be retiring in the near future and their know-how must be recorded and shared.
- Specialist know-how in this particular context develops by learning on the job and it cannot be acquired by training.
- Know-how is not being transmitted from groups and construction sites to others; knowledge is very often withheld.
- Know-how does not always enjoy sufficient recognition or appreciation.
- Many development projects are under way, but they are not coordinated with each other; an overall view seems to be missing.
- Construction work is project based and so development work has not been sufficiently long term.
- The company's secure position in the market and strong economic performance has discouraged risk-taking and innovation.

The phases of collaboration

In the following, the phases of the collaboration between the experts and the researchers are reconstructed. The core and sub-processes fostering learning and knowing in the work organization are presented as results of the collaboration including six phases. We then present the theoretical basis of the process model of learning at work. Finally, we give an example of tracking the suggestion scheme (fostering and developing initiatives) in the work organization.

The first phase was the recognition of problems and the setting of goals. The goal of the research and development project was the planning of strategies and action models for managing learning at work in YIT Construction on the basis of the authors' process model. The second goal concerned the collaboration between the experts and researchers; cooperation required an operations model in which the development of a shared set of concepts and a shared language was an important component. The work was done in workshops and was documented by the researchers.

The second phase was the finding and development of a set of concepts to be shared by the researchers and the experts. Using articles, examples of applications and metaphors, the expert members gained an understanding of the process model of learning at work. The experts for their part produced descriptions of YIT Construction's operations, strategic goals, core processes and above all processes connected with know-how. This familiarization phase took place in four 2–4 hour workshops during spring 2002.

The third phase can be called the concept-testing phase. Both parties tried to use the other party's concepts in their own descriptions of relevant matters. These descriptions were dealt with in several sessions during autumn 2002. In this phase the participants tried to identify company activities that matched the social, reflective, cognitive or operational processes, depicted in the process model of learning. The manifestations of these processes were examined in the activities of an employee, group or the entire organization.

The fourth phase was the analyzing of the current state of the production of know-how by using the process model. The development projects and activities in progress were analyzed and related to the goals of this project. The participants sought to identify impediments and problem areas; they wanted to find the *critical points* in activity producing learning and know-how.

The fifth phase was a critical scrutiny of the applicability of the process model. The experts tried to use the model for describing the activities in a concrete form. This was the *first round of modelling*, which took place at the end of autumn 2002. It produced some crude applications, but the cyclical nature of the model had not yet been understood, nor had the simultaneous nature of the processing of learning by the individual, group and organization. Phases 3–5 were accomplished in five 2-hour workshops during autumn 2002.

The sixth phase involved the remodelling of the development activities by the experts in the light of the feedback they had received from the researchers. In spring 2003, during the second round of modelling the participants reached agreement about what are the core processes producing learning and know-how that have to be managed. The core processes with their sub-processes are:

Research and development
- initiatives, suggestion scheme
- project scheme

Development of know-how
- skills mapping
- performance appraisals
- supervising learning at work

Continuous improvement of the activities
- auditing of core processes and work practices
- development of measures

An idealized description of each sub-process showing the learning cycles of the individual, group and organization was produced with the aid of the process model. Before giving an example, we clarify the background and the theoretical basis of the model.

Experience as a source of learning at work

The idea of experiential learning has its roots in many of the approaches to the study of cognitive development, but above all it has been built on Dewey's (1910, 1938) and Lewin's (1951) views of learning. Dewey's progressive view of education represented a challenge to traditional school teaching. He emphasizes the central role of experience in the learning process, but at the same time he also describes the problematic nature of the experiential process (Dewey, 1910, p. 156). Experience can be a matter of routine, which is based on tradition, external authorities or circumstances, but experience can also be reflective activity (Jarvis, 1987). The 'here and now' nature of experience and the role of feedback processes are very essential factors for understanding and guiding learning activities at work. Lewin (1951) developed this view of learning in the context of training intended to improve employees' skills in group dynamics and in the evaluation of their activities.

Kolb's study of experiential learning (1984) relies heavily on Lewin's views. Kolb does, however, mention that Piaget's theories of learning have influenced the evolution of his own ideas. Kolb sees experiential learning as a process that combines education, work and personal development.

Experiential learning is considered by Kolb to represent the workplace as a learning environment, which can be linked to formal education (Kolb, 1984, pp. 4–5). Together with his colleagues in Case Western Reserve University, Kolb later applied his experiential learning approach to the refashioning of management training (Boyatzis *et al.*, 1995).

The work of Dewey, Lewin and Kolb contains a critique of formal education; for them experiential learning is a powerful alternative. Nevertheless, they have not actually studied informal learning that takes place at work. In some less well-known research, however, Kolb (1988, pp. 68–88) does present the role of experiential learning working methods in the development processes of advanced professionals.

Many of the developers of experiential learning theory have concluded that reflection is the crucial stage of the experiential learning cycle (see later in this chapter), and it requires thorough-going analysis (see, e.g., Boud *et al.*, 1985). Reflectivity has been studied as a major factor in the learning and development of adults in both critical education (see, e.g., Mezirow, 1981; Kemmis, 1985) and activity theory research (see, e.g., Engeström, 1987). Experiential learning theory is criticized for studying the reflective process too lightly, for making the relationship of reflection with experience seem unproblematic and for detaching experience from its socio-historical context. One critique against experiential learning approach is that it passes an emotional dimension of learning. Illeris (2002, p. 37) disagrees with Kolb for paying attention exclusively to the cognitive dimension of learning. However, in Wolfe's and Kolb's earlier research work from the beginning of the 1970s, they found that an affectively complex learning environment supports best a learning approach relying on experience (Kolb *et al.*, 1984, pp. 137–40). Also the phenomenological approach in experiential learning (see, e.g., Boud *et al.*, 1985) attaches great importance to the analysis of the emotions in experience.

We see experiential learning as its own theoretical orientation and because of that it is understood as the basic idea for understanding learning at work. Experience is the starting point for learning, but also the result of learning activity. Moreover, learning is in itself experience. Recognizing, conceptualizing and managing learning at work is linked to the ability of the actors to reflect, which is to observe, find and be aware of the organizational processes that generate learning and knowing.

Learning contexts in a work organization

In this section we present a background of our process model (Järvinen & Poikela, 2001). We first describe the three contexts of learning in a work organization with the aid of Kolb's (1984) experiential learning model, Nonaka and Takeuchi's (1995) knowledge creating model and Crossan *et al.*'s (1999) organizational learning approach. After this section we present our own process model of learning at work, where we have combined the earlier mentioned approaches. This theoretical model has been tested in analysis of empirical studies performed in different organizations (Poikela *et al.*, forthcoming).

Learning in the context of an individual's work

The experiential learning model forms the basis for analyzing learning at work (see Figure 11.1). It says that a learner's prior experience and skills constitute the base for continuous learning at work. The employee usually uses his/her skills in a routine fashion when doing his/her work, but every now and then he/she has to think about new problems and solutions when old routines and skills are found wanting. Then the employee observes and considers earlier solutions, seeks out and receives feedback, and analyzes critically what the problem is and how he/she should act. Put in the language of theory, he/she *reflects* on his/her action.

When necessary, this is followed by the acquisition of new knowledge, for example by asking workmates or using other sources of knowledge, as well by attempting to find new ways to understand and conceptualize the

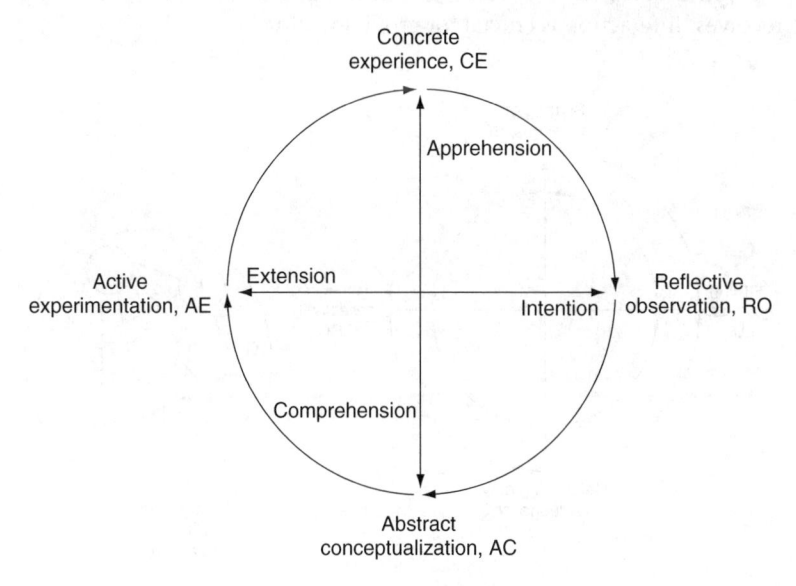

Figure 11.1: Learning in the context of an individual's work

problem at hand. This is a matter of finding new expressions, models or concepts that make possible the development of a new activity, model, prototype, tool and so forth. The new model is experimented with in practice, which in turn produces new experience, and so the experiential learning cycle continues. Thus Kolb's model can be regarded as the starting point for the description of learning at work and its management.

Learning in the context of shared work

In the same way as an individual, a work group or team learns collaboratively using the principles of experiential learning (see Figure 11.2). The group encounters a new problem or challenge, which cannot be tackled with its existing knowledge and work practices. The employees *share* their experiences and knowledge of the matter among themselves. They then proceed to jointly *reflect* on what the problem really is. Together the group starts to collect new knowledge, models and concepts so as to be able to understand the phenomenon in a new way. Newly acquired knowledge and knowledge, which has previously proved to be valuable, will be *networked* in the form of a conceptual model, plan or some other model.

The plan of action, prototype, tool or whatever is experimented with in practice. In other words, the group and its members learn in practice *by doing*. Experiences are gathered once more, this time about how well the new method or tool works in practice, and so the cycle of learning revolves. Interaction is crucial for group learning.

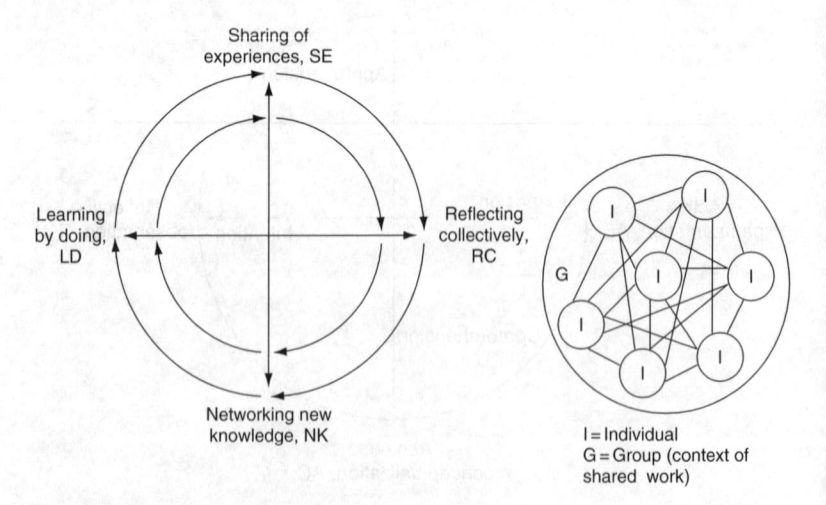

Figure 11.2: Learning in the context of shared work

The above description bears an analogous relationship to Nonaka and Takeuchi's (1995) well-known organizational knowledge creation model. The difference lies in the perspective: instead of learning, Nonaka and Takeuchi analyze what they call SECI processes (Socialization-Externalization-Combination-Internalization). Corresponding concepts (sharing members' experiences – dialogue or reflecting collectively – networking new knowledge – learning by doing) can be found in some writings by Nonaka (1994) or Nonaka & Takeuchi (1995, pp. 70–72). They cannot be found in the diagrams they drew to illustrate their ideas, the function of which is primarily to delineate the processing of knowledge.

Nonaka and Konno (1998) tried to show also the context, time and place for the realization of the SECI processes, which they describe with the Japanese term 'Ba'. It means a physical, virtual and mental state in which the creation of organizational knowledge becomes possible.

Socialization is a person-to-person occurrence, in which implicit knowledge is transferred from one employee to another in various face-to-face situations. In the externalization phase, the group plays the decisive role. In the combination phase the group systematizes what it knows and joins new knowledge to it in line with the common goals, and then knowledge moves between groups in a network. In the internalization phase, the individual has the leading role once more, but the new action model becomes established as a modus operandi for the groups and the whole organization, thus embracing the entire organizational culture.

In Nonaka's thoughts, the key group in the processing of knowledge is the organization's middle management, which must be able to function in both hierarchical and non-hierarchical fields of organizations (Nonaka, 1994). Middle management's role is critical because information flows from it to both the higher and lower levels of the organization. Senior managers are dependent for relevant information about the organization's activities on the middle managers, on whose leadership and guidance the development of employees' know-how also depends. Zuboff (1988, pp. 396–9), who sees learning as a new form of work, also assigns to middle management the duty of leading learning and directing of information functions.

Learning in the context of the organization's work

When talking about learning at the level of the whole organization, it is no longer possible to speak just about analyzing experience, something that is crucial in the learning of individuals and groups. This is actually more a matter of organizing the distribution of know-how and new knowledge throughout the whole work community (see Figure 11.3). Collective knowledge and know-how, which is often manifested through *intuition*, is *interpreted* in the group from the perspective of the whole organization. Knowledge, which is acquired through an initiative or the elaboration of some innovation, is *integrated* with existing knowledge and the organizations' databases. Then management tries to establish the new working practices as knowledge accessible by all. In other words, the new activity is *institutionalized* as a part of the whole organization's operations. The acquisition of new experience and its evaluation is the next step.

The main task of the organization's management is to take care of the assessment of new organizational practices, create channels and forums for feedback and assessment knowledge and the acquisition and interpretation of new knowledge. Thus the cycle of organizational learning continues. At the same time, management must see to it that the information supporting learning in the organization and the organization network flows without impediment.

The description of shared learning developed from Nonaka and Takeuchi's (1995) model bears an analogous relationship to Crossan *et al.*'s (1999) organizational learning model. According to them, organizational learning begins with intuition formation and continues within the subsequent stages that are intuition interpretation, integration into shared activities and institutionalisation as an established practice.

Intuition formation is very closely connected with the latent or preconscious action processes going on in the organization. It cannot be explained from the viewpoint of a single individual's action because

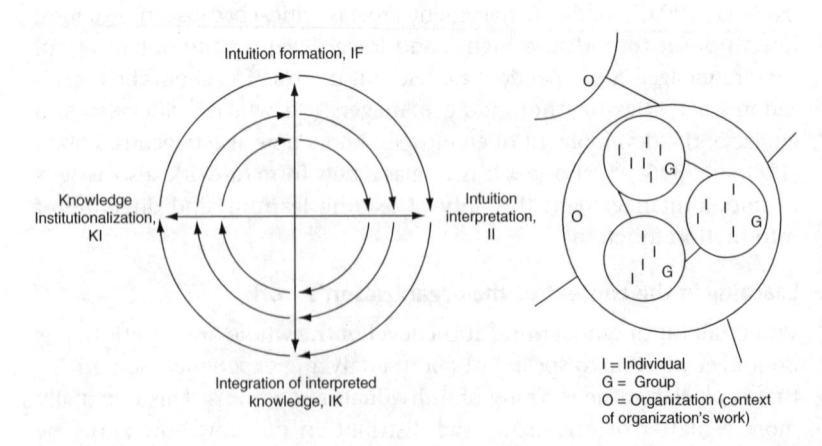

Figure 11.3: Learning in the context of an organization's work

work processes are shared between only individuals and work groups. Intuition interpretation begins with the charting of an action's conscious elements. The interpretation process also affects tacit knowledge, which has to be transmuted into linguistic form. On the individual level, interpretations contain contradictions, and these have to be resolved in the group in a way that everyone can understand and approve.

It is the shared language and shared interpretation that make knowledge derived from intuition the property of the organization, which means the *integration* of the interpreted knowledge as a part of collective activity. Integration expresses the work community's continuous internal communication through shared work practices. The establishing of new work practices results in their institutionalization, by which is meant the routines, structures, systems, strategies and formal frameworks, which ultimately direct the organizational behaviour of individuals.

Crossan *et al.*'s model fills in what was missing from Nonaka and Konno's earlier mentioned 'Ba' description. The model emphasizes the role of learning's feed-forward and feedback processes, which form the links between the levels of an individual, a group and an organization. However, they see the links as if these were only a matter of systematic input and feedback mechanisms. In our view they need to be understand as the processes fostering learning and knowing simultaneously between and within the different contexts of the work organization. In the next section we try to clarify this view.

Learning processes in the work organization

The models of Kolb (1984), Nonaka and Takeuchi (1995) and Crossan *et al.* (1999) intersect in a way that makes it possible to outline the process model of learning at work (cf. Järvinen & Poikela, 2001). Kolb's cycle aims at universality, in that its purpose is to explain the learning activity of an individual in any context whatsoever. Nonaka and Takeuchi's description illuminates the knowledge formation processes, which are essential for individual and collective learning. In Crossan *et al.*'s model, the individual's intuition needs the group as its interpreter and transmitter, after which the knowledge acquired can be integrated and institutionalized as the property and a characteristic of the whole organization. Learning at work can be condensed into the form of a process description, in which social, reflective, cognitive and operational processes follow, affect and refashion each other in a continuous process of learning (see Figure 11.4).

The social processes (concrete experience – sharing experience – intuition formation) mean the sharing of know-how knowledge and

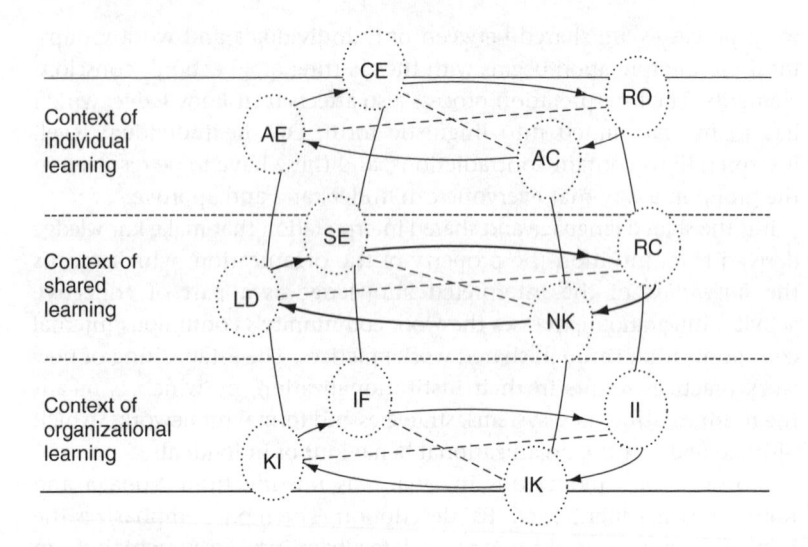

Social processes: concrete experience (CE) – sharing experience (SE) – intuition formation (IF)

Reflective processes: reflective observation (RO) – reflecting collectively (RC) – intuition interpretation (II)

Cognitive processes: abstract conceptualization (AC) – networking new knowledge (NK) – integration of interpreted knowledge (IK)

Operational processes: active experimentation (AE) – learning by doing (LD) – knowledge institutionalization (KI)

Figure 11.4: The process model of learning at work

experience between the individual, the group and the whole organization. Learning requires participation; it also requires that the participants are able to influence to developing activities.

The reflective processes (reflective observation –reflecting collectively – intuition interpretation) encompass the factors relating to the obtaining and giving of individual feedback, the assessment discussion of groups and the drawing of conclusions as well as the continuous evaluation for promoting the development of the whole organization. It is important that the managers of learning at work ensure that the assessment practices really are used and flow smoothly.

The cognitive processes (abstract conceptualization – networking new knowledge – integration of interpreted knowledge) concern the production, sharing, transfer and recording of knowledge and new models or concepts coming from the employee, the group and the whole organization. Experience-based knowledge, to which has been added externally acquired knowledge, is at this stage refined into more general knowledge for the organization's databases.

The operational processes (active experimentation – learning by doing – knowledge institutionalization) contain continual experimentation and testing of new practices on the part of both individual employees and work groups and departments. From the perspective of the organization, this means that the new practices become firmly established.

The new description produces a new kind of modelling, in which the organization is seen as being formed of processes instead of levels and hierarchies. This makes it possible to understand, handle, combine and lead processes in an appropriate way. In the following, there is an account of an application of the model within the suggestion scheme in the work organization. The example gives a close-up of initiative processes were modelled between the developers of the model and experts from the construction company YIT.

An example of an implementation: an initiative process in YIT

An initiative that is born in a work organization is usually the result of a concrete development need felt by many people. At its simplest, it might be a technical improvement, the correction of a fault, a precautionary measure or a proposal for doing certain things in a different manner. Many might be aware of the need to do something differently, but someone has to take the initiative. Of course, the person who took the initiative should be rewarded, so that employees are encouraged to draw attention to shortcomings and to make suggestions on how to deal with them. An initiative is, however, by nature a collective matter, but its presentation depends on the inspiration of a single individual.

An initiative might have far-reaching consequences. It is not a question of just a simple corrective measure for some problem and of 'single-loop learning' (cf. Argyris & Schön, 1978); an initiative can lead to re-examination of the bases for the activity of the whole operational unity or even of the entire organization. The solution to a problem can call for strategic measures. Using Agyris and Schön's terminology, it is then a matter of 'double- or teutero-loop learning'. In such a case, the problem cannot be corrected by any simple technical or managerial means; the improvement might affect not just everyday working practices but also the governing principles, strategies and objectives of the organization.

The first critical stage in the initiative process is when no one dares or is able to frame the idea in words. Such a situation can be found both in work climates and organizational cultures that promote learning and professional development and in those that hinder it. The second critical stage comes in the work practices in which initiatives are treated. Typically

184 *Learning and Knowing in Work Organizations*

the initiative-taker loses any further role in the treatment process once he/she has taken the reward for the idea. Later, if the initiative is put into practice, it usually appears in the form of a new set of guidelines.

A middle manager or someone else with responsibility for initiatives, serves as gatekeeper, and, insofar as his/her understanding and expertise allows, separates the sheep from the goats. He or she decides which initiatives the initiative committee, which then continues the sifting, will deal with; attention is paid especially to the relevance of the initiative for the unit's and the organization's tasks and goals. At the same time the committee inadvertently assumes only for itself the learning possibility contained in the initiative process, because the people who originally experienced the development need and problem are no longer involved in the development process producing learning and know-how. From the perspective of learning the ideal initiative process unfolds as follows (see Figure 11.5):

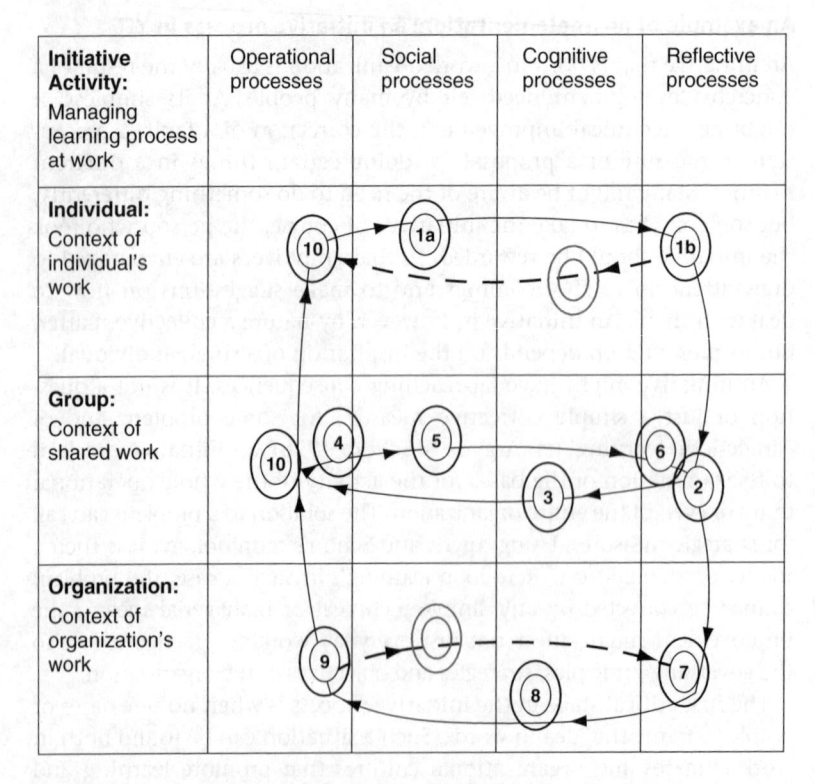

Initiative Activity: Managing learning process at work	Operational processes	Social processes	Cognitive processes	Reflective processes
Individual: Context of individual's work	10	1a		1b
Group: Context of shared work	10	4	5	6 / 3 / 2
Organization: Context of organization's work	9		8	7

Figure 11.5: Processing initiatives (an example of a sub-process)

- An employee presents an initiative (a) which has been simmering in the work community and which could lead to a significant improvement in their work. The employee must fill in a section on the initiative form, which asks what the purpose of the initiative is and how it is to be realized.
- The initiative is dealt with by the team led by the employee's senior or some other responsible team person; they consider the background and the possibilities for developing and applying the idea. The goal is to generate ideas, which will further refine the initiative and to chart the adequacy of existing know-how. The group defines explicitly the problem that the initiative is intended to solve. Next comes planning and experimenting and arranging the necessary resources.
- Group members acquire the knowledge needed for solving the problem from various sources. The aim here is to model the solution required by the problem and to draw up an action programme for its execution. Every group member must understand the rationale for the solution and his/her own role in putting the solution into effect.
- The group tests the model that has been thus produced in a practical application. The test is repeated as much as is necessary or possible. A record is kept of the initiative's strong and weak points as revealed in the experiments for later evaluation.
- Experience has been gained from the experiment, but among the members of the group there is a variety of views arising from differences in the observations they made during the experiment. It is vital that the group exchanges experiences so that they can kick them around.
- The group assesses the result of the process of their development efforts. If they are not satisfied with the result, stages 2–6 can be repeated by focusing the development process more precisely.
- As the initiative and its development process has required resources the organization's management is aware of it, has monitored its progress and evaluates the innovation's potential from the perspective of the whole organization.
- Management ensures that the principle of the innovation, its development model and other knowledge is documented in an information system, which can be accessed by all interested groups and employees in the organization.
- Management takes decisions about putting the applications into use, monitoring and distributing information gathered from the testing throughout the organization; at the same time management must see to it that their own knowing grows continuously.
- The groups and individuals responsible for the practical applications develop continuously their own know-how.

Conclusion

A big challenge to the researchers in the development project described in this chapter was to share the theoretical concepts of the process model of learning at work with the practitioners. In the current literature it is seldom described which kind of phases it is needed during a sharing procedure. In this chapter we reconstructed six phases of the conceptual sharing process. However, a big challenge to the practitioners in the development project was to construct the processes, which produce learning and know-how in a construction company. With the help the process model, three core processes and seven sub-processes were founded and modelled by the practitioners together with the researchers. This kind of modelling helps managers to recognize workplace-learning processes and to make them visible. The next challenge for both the researchers and the practitioners is transferring the core and sub-process models to work practice. The following stage in the development project will be the pilot programme, which involves dissemination of the action models, organizing the management of the processes, the development of evaluation and the measurement of results.

References

Argyris, C., & Schön, D. A. (1978). *Organizational Learning: A Theory of Action Perspective*. Reading, MA: Addison-Wesley.
Boyatzis, R., Cowen, S., Kolb, D. (1995). *Innovation in Professional Education: Steps on a Journey from Teaching to Learning*. San Francisco: Jossey-Bass.
Bushe, G. R., & Shani, A. B. (1991). *Parallel Learning Structures. Increasing Innovation in Bureaucracies*. Reading, MA: Addison-Wesley.
Boud, D., Keogh, R., & Walker, D. (1985). Promoting Reflection in Learning: A Model. In D. Boud, R. Keogh & D. Walker (eds), *Reflection: Turning Experience into Learning* (pp. 18–40). London: Kogan Page.
Crossan, M. M., Lane, H. W., & White, R. E. (1999). An Organizational Learning Framework: From Intuition to Institution. *Academy of Management Review*, 24(3), 522–37.
Dewey, J. (1910). *How We Think*. Boston: Heath.
Dewey, J. (1938). *Experience and Education*. London: Collier Macmillan.
Engeström, Y. (1987). *Learning by Expanding. An activity-theoretical approach to developmental research*. Helsinki: Orienta-Konsultit.
Illeris, K. (2002). *The Three Dimensions of Learning*. Roskilde: Roskilde University Press.
Järvinen, A., & Poikela, E. (2001). Modelling Reflective and Contextual Learning at Work. *Journal of Workplace Learning*, 13(7/8), 282–9.
Jarvis, P. (1987). Meaningful and Meaningless Experience: Towards an Analysis of Learning from Life. *Adult Education Quarterly*, 37(3), 164–72.

Kemmis, S. (1985). Action Research and the Politics of Reflection. In D. Boud, R. Keogh & D. Walker (eds), *Reflection: Turning Experience into Learning* (pp. 139–63). London: Kogan Page.

Kolb, D. (1984). *Experiential Learning. Experience as the Source of Learning and Development*. Englewood Cliffs, NJ: Prentice-Hall.

Kolb, D. (1988). Integrity, Advanced Professional Development and Learning. In S. Srivastva *et al.* (eds), *Executive Integrity. The Search for Human Values in Organizational Life* (pp. 68–88). San Francisco: Jossey-Bass.

Kolb, D., Rubin, I. M., & McIntyre, J. M. (1984). *Organizational Psychology. Readings on Human Behaviour in Organizations* (4th edn). Englewood Cliffs, NJ: Prentice-Hall.

Lewin, K. (1951). *Field Theory in Social Sciences*. New York: Harper & Row.

Mezirow, J. (1981). A critical theory of adult learning and education. *Adult Education*, 32(1), 3–24.

Nonaka, I. (1994). A Dynamic Theory of Organizational Knowledge Creation. *Organization Science*, 1(5), 14–37.

Nonaka, I., & Konno, N. (1998). The Concept of 'Ba': Building a Foundation for Knowledge Creation. *California Management Review*, 40(3), 40–54.

Nonaka, I., & Takeuchi, H. (1995). *The Knowledge-Creating Company*. New York: Oxford University Press.

Poikela, E., Järvinen, A., Heikkilä, K., & Tikkamäki, K. (forthcoming). Contextual Knowledge and Learning Processes at Work. In R. Gerber *et al.* (eds), *Improving Workplace Learning*. Nova Scientific Publishers.

Sanchez, R., & Heene, A. (1997). Reinventing Strategic Management: New Theory and Practice for Competence-based Competition. *European Management Journal*, 15(3), 303–17.

Senge, P. M. (1990). *The Fifth Discipline. The Art and Practice of the Learning Organization*. London: Century Business.

Zuboff, S. (1988). *In the Age of the Smart Machine. The Future of Work and Power*. New York: Basic Books.

12
Conditions for Learning During a Period of Change. Dilemmas and Disturbances on the Production Floor

Gun-Britt Wärvik and Per-Olof Thång

According to powerful rhetoric, economic competition within the industry, related to globalization and new technology demands 'something different' – traditional solutions do not work any more. The traditional solutions are often related to Frederic Taylor and scientific management and a production system connected to mass production. A Tayloristic top-down command and control system where the work is planned in the office and carried out by the workers on the production floor should be replaced by flexible and competent workers in self-directed work teams (Karlsson & Eriksson, 2000; Sandkull & Johansson, 2000).

It is the employers who seek regeneration from the employees. The management conditions are described as something utterly unstable and changing, it is a management responsibility to create a sustainable work system (Docherty *et al.*, 2002). A competent and flexible production workforce is emphasized as a means to handle the unstable and uncertain conditions (Wilhelmsson & Döös, 2002), which also draws attention to learning aspects. In this article, the aim is to discuss conditions for learning during a period when management actively strives for changing the working conditions on the production floor. As a source of inspiration, we have turned to activity theory as developed by Yrjö Engeström (1987).

The background is interviews with two production managers in the engineering industry. Both have actively tried to restructure work on the production floor but they say that the workers 'don't want to learn', that they continue to work as usual. We will argue that this is not a story about production workers who do not want to learn; it is a story about artefacts with different meanings in different activity systems. The intention is to make the division of labour visible, and to show how artefacts work concerning boundary setting and boundary crossing

(Engeström *et al.*, 1995; Star & Griesemer, 1989). Our point of departure is, therefore, artefacts developed by the management, whose aim is the transmitting of their intentions to the production floor and also how these artefacts work on the production floor.

In Sweden, there is a long tradition of cooperation between the parties on the labour market and the Social Democratic government concerning the question of how to adapt the production workers to 'something different'. During the past three decades, different developmental programmes have been carried out with the aim of supporting local change processes in different work places (Cole, 1989; Hamde, 2000). The programmes have been built up around the idea of facilitating the transfer from 'something' to 'something different'. Increasingly, competence and learning have come into focus and a lot of money has been invested in the projects (Docherty, 1996; Thång & Wärvik, 2001). However, a sustainable and long-term development seems to have been hard to achieve (see, e.g., Svensson and Randle, this volume). By a concrete example from one of the workplaces mentioned above, here called 'Gear', we will emphasize the complexity in the situated practice and the related conditions for learning. Activity theory offers conceptual tools that make this possible.

Analytical concepts

In their theory of informal and incidental learning, Victoria Marsick and Karen Watkins (1990, 1999) discuss learning in the workplace related to organizational changes. Their reasoning comes close to the problem area described here. Informal and incidental learning are defined by their contrast to formal learning. Formal learning often takes place in classrooms and is normally organized by institutions, whereas informal learning is commonly planned or intentional, but not so highly structured and is often integrated with daily routines. Incidental learning is unintentional – 'a by-product of some other activity, such as task accomplishment, interpersonal interaction, sensing the organizational culture, trial-and-error experimentation, or even formal learning' (Marsick & Watkins, 1990, p. 12). Marsick and Watkins (2001) define a model of a learning organization where informal learning is triggered by stimuli, for example, non-routine situations, leading to dissatisfaction with current ways of thinking and acting.

By reflecting upon the situation and problemizing what apparently seems to be obvious, and thereby surface tacit theories, the individuals or groups within an organization can use the situation for personal and professional development. This is also described as a reflective conversation with the situation. However, informal learning can also be dysfunctional when 'some aspect of the situation is either blind or hidden from the key person or persons' view' (Marsick & Watkins, 1990, p. 204). In addition, what people learn incidentally is regarded as not 'inherently correct'.

To follow in Marsick and Watkins' footsteps, the analysis could be concentrated on conditions in the social setting that will enhance the effectiveness of informal and incidental learning. According to Marsick and Watkins, these are conditions that will stimulate pro-activity, critical reflectivity and creativity. This would also create conditions for an analysis with the preconceptions of the production workers as a starting point and also how they frame the problems they face.

Marsick and Watkins' approach has a focus on the individuals in their social context, which also points towards the importance of collective processes. However, they leave the artefacts outside the analyses. To quote Bo Dahlbom and Jan-Erik Janlert, 'just as you cannot do very much carpentry with your bare hands, there is not much thinking you can do with your bare brain' (unpublished, cited in Dennett, 2000, p. 17). The point of departure here is that we do not have a direct and immediate access to the world around us; the relation between a subject and an object is mediated by artefacts. The mediating artefacts are tools, which help us perceive and act in and on the world according to specific criteria (Säljö, 2000). Described in this way, artefacts have an inscribed purpose; they are stored with intentions, shaped as they are in a specific social, historical and cultural context. Miettinen (1998) states that, 'the mediating artefacts are laden with "intentions", which cannot be attributed only to the subject'. Mediating artefacts shape actions but neither decide nor are the cause of any specific actions. They are not physical devices that can be separated from our understanding of them; they are material as well as conceptual. This also means that human beings cannot be separated from neither the artefacts nor the social context.

The individual and the context as an inseparable unit is made explicit by Engeström (1987, 2001) in his model of an activity system. An activity system consists of the subject, that is, the individuals whose agency are the point of departure in the analysis, and who direct their attention toward the object, that is, the raw material or the problem space that is transformed into an outcome and motivates the existence of the activity system. The relationship between the subject and the object is mediated by artefacts, which can be material tools as well as signs and symbols. Rules and division of labour between people who share a common object, that is, the community, also socially mediate an activity system. The object is understood as something imprecise and not quite reachable, a horizon that is always moving and constantly is (re-)produced and negotiated (Engeström, 2001; Engeström & Escalante, 1996). Human beings not only use tools, but also develop and renew them. Likewise, we not only follow rules, but also form and reformulate them. In one sense, the object can be understood as stabilizing and as setting the limits for possible actions. However, in the multivoiced activity system the stabilizing is constantly exposed to negotiations and reconsiderations, which lead to a motion. It is about a motion that constantly strives to stabilize, and both aspects work at the same time. Activity systems are therefore dynamic systems, always in a state of imbalance and change which results in dilemmas and disturbances within the activity system itself and in the encounter with other activity systems that are also a source of development and learning (Engeström, 1987, 2001). This means that the intentions mediated by the artefacts cannot be regarded as separated from the activity system of which they are a part. It is not possible to predict how artefacts will work on the production floor only by noticing the intentions that at first sight seem to be inscribed in them. In and through the situated practice, they both appear as something and are shaped to something.

Thus, the activity system as a unit of analysis does not only include individuals and collectives, but also embraces a complex mediational structure. They are open systems and must by necessity be regarded as such. It is impossible to isolate and keep social aspects constant and thereby study a closed system (Sayer, 1992). According to Russel (2002), the world is 'not neatly divided into activity systems. It is up to the researcher or designer to define the activity system based on the purposes of the research study or design task, to focus the theoretical lens AT provides' (p. 67). The activity system is an abstract model that can be used analytically to make visible processes not directly observable. In this case, to make visible dilemmas and disturbances as a potential source of learning and development.

To collaborate, different activity systems have to create a joint context so that the information they share makes sense (Bowker & Star, 1999; Engeström, 2001; Engeström *et al.*, 1995; Star & Griesemer, 1989). The processes analyzed here concern production workers who have to work on a border between areas with which they are not so comfortable. They have to touch upon or even cross the borders into other activity systems which, for example, have other tools and other rules. The borders can be bridged through the production of new mediating concepts (Engeström *et al.*, 1995). Susan L. Star has coined the concept of boundary objects, which can be understood as such mediating artefacts.

'Boundary objects are those objects that both inhabit several communities of practice and satisfy the informational requirements of each of them. Boundary objects are thus flexible enough to adapt to local needs and constraints of the several parties employing them, yet robust enough to maintain a common identity across sites. They are weakly structured in common use and become strongly structured in individual-site use. These objects may be abstract or concrete' (Bowker & Star, 1999, p. 297).

Boundary objects make it possible for people from different activity systems to understand each other and to coordinate (Engeström, 1999) their work. They constitute a kind of a crossing point between different activity systems. Through their vague and unspecified nature, boundary objects can easily adjust to specific circumstances and also acquire a more specific meaning.

Gear

Gear is a unit within Service AB, which in turn is a company within a multinational engineering company. The manufacturing at Gear consists mainly of one-piece production, sometimes with numerically controlled machines, and always with high precision demands. In most cases, the customers come from Production AB, another company within the multinational. When the study began in 1999–2000, Gear had approximately fifty employees. Together with the operators on the production floor and the production manager, there were two planners, two foremen, and an orders clerk. The unit was facing a major change. Up to this time Gear had been a part of Production AB but from then they were expected to belong to Service AB, which also incurred a responsibility for creating financial accountability. Besides, Gear had to be competitive on the market. All this was something new. The relationship between Gear and Production AB was no longer an assumed client. One problem for Gear was the difficulties it had in meeting delivery deadlines and this placed pressure on the unit because of the new demands to become profitable.

How to understand 'something different'

The question then is, how to understand 'something different'. The situation described by the production manager at Gear can be likened to what Victor and Boynton (1998) term 'mass customization'. In short, mass customization is to produce what the customer wants, no more and no less, quickly and with high quality, and competitively priced. 'Getting information from the market, interpreting market needs, and rapidly organizing resources – these are the keys to mass customisation' (Victor & Boynton, 1998, p. 98). Flexibility is of central importance and the employees are described as 'hubs in complex web of activities' (ibid., p. 104), self-governed, but capable of cooperating and eager to change. In mass customization, the company asks for the production workers' close knowledge about the architecture of the production system. This in turn highlights a control dilemma and it is in relation to this the expressed need of competent and flexible production workers can be understood. Strategies for flexibility can be of different kinds, for example flexibility for predictability and tight control and flexibility for adaptability and innovation. The former is about production workers that can easily be moved around to where they at any given time are best needed. The latter is about production workers encouraged to be independent and act on their own initiatives without anyone giving an order (Watson, 1995).

Most likely, a company can experience pressure for both strategies and the tension that then is the result must be handled. Flexibility for predictability and tight control undermines flexibility for adaptability and innovation. Tightly controlled production workers cannot be induced to be innovative (Watson, 1995). The situation can be potentially contradictory and can only be understood in the situated practice. However, it will not be enough to study discursive practices only but also the stabilising conditions. A production-planning meeting offers an opportunity to study how the management develops artefacts with the aim of transmitting their intentions to the production floor. The idea is to grasp something that is always moving but at the same time tends to stabilize.

The production-planning meeting

In production-planning meetings, production workers with a special responsibility for production planning participate together with the production manager, the two foremen, the orders clerk and the two planners. The production workers with this responsibility are called logistics agents, and Gear has five of them, one in each work team. The logistics agents are expected to get involved in the production planning besides their ordinary job as operators. A closer look at this production planning meeting presents an opportunity to study the transformation from mass production to 'something different' as a learning process, that is, how to cope with new demands from customers.

Lists with information about metal pieces play a central role during the meetings. The lists are printed from Monitor, a computer-based system for production planning. The analysis is directed towards the expected normal flow of events during the production-planning meetings and to the dilemmas and disturbances that appear in relation to this, and also to solutions that come up during the meetings. The analysis is therefore also focused on the crossing points between the two activity systems and on mediating tools, which can be connected to a boundary object.

One conclusion from the analysis is a division of labour between the planning of the work and the work on the production floor so total that a suggestion is that the situation can be studied as a meeting between two activity systems. However, the two activity systems have something in common; within both, the object is related to metal pieces. Among the workers on the production floor, the object can be described as 'to change metal pieces concerning form and properties'. The object of the activity of planning, as exposed during these meetings, appears in a different way. It is about 'planning and controlling the flow of metal pieces during their way through the production floor'.

A dilemma of delay

The lists printed from Monitor present the production process in ways that require a certain infrastructure. Monitor's logic is built upon notions of central control, of division of labour, and of an unproblematic transfer from the planners' intentions to the production workers. Disturbances and dilemmas appear in relation to, on the one hand, Monitor's infrastructure and on the other hand, the demands from customers, who want fast deliveries and the management who want economic surplus.

During a meeting, under the topic 'capacity', a planner shows that the numbers of metal pieces on the production floor, in terms of hours, are decreasing. The planners have also difficulties to get on well with their work, every week a lot of orders are not planned. The backlog of orders result in delayed delivery and in the long-term lost customers. However, the solution is not just to plan the entire backlog.

The list of 'capacity', printed from Monitor, reveals that one of the machines (number 316, see extract below) has been assigned too many production hours. The capacity of the machine measured in terms of production hours is not enough. This is about hours assigned to the machine by the planner when he planned for the tracks of the different metal pieces. It is not about the real production time, that is, the time it takes for the production worker to choose the suitable tools, fasten the metal piece in the machine, and to carry out the operation.

> Log.agent 1: but there's a lot in 316 (*the machine*)
> Foreman 1: but it's double planned...
> Planner 2: we must get jobs out to the production floor too, when we run simulation, it's low on the production floor... it must be overloaded somewhere...

Gear must quickly plan all of the orders to be able to handle its economic situation, and quickly deliver in time the unique metal piece ordered by the customer. But if it does, some machines become overloaded and delayed delivery, lost customers, and low revenue will follow. If the planners do not overload the machines, the backlog of orders will increase and the result will be the same. Whatever the planners do, it will be wrong. The ordinary solutions do not work any more because nobody wants capital tied to metal pieces in a stock room, which means that customers only order metal pieces when they need them, and Gear has to make a profit. The situation can also be seen as a basic dilemma from the perspective of the management. A strategic managerial solution to the dilemma is to introduce the position of logistics agents. Thereby, a transformation pressure is expected to affect the production floor.

The logistics agents

During the production-planning meeting, the logistics agents appear in relation to three situations. One situation is to help the planners with the backlog of orders, to be the substitutes. The two others are focused on the work on the production floor, but can be regarded as attempts to improve the lists from Monitor so that they will correspond better with reality. It is about run schedules that have to be followed, and about the production workers' reports of performed work – the re-reporting. All of the situations can be related to planning work and they also involve border-crossing situations for the logistics agents, even if many situations physically are taking place on the production floor. The three situations are here seen as crossing points where the different activity systems meet and intersect.

Then the question is, 'What makes border-crossing possible, how can a boundary object be described?' A suggestion is that production time can be regarded as such a boundary object. It is in relation to production time that the position as logistics agent is developed and accords with the planning as well as the customers and the management/owners. However, within the different activity systems different tools and rules are developed related to production time.

The substitutes – lack of capacity among the planners versus lack of capacity on the production floor

When the backlog is growing, the logistics agents should help the planners to plan, to be the substitutes. However, the solution to let the logistics agents do planning work immediately triggers a new problem. To take two people away from operators work with a machine causes more trouble: a lack of capacity on the production floor. This will also result in delivery delays. The dilemma, to choose between lack of capacity on the production floor or in the planning, remains.

The run schedule – the replaceable worker versus the skilled worker

The run schedule is a print from Monitor. Every logistics agent prints his/her own run schedule and brings it to the production-planning meetings. After the meeting, they put the run schedule on the wall beside the shelf where the work team keep metal pieces waiting for the next operation. The intention is that the production workers should choose the metal pieces according to the list. However, the planners cannot control the production workers when they pick up a metal piece from the shelf. In the following extract, the production workers are described as disturbing the order by taking two pieces at a time from the shelf to the machine. The workers do not follow Monitor's directions.

> Planner 1: ...maybe they take one or two jobs, one cannot know
> Log.agent 1: yes, it happens sometimes that they do...when the pieces are similar and such things

The production work at Gear is characterized by 'one man-one machine'. Occupational skills, related to several years of operators work with metal pieces by the machine, are highly valued among the production workers. This strong focus on the highly skilled worker in his machine is something that has been developed during decades of piece rate. In the current team-based work organization, the wages are monthly and not based on individual results, but Gear had piece rate until the beginning of the 1990s. During the period of piecework, the production workers had to be smarter than the planners, to perform a piece of work faster than the planner thought was possible. If a production worker was able to do this, he could raise his pay. Those who made a mistake sometimes did not get pay for this particular piece and had to work on weekends to catch up.

A clear dilemma is the signal of replaceable workers expressed by the run schedule in relation to the norms of the highly skilled worker that are expressed among the workers on the production floor.

> 'It takes a long time to become skilled. Nobody will let one cross the border to something else until one is skilled in something and then one doesn't dare. Because, then one has to start from the very beginning and again become unskilled. And one doesn't want that either' (talk with a production worker).

From the point of view of the production workers, to strictly follow the run schedule can be the same as to become unskilled, despite occupational skills developed during decades. They can maintain their occupational pride by choosing a metal piece, maybe the trickiest one, by the shelf and neglect the run schedule.

Re-reporting – control from above versus autonomy

The lists from Monitor are not reliable because the re-reporting seems to be late.

> Someone: yes... maybe five or six jobs are not re-reported
> Log.agent 2: they carried out the operation last Monday or Tuesday
> Log.agent 1: then they (the actual metal pieces) should be re-reported...
> Planner 2: It's your business, see to that (the re-reporting)

Quite a few operations are not re-reported. Planner 1 says that the logistics agents must see to it that the re-reporting is done. He therefore tells the logistics agents to control their workmates, to ensure that all the production workers do the re-reporting as soon as the work with the actual operation is completed. From a management perspective, delayed re-reporting is problematic. The management will not get a true picture of the situation on the production floor. On the whole, the possibility of controlling production is strongly related to re-reporting, according to Monitor's logic. Monitor is build upon the assumption that production information can easily be gathered by a central control function, and then, with the help of the lists presented during the meetings, the employees within planning and production can easily be directed by the management.

On the production floor, among the workers, re-reporting is something different. Re-reporting once was a tool in the service of individual piece rate and the MTM-method (method-time-measurement). Only a few of the workers have personal experience of MTM, used during a few years in the 1960s and the 1970s, but they all 'know' how it was. The traces are still there. They point to big cupboards that are (still) placed very close to some machines. Unnecessary steps between the cupboard and the machine should be avoided by this arrangement. A central stock room with a sign still exists even if it is not a central stock room any more. Earlier, the production workers did not have access to the stock room; they had to go to a desk to get the tools someone else had decided should be used for the particular work. Today, the workers themselves select the most suitable tools. It is difficult to grasp if the stories told are related to MTM or to the piece rate. Maybe this is not so important. In both cases there is a need of autonomy and freedom from control, to have the opportunity of minding one's own business, without every minute of one's activities being transformed to management information.

Conclusions

The transformation pressure clarifies the division of labour as well as weak crossing points between the different activity systems. The crossing points were earlier built upon 'time clock and whip'. The new situation requires alternative solutions. With the intention of letting the transformation pressure affect the production floor, positions as logistics agents are introduced. The logistics agents are expected to act in such a way that the infrastructure required by Monitor can be maintained as a way of handling the tension between flexibility for tight control and predictability and flexibility for adaptability and innovation. However, this does not solve the problem of late deliveries and the dilemma of the lack of capacity within the activity on the production floor or within the planning activity itself.

The different activity systems seem to be difficult to combine; they are driven by different motives. The weak crossing points between them become visible in relation to the different tools and rules related to 'production time' as a boundary object. During the production planning meetings, the logistics agents and the planners can coordinate their work through the boundary object, however, without changing the basic conditions. 'Production time' partially connects the objects of 'changing metal pieces concerning form and properties' and 'planning and controlling the flow of metal pieces on their way through the production floor', and also the artefacts 'run schedule' and 're-reporting'. However, this is not about an unproblematic transfer of ideas from the planners to the production floor. The artefacts and how they are developed in a historical sense are of great importance for what is going on. The run schedule, as an outcome of the planning activity, is meant to function as a tool within the activity on the production floor. The schedule can also be described as an artefact with the aim of transferring the planners' intentions to the production floor. The run schedule and re-reporting are changed to something else on the production floor. Within the activity system of planning, they are artefacts with a rational meaning.

The intention is that the operators shall follow the run schedule when they pick up a metal piece from the shelf. Then Monitor's lists will show a picture of a well-functioning production process if the operators re-report after they have finished an operation. Run schedule as well as re-reporting is then a matter of controlling the transportation of metal pieces on the production floor. On the production floor, however, run schedule and re-reporting are closely connected to occupational skill as opposed to a replaceable worker and to autonomy as opposed to control from above.

The knowledge created within an activity system is not a transparent reproduction of a given reality; it is about knowledge related to a certain activity system and where the object and the mediating artefacts constantly are (re-)produced. The runs schedule and re-reporting are artefacts that acquire different meaning within different activity systems and create dilemmas and disturbances on the production floor.

The lack of mediating tools that can bridge the two activities and the division of labour is apparent. It is obvious that neither the planners nor the production workers can take in the whole production process, they can only take in a part of it; some aspects are 'hidden from the key person or persons' view' (Marsick, 1990, p. 204). The situation can also be described in terms of informal and incidental learning. However, there is more in this than a possibility to reflect upon the situation and thereby surface tacit preconceptions. It is the workings of the material artefacts that are hidden. To conclude, this is neither a story about single individuals who 'don't want to learn', nor an account of how the situation can be explained by collective norms of workers' resistance only. The artefacts and their historical development are also important.

References

Bowker, C. G., & Star, S. L. (1999). *Sorting Things Out. Classification and Its Consequences.* Cambridge, MA and London: MIT Press.

Cole, R. E. (1989). *Strategies for Learning. Small-Group Activities in American, Japanese, and Swedish Industry.* Berkeley: University of California Press.

Dennett, D. C. (2000). Making Tools for Thinking. In D. Sperber (ed.), *Metarepresentations. A Multidisciplinary Perspective* (pp. 17–29). Oxford and New York: Oxford University Press.

Docherty, P. (1996). *Läroriket – vägar och vägval i en lärande organisation.* [The Learning Domain – Ways and Alternatives in a Learning Organization]. Stockholm: Arbetslivsinstitutet.

Docherty, P., Forslin, J., & Shani, A. B. R. (eds) (2002). *Creating Sustainable Work Systems. Emerging Perspectives and Practices.* London and New York: Routledge.

Engeström, Y. (1987). *Learning by Expanding: an Activity-Theoretical Approach to Developmental Research.* Helsinki: Orienta-Konsultit.

Engeström, Y. (1999). From Iron Cages to Webs on the Wind: Three theses on themes and learning at work. *Lifelong Learning in Europe*, 4(2), 101–10.

Engeström, Y. (2001). Expansive Learning at Work: toward an activity theoretical reconceptualization. *Journal of Education and Work*, 14(1), 133–56.

Engeström, Y., & Escalante, V. (1996). Mundane Tool or Object of Affection? The Rise and Fall of the Postal Buddy. In B. A. Nardi (ed.), *Context and Consciousness. Activity Theory and Human-Computer Interaction* (pp. 325–73). Cambridge, MA and London: MIT Press.

Engeström, Y., Engeström, R., & Kärkkäinanen, M. (1995). Polycontextuality and Boundary Crossing in Expert Cognition: Learning and Problem Solving in Complex Work Activities. *Learning and Instruction*, 5, 319–36.

Hamde, K. (2000). *Shifting Identities. Teamwork and Supervisors in Swedish Change Programmes for the Last Three Decades.* Stockholm: School of Business. Stockholm University.

Karlsson, J. C., & Eriksson, B. (2000). *Flexibla arbetsplatser och arbetsvillkor. En empirisk prövning av en retorisk figur.* [Flexible Workplaces and working conditions. An empirical test of rhetoric]. Lund: Arkiv.

Marsick, V. J., & Watkins, K. E. (1990). *Informal and Incidental Learning in the Workplace.* London: Routledge.

Marsick, V. J., & Watkins, K. E. (1999). Looking Again at the Learning Organization: a Tool That Can Turn into a Weapon. *The Learning Organization*, 6(5), 207–11.

Marsick, V. J., & Watkins, K. E. (2001). Informal and Incidental Learning. *New Directions for Adult and Continuing Education*, 89, 25–34.

Miettinen, R. (1998). Object Construction and Networks in Research Work: The Case of Research on Cellulose-Degrading Enzymes. *Social Studies of Science*, 28(3), 423–63.

Russel, D. R. (2002). Looking beyond the Interface. Activity Theory and Distributed Learning. In M. R. Lea & K. Nicoll (eds), *Distributed Learning. Social and Cultural Approaches to Practice* (pp. 64–82). London and New York: Routledge Falmer, The Open University.

Säljö, R. (2000). *Lärande i praktiken. Ett sociokulturellt perspektiv.* [Learning in Practice. A Socio Cultural Perspective]. Stockholm: Prisma.

Sandkull, B., & Johansson, J. (2000). *Från Taylor till Toyota. Betraktelser av den industriella produktionens organisation och ekonomi* [From Taylor to Toyota. Reflections on the Organization and Economy of Industrial Production]. (2nd edn). Lund: Studentlitteratur.

Sayer, A. (1992). *Method in Social Science: A Realist Approach*. London: Routledge.

Star, S. L., & Griesemer, J. R. (1989). Institutional Ecology, 'Translations' and Boundary Objects: Amateurs and Professionals in Berkeley's Museum of Vertebrate Zoology, 1907–39. *Social Studies of Science*, 19, 387–420.

Thång, P.-O., & Wärvik, G.-B. (2001). *Kompetensutveckling för yrkesverksamma inom den västsvenska verkstadsindustrin – är det möjligt?* [Competence Development for employees within the West Swedish Engineering Industry – Is it Possible?]. IPD-Rapport 2001:04. Göteborg: Göteborgs Universitet.

Victor, B., & Boynton, A. C. (1998). *Invented Here. Maximizing Your Organization's Internal Growth and Profitability. A Practical Guide to Transforming Work.* Boston, MA: Harvard Business School Press.

Watson, T. J. (1995). *Sociology Work and Industry* (3rd edn). London and New York: Routledge.

Wilhelmsson, L., & Döös, M. (2002). Sustainability in a Rapidly Changing Environment. In P. Docherty, J. Forslin & A. B. R. Shani (eds), *Creating Sustainable Work Systems. Emerging Perspectives and Practices* (pp. 101–13). London and New York: Routledge.

13
A Context of Learning in the Workplace

Hanne Dauer Keller

It seems to be generally acknowledged that the efficiency of knowledge-based organizations depends upon a continuous development of the competence of the employees. In social work too, the continuous development of competence is crucial. The general conditions on which social workers try to provide help to the citizens are marked by frequent changes of laws and regulations. In addition to this instability, social workers' expertise is often exposed to criticism from several sides. Furthermore, it can be demonstrated that – whatever the reasons might be – many clients do not benefit from the help provided by the social system and mediated through the interpretations and actions of the social workers. The continuous change of tasks and work conditions together with the recurrent criticism of social workers' professionalism point to a general need for development of competence in social work.

Competence develops through a process of learning. Competence implies a 'what' and a 'how' of learning: something that is learned together with a way in which the learning takes place. However, this point is often misunderstood. Widespread notions of competence are about abstract categories of individual-bound entities, such as conscious knowledge or cognitive skills. In consequence, the development of competence is understood as an improvement of such resources that are distinct and general at one and the same time. For instance, 'knowledge about mental illness' is supposed to be acquired like an exact entity, or precisely 'the ability of empathy' is supposed to be improved. In contrast to this prevailing understanding, a notion of competence as the social workers pre-conscious conception of their work is presented. This notion implies that the development of competence is closely related to the shared articulation and reflection of the practical experience of a community. It is not just (and not even primarily) an acquisition or improvement of individual abilities.

On the theoretical arena, two contrasting views of the learning that develops competencies are at play. At one side, formalized learning (for instance through institutionalised supplementary training) has traditionally been promoted. At the other side, one can argue for the importance of informal learning and for supporting the learning conditions of the community of practice. These opposite notions of learning and development seem to imply correspondingly different conceptions of competence. In the first case, competence is understood as a context-independent personal capacity that can be acquired through education and transmitted to practice. In the last case, competence is understood as tightly associated with the performance of practice and the participation in a community of practice. So, in both cases, there is coherence between the concept of competence and the idea of learning. The problems of both the educational and the practical orientation are well known. The educational approach runs into the problem of transfer when it repeatedly turns out that knowledge acquired under education is not directly transferable to practice. In the practical oriented view, there is a problem of getting at a sufficient distance to the practice in which one is about to develop practical knowledge. In this chapter, I argue for a practically oriented perspective on the development of competence. The problem of the lack of distance is overcome by introducing group supervision as a method for reflected development of competence. In group supervision, the connection to practice is maintained in the contents of the supervision, namely the immediately experienced problems of practice. At the same time the distance to practice is created through the use of dialog that encourage reflection.

The concept of competence

Across many discussions of learning and competence as matters that are closely related to the performance of practice, three different concepts of competence can be distinguished. With one of these concepts, competence is regarded as something inner that belongs to the individual, for instance his or her knowledge or skills. A second type of understanding of competence focuses on what is demanded by the employer in order to accomplish the work. It is this kind of interest in the subject that is taken in the numerous surveys of managers' views on what kind of competence their employees need in the future. A third kind of understanding tries in different ways to build a bridge between these 'inner' and 'outer' oriented approaches: competence is viewed as 'action competence', that is, defined as the transformation of personal capabilities into the ability to work. Following this point of view, competence can be understood as the ability to work that the staff member puts into play when he/she meets the demands and expectations of the work situation. Thus the competence we speak of here is neither a phenomenon that exists solely in the inner of the staff member nor a phenomenon that can be clearly defined by managers, customers, clients, colleagues or engineers. This view indicates an understanding of the staff member's actions as not (totally) determined by the demands of work. The staff member perceives and acts in the light of an interpretation of the demands, possibilities and dilemmas of the surroundings in relation to his/her own experiences. The staff member makes sense of his/her work while doing it (Weick, 1995). As we apply this third approach, it is stressed that the staff member is basically regarded as an active *interpreter* of his/her environment.

The concept of competence applied in this chapter is about work conceptions, which groups and individuals construct in coherence with their practice. The staff member's conception of their own work is a meaning structure that is basic to their competence, that is, crucial to how they perform their job (Sandberg, 1994). Understanding and reflection *in practice* integrate specific knowledge and skills into the concrete way that the task appears. Knowledge and action are seen as mutually connected – we act on the basis of our knowledge and we develop our knowledge through action. Therefore, we form experience and develop competence through practice. The concrete sense making in relation to the handling of ambiguous work settings and situations is often an inter-subjective process that implies the negotiation of meaning in a community of practice, where the knowledge and skills of individuals are transformed and mediated in relation to the organizational context of action (Jensen & Prahl, 2000). But sense making also occurs as an individual's immediate structuring of the meaning of a work task, for instance the 'reflection-in-action' as described by Schön (1983). In both cases, the sense-making process must establish an understanding of the work that dissolves ambiguities sufficiently for action to take place, that guides the way of carrying out the work, and that remains open for change through feedback from the world, that is, open to learning.

Sense making in social work

This chapter relates to empirical material from the field of social work (cf. Keller, 2003). The focus of the empirical material is the practice of

Danish social workers occupied with activation of social welfare recipients, that is finding activity or job training for the client to attend. 'Activation' is a practice developed in particular in the 1990s in the light of a change in the politicians' view of the most helpful support to social welfare recipients. There has been an increasing approval to the viewpoint that social security must be connected with demands on the client to make an active effort to regain a footing on the labour market. There is now a legal foundation to improve the client's chances of getting a job by qualifying the client. The purpose of social workers' efforts with the social welfare recipients is clearly to improve the rate of employment among the clients. Ideally, the task is to integrate the requirements of the labour market into clients' experiences, wishes and possibilities. In fact, the work mainly consists in trying to combine the individual experiences and wishes of the clients with the rather limited possibilities of municipal activation projects or job training. Thus, the job contains several dilemmas, for instance the dilemma of serving clients on an individual basis, while there are many rules and regulations to follow in the administrative system, and as a result the clients are to a large extent treated alike.

In connection with the discussion of competence, sense making and learning in practice, this state of affairs within the field of social work raises some interesting questions: Does the practice of the social workers at all contain a latitude for acting in different ways? To what extent it is reasonable to understand social work as a non-routine practice open for competence development? Is it in fact adequate to maintain that social workers have to interpret their work situation in order to get their job done? Social work is, on the one hand, performed extensively by routine, as actions and decisions must be in conformity with the law. On the other hand, the core of social work is to help people with specific problems, that is, to organize help on an individual basis. Resent research indicates that job demands within the social and healthcare professions are *not* (completely) defined by technology, regulations and routines (Larsen *et al.*, 2001). The tasks are not associated with a single well-defined goal, but indicate several possible solutions and differing procedures to attain them. There is some objective autonomy for staff members' assessment and discretion as to their job performance. So, the active utilization of this autonomy is in fact a job demand – as well as a stimulating aspect of the psychosocial work environment. This active interpretation is a formation of meaning that coheres closely with the actual undertaking and accomplishment of the practice as well as with staff members' application of personal knowledge and skills.

Development of practical knowledge

Knowledge of practice develops through practice. Work consists of more than the application of a profession's formalized knowledge on practical problems, and more than the use of the methods and techniques of the profession. For a social worker to be confronted with a client and trying to understand that person, in order to plan how he/she can be helped, is of course quite different from being in an educational context where one learns about a helping relation. In education one learns about models and the complexity of the studied problems is under control. But in the real world problems do not fit the models very well and the complexity, ambiguity and level of dilemmas can be overwhelming. I have met newly educated social workers that – in the light of practical experiences that stimulated their learning – jumped to the conclusion that they had not learned anything through three and a half years of education.

What characterizes competent work performance is – as it has often been emphasized – that the performance is intuitive rather than according to rules, artistic rather than clearly explicable. Such performing develops, it is claimed, through experiences with several cases from which a recognizable figure gradually emerges as it assumes a characteristic pattern (cf., e.g., Wacherhausen, 1991; Dreyfus & Dreyfus, 1999; Schön, 1983). In more general terms, our understanding of the social world can be described as founded on *common sense constructions* of social life (Schütz, 1975). People who live in the same social context share the meaning of this context. It has a special structure of relevance to them. Common sense constructions are a set of abstractions, generalizations, formalizations and idealizations of the reality of everyday life that function as interpretations of the social world. They are constructions of the *typicality* of the world.

This emphasis on typicality does not mean that members' constructions of the typicality of the world are regarded as fully developed to grasp every situation. On the contrary, the typicality operates as a schedule of reference, which makes it possible for us to distinguish what is different from the typical. However, it is in our nature to develop common sense constructions, that is, to understand the social world with an emphasis on typicality. Unfamiliar experiences that differ from the typical have a tendency to be either contained by commonsense constructions or to result in the development of new common sense constructions in relation to the specific social practice.

The process of development from newcomer to competent staff member can be described as follows. At first, practice will seem very open. On example of this (cf. Keller, 2003) is that several social workers have the impression that newcomers seem to be aware of more possibilities in the concrete work with a client than more experienced social workers recognize. For the newcomer, it seems relatively open on what to focus in the dialogue with the client and it also seems open what kind of help is needed and what kind of help that can be provided. Gradually, the newcomer will get practical experience and through repeated experiences with situations – that have something in common but also differ in some ways – a perspective on practice is constructed, and this allows for some features of a situation to stand out while others remain in the background. An understanding of the typical features of the situations is constructed. With additional experience, the situation is seen as a unified whole, a pattern or a *Gestalt*. The recognition of the pattern makes it possible immediately to experience certain purposes in the situation and certain actions as relevant. The staff member no longer needs to formulate in a conscious way the purpose of the task in order to determine which actions to perform. The situation itself calls upon certain actions. As a result, staff members build up a repertoire of ways of performing practice through experience.

The suggested approach emphasizes that in our work we draw on our stock of social knowledge. At the same time we build up experiences with practice and make commonsense constructions of the typicality of practice. Social workers for instance develop typical concepts for types of tasks, clients and patterns of actions. The commonsense constructions associated with our stock of social knowledge structure our conception of the work. Drawing on experiences, we immediately sense how the present problem must be constructed and solved. The concepts of the social world, which are based on experiences, can be described as pre-conscious. This means that the commonsense constructions of the social world work without involving a reflective consciousness and that they are difficult to delineate explicitly. However, this approach maintains that it is possible to a certain extent to express or indicate the tacit notions of practice, especially to people who hold comparable kinds of experience (Wacherhausen, 1991).

Learning through being part of a community of practice

The individual does not learn from experiencing practice alone. In addition, the individual's experiences are negotiated in a community of practice. Through the collective negotiation of meaning the regime of competence belonging to the community of practice comes into existence

(Wenger, 1998). Learning is a part of practising social practice and is connected to the changes, demands and possibilities of the social practice. The purpose of learning is to master a social practice (Lave & Wenger, 1991; Nielsen & Kvale, 1999). In this way, learning is about a lot more that just acquiring formalized knowledge. It is also about acquiring identity, skills and knowledge about social norms. You must learn to progress and become a full member of a social context.

Since social practice is carried out by a community of practice, the community possess some knowledge about practice, which the novice does not. Thus, for the newcomer, learning means to get access to the knowledge of the social practice that the community holds and to get access to the negotiation of meaning, in which the community continuously engages. This learning includes to get a good grip of social relations, of who knows what and of who has which (informal) position in the community of practice (Wenger, 1998). Although the newcomer learns by getting access to the knowledge of a community of practice, for instance through legitimate peripheral participation (Lave & Wenger, 1991), the experience of the individual can also have an effect on the knowledge of the community of practice.

Through the life of the community of practice solutions to problems are created with the purpose of conducting the work of the community in the best way. Thus, the practices and the ways of acting belonging to the community can be understood as a kind of learning history, a story of what answers to what problems the community has developed. Learning in this sense is highly incidental, as pointed out by Marsick and Watkins (1990). It is a by-product of the community performing its social practice.

The learning that takes place in communities of practice can only be facilitated, never controlled. Initiatives that are being organized for learning to take place might facilitate certain learning processes of the community, potentially leading to defined goals. But there is no guarantee. For instance, if a course is organized for the members of a community, what determines the success of the learning is to what extend the community will organize its learning around that resource. New ways of thinking and acting, new ways of organizing or new technology is incorporated in practice only if they show themselves useful for the purpose of conducting the social practice that the community holds (Wenger, 1998).

Learning as adaptation and renewal

The emphasized approach to learning illustrates how the newcomer develops qualifications to conduct the existent practice. It emphasizes how the newcomer can get hold of the knowledge that already exists in the community and thereby become a full member of it. In a way the 'community of practice' approach is not occupied with innovation and creativity.

Is this focus on acquiring already existent knowledge an advantage or a problem? One might argue that when society changes rapidly it is no advantage to take over the practice of last year. However, there is a danger that the present focus on change and development makes us forget the kind of knowledge, which is not constantly changed or replaced. Most of our knowledge is the same tomorrow as today. Even though we might get into trouble if we too doggedly resist the change of knowledge and skills, it is also an advantage that everything is not open for discussion, negotiation and change at all times. Thus, it seems reasonable to focus on how we acquire the already present knowledge, which in a sense is a necessity for change and development in the future. If the aim of the learning process is adaptation, we should not automatically consider it as problematic or normatively judge it as a less important way of learning.

Like informal and incidental individual learning, collective learning can be described as adaptive. When the community of practice collectively learns in an incidental way, the underlying aim of the learning process is to adapt social practice to the influences of the environment. However, the reaction cannot be described as determined, but must be understood as negotiated and interpreted response to the circumstances. Still, the learning described is highly adaptive. Communities of practice 'make the job possible by inventing and maintaining ways of squaring institutional demands with the shifting reality of actual situations' (Wenger, 1998, p. 46). Communities of practice are thus very good at developing and preserving solutions to conflicting demands in their practice, and they are especially good at transferring, informally, the accumulated practical knowledge to newcomers. This of course has certain advantages. Things get done and newcomers will quickly become efficient. However, adaptive learning can lead to unintended consequences because it is directed towards practical solutions. To give an example, a well-known problem in the social and health professions is, that there are too many duties and too little time. In practice, this dilemma is often solved by the actions of clients or patients. The clients who frequent the social security office often or behave in a problematic manner are 'serviced', while low priority is given to the 'invisible' and quiet clients. Of course this 'solution' is problematic, because priority is not based on professional criteria, and the short-term 'solution' to the problem might result in untreated clients developing more serious social problems in the long run.

So, the effective adaptation of a practice to the given, environmental conditions of change can have unintended consequences. Therefore, it can be important to facilitate the negotiation of meaning and the learning of the community of practice, so that the development is to a larger extent build upon reflection and a proactive attitude, and not just the spontaneous and reactive adaptation to 'external' changes.

If we want to promote other kinds of learning processes than the pragmatic adaptation to the circumstances, it may be necessary to create a specific context – to delineate a distinct space – for learning, which in a sense is distanced from practice and the incidental learning that goes on in the practice. Of course, the risk is present that what is learnt in this specific context for learning is too distanced from practice. This would mean that staff members are unable to apply 'the learning' to the work context. It is therefore important to discuss the possible advantages and disadvantages of such a more 'formalized' learning context and pay attention to the correlation between this kind of specially arranged context and the working life. The more formalized context for learning provides a *possibility* for individuals as well as the collective to structure their negotiation of meaning.

In the following, I refer to results from my study of a specific context for practice-oriented learning, a course on group supervision. The aim of the research was to investigate in how far and in what ways the development of the staff members' competencies could be supported through their participation in an arranged learning-oriented course.

A study of the development of social workers' competences

The study aimed at investigating if and how a course on group supervision would facilitate the development of the competences of social workers. The focus was on changes in the staff member's pre-conscious structuring of his/her work task and his/her work role. You might say that the attention was on the changes in the staff member's theories-in-use (Argyris, 1990) or taken-for-granted assumptions.

Two groups of social workers were part of the study. Each group consisted of four social workers whose job function was to activate social welfare recipients, that is, to find an activity or job training for the client to attend. The social workers pre-conscious structuring of their task and role was studied *before* the course on group supervision and again *after* the ending of the course.

The reason for choosing a course on group supervision in preference to other learning settings was that it offers a particularly fine opportunity to combine (or balance) the two – in many ways contrasting – perspectives of practice and learning. On the one hand, it establishes such a distance from the intrusive immediacy of the practice that collective and individual latitudes for critical reflection can emerge. On the other hand, this learning through thematic discussions remains firmly associated with the crucial challenges and the experienced details of the members' shared practice. In general, the advantages that characterize group supervision may be stated as follows:

- In this kind of course it is possible to handle problematic situations that at first seem vague, ambiguous or uncertain to the supervised. The role of the helping supervisor (i.e. a member of the group) is handled according to the principle of process consultation (as defined by Schein, 1999). When the supervisor works in a way that facilitates the process of reflection of the supervised it is possible to start from more vague formulations of the problem.
- It is possible for the supervised to discover the premises for action and to explicate his/her tacit knowledge of the practice. This is possible because the participants share a deep and problem oriented experience of the practice and because of the particular setting of the group supervision in which sufficient time is provided, different questioning techniques are used to change perspective, and the participants engage in reflecting teams.
- The contents of the supervision are controlled by the participants, and the themes taken up are always problem oriented. The problems to be handled in supervision always stem from a need on the side of the supervised for some help in handling problems in his/her job. In this way the learning is self-directed.
- It is possible to facilitate personal growth in this context. In the course of colleague supervision it is possible to focus on mutual relations, so an atmosphere of safeness and confidence is created, making it possible to also support learning in a personal dimension.

In this kind of supervision, the problem of the supervised is put into words. The participants engage in critical reflection upon the problem, and through feedback from supervisor and the reflecting team the supervised attains new perspectives on his/her practice together with new opportunities of action in his/her practice.

In my research project, different qualitative methods were applied. An important method was observations of social workers' counselling for 'difficult' clients, followed by an interview with the client about his or her experience of the counselling and then by an interview with the social worker about his/her practice. Subsequently, the dialogue between the social worker and the client was analyzed. The idea was to describe the social worker's implicit understanding of the problem of the client, and also the mutual relationship as it appears from the way the social worker handles the counselling. The aim of the analysis was to describe the sense making in which the social workers engage during their work. To describe the process of sense making, I used Schön's description of the structure of reflection-in-action as a model to uncover the process of sense making in the counselling. The process of sense making is a concrete expression of how the person relates to the dilemmas of work and chooses (often unconsciously) to solve them.

Some dilemmas of social work

In an operational perspective, we may say that the way in which the individual social worker handles central dilemmas and conflicts of his/her work constitutes his/her competence. One of the important dilemmas of social work is to unite the individual needs of the client with the demands and possibilities of the administrative system. An unproblematic match is seldom found. Often the client is in need of a kind of help that cannot be offered by the system, and likewise the system has some demands and possibilities, which from the client's point of view do not seem meaningful ways of being helped. When the work is stretched between the considerations of the instructions of the administration, what Habermas (1997) has called *a system world*, and the considerations of the unique needs of the client, which could then be named *the lifeworld* of the client, it is possible that different social workers understand their work with different emphasis on the balance between consideration of the system world and the lifeworld of the client respectively. In the one extreme, the social worker counsels according to the system world, which means that he/she structures the social problems of the client identically with the system's way of structuring the task. In the other extreme, the social worker acts exclusively according to the wishes and needs formulated by the client. Thus one important category of analysis related to how each of the social workers in their practice solved the conflict between the demands of the political and administrative system and the needs of the unique client. In addition, there was a research focus on how the social worker made sense of the interaction with the client and transformed – during the work process – an ambiguous and complex situation into a problem that he/she could handle.

The dilemmas of the social work imply different possibilities for acting in the helping roll. If the social worker is mostly engaged in the administering of a law, he/she might adopt the role of a specialist or an expert, which means that he/she, on the basis of his/her experience, decides the contents of the social problem and the appropriate intervention to solve the problem. If the social worker is more focused on the clients needs, he/she might adopt a role as the client's advocate (against the 'system') (Høilund, 2000). Resent research points out that social workers often solve the dilemma by accepting a mediating roll, which means that the social worker understands his/her job largely as the 'translation' of demands from the system to the client in a way that the client can accept, but also to mediate the client's wishes in ways acceptable to the system (Berg Sørensen, 1995). One last alternative should be mentioned, namely the possibility of surpassing the dilemmas by assuming a helping role constructed on the principles of process consultation. The fundamental assumption in process consultation is that the helper can only assist the client in helping himself. Thus, to assist means to establish a helping relation in which the social worker and the client jointly diagnose the situation and develop adequate solutions. The helper does not in advance have a definition of the problem, but joins the client in an inquiry of the situation (Schein, 1999).

The results

The results of the study were not unambiguous and call for an interpretation. During the course on group supervision (which I observed), it was obvious that the supervised learned something about their practice and the way they related to it. It was not unusual that a supervised declared that the supervision 'really' had been of great help and had given him/her new opportunities to move on with a difficult case. In the groups, they also spoke of supervision as 'really good' and as something in which they should engage much more. Contrary to this generally positive impression, there were great differences in the evaluation given of the two groups after the completion of the course. One group gave much positive response and the members gave different descriptions of how they applied the learning to their work. In the other group, they thought of the course as 'almost wasted'. As a parallel to these differences, my study of the social workers' competencies showed two different trajectories of development. In the 'positive' group, a social worker's development could be described as a development towards working more client oriented and adopting a role resembling the role of a process consultant, while she was trying to facilitate the potential for development of the client and strengthen the inner motivation of the client. In the 'negative' group, the development of a social worker could be described as a development towards working more system oriented, and consistent with that his/her role was changed towards the role of the expert. This attitude involves a risk of 'freezing' the client in a role of dependence on the social system, without any chance to influence the system's discretion and measures to intervene on his problems.

The two different and contrary developments cannot both be meaningfully understood as a result of social workers' participation in the course on group supervision. Certainly, group supervision – in particular on a systemic theoretical basis, such as in the course in question – does not have a narrow aim for development. The aim is that social workers develop a better understanding of a typical work situation through a change of perspectives. Still, certain developments of understanding are more than others in line with the activities and implicit norms of the group supervision. The emphasis on the change of perspectives tends to imply that social workers would also try to view the problem situation in the perspective of the client. Therefore, it seems reasonable to assume that a stronger focus on the client's perspective is a likely result of the learning process. In the group supervision, reflection on actions is emphasized in association with the opening and widening of spontaneous perspectives and approaches, and this is regarded as something contrary to the correct analysis and good advice of traditional 'experts'. Thus, it is important that everybody in the group supervision contributes to the understanding of the situation. It is, therefore, most likely that the social worker develops his/her role of counselling toward that of a facilitator, resembling a process consultant who supports the development processes of the client, and it is not probable that he/she will develop his/her role in the direction of something like an expert.

Based on the above, it is possible to conclude that the social workers in the 'positive' group actually had made use of the course of group supervision as a context for learning, which supported them in conducting their work, while the 'negative' group had not been able to do the same, despite positive experiences during the course and a general attitude towards group supervision as good and necessary.

Even though the social workers in the 'negative' group had not really been able to use the course on group supervision as a context for learning and did not develop their competencies in line with the expectations, the closely analyzed member of the group had, however, in the same period changed her conception of task and roll. Alterations in the collective practice as well as in the attitude of the individual social worker had taken place during the period from the first to the last observation. Taking into consideration the suggested theoretical understanding of learning, one would expect this kind of result because learning is conceived as a part of social practice: if practice changes, the staff members are most likely engaged in learning processes. To be more specific, first, about the individual social worker, her competence had changed from a certain degree of client orientation to a system orientation, and her conception of the work role had changed from mediator to expert. In line with this development, her conception of the client's awareness of his/her own problems, needs and wishes changed from a recognition of the client as having a certain (but limited) awareness of own needs to a conception of the client as being in need of experts to define his/her needs.

Developments of social practice

Taking into consideration the suggested theoretical approach to learning, it is obvious to connect the two different trajectories of development of competence with the fact that the social practice of the two groups changed in very different directions during the period. The 'positive' group's social practice had changed in a favourable way. When I first met the group, they could scarcely be characterized as a community of practice. But during the research period the group had developed a strong community in which they supported and developed each other professionally and also did relate to each other personally. In the same period, the psychosocial work environment had changed from highly stressful to a more regular level, because of a decline in the number of clients and in addition an extra group member and a full-time manger of the group had been engaged. In the 'negative' group, almost opposite changes occurred. The original group disintegrated and at the end of the period the passages of members in and out of the community was so striking that the remaining members had temporarily given up on playing any particular role in the introduction of the newcomers to the social practice. During the period the workload had changed from high to enormous. The increase in workload arose because of a coincidence of longer periods of illness among staff members together with new and additional tasks. Furthermore, assigned to the group was a new manager, who was highly interested in getting the social workers to initiate activities for a larger part of the clients. Moreover, the autonomy of the work had changed. The group got more routine tasks and as a consequence the part of work containing professional content had decreased.

The described change in the competence of the social worker from the 'negative' group (toward a system orientation and an expert-like role) is understandable when it is viewed in light of the development of practice towards increase of demands on effectiveness and decrease of autonomous discretion. One can imagine that the result of the increase in workload is that the social worker gives up time-consuming conceptions of and attitudes towards the work and adopts a less time-consuming role and conception of the work. A system-oriented way of working is predicted in the organization by regulations and routines. In addition, by adopting the role of an expert, the complexity of the tasks is reduced. An increase in the intensive demands of the job will probably mean that staff members must reduce their qualitative and professional demands. The time for dialogue with the clients is cut down and the activity for the client must be found very quickly. Consequently, the social worker acts as an expert and makes sense of the situation without involving the client very much.

Conclusion

Group supervision seems to function as an organizational context dedicated to learning, that is, a specific context of learning, which allows for collective explication and reflection while remaining highly or entirely practice-related. The mediation between pre-conscious competence and reflected competence development, between practice and learning that takes place in group supervision, is reciprocal. Far beyond what is explicitly said in this learning space, practice brings its influence to bear through the competent interpretation of *typical* cases and difficulties. And far beyond what is explicitly intended, the reflections and discussions within the learning space are smoothly integrated as new perspectives, procedures and techniques in the everyday work practice.

The above results from my study put into focus the complex connections between the individual learning, the community of practice, a specific organizational context for learning, and the psychosocial work environment. An important point is that an arranged context of learning can explicate – closely and adequately – the member's own experience as a community of practice. Still, the development of staff members' competencies does not seem to be fully understood until the factors of the psychosocial work environment are taken into consideration. The psychosocial work environment includes the individually and collectively experienced work practice together with the problems, dilemmas and challenges that it presents. Some of the most important conditions at the task level are about complexity, autonomy, participation, required competence, stress, latitude for reflection and action. At the collective level, conditions as sharing knowledge and joint negotiation of meaning are of importance.

More generally, the results emphasize that it is not sufficient to understand working life learning from a pedagogical angle. In addition, we must pay attention to how competence and learning are actively promoted and hindered through work conditions. In this study, the results of the 'negative' group became understandable when the changes in the work environment were taken into consideration. But also the results of the 'positive' group should be interpreted in the light of work environment changes. There seems to be a fairly close coherence between the benefit of the context of learning and a sound work environment, which in the future ought to be investigated in much more detail in order to enhance learning at the workplace.

References

Argyris, C. (1990). *Overcoming organizational defences. Facilitating Organizational Learning.* Boston: Allyn & Bacon.

Berg Sørensen, T. (1995): *Den sociale samtale – mellem klienter og sagsbehandlere.* [The social dialogue – between clients and social workers]. Aarhus: Gestus.

Dreyfus, H., & Dreyfus, S. (1999). Mesterlære og eksperters læring. [Apprenticeship learning and experts' learning]. In K. Nielsen & S. Kvale (eds), *Mesterlære – læring som social praksis.* København: Hans Reitzels Forlag.

Habermas, J. (1997). *Teorien om den kommunikative handlen.* [The theory of communicative action]. Aalborg: Aalborg Universitetsforlag.

Høilund, P. (2000). *Socialretsfilosofi – retslære for socialt arbejde.* [Philosophy of social law – jurisprudence for social work]. København: Nordisk Forlag.

Jensen, I., & Prahl, A. (2000). Kompetence som intersubjektivt fænomen. [Competence as an inter-subjective phenomenon]. In T. Andersen, I. Jensen & A. Prahl (eds), *Kompetence – i et organisatorisk perspektiv.* Roskilde: Roskilde Universitetsforlag.

Keller, H. D. (2003). *Læring i arbejdslivet. – Om kompetenceudvikling i socialt arbejde.* [Learning in working life. – On competence development in social work]. Institut for Læring, Aalborg Universitet.

Lave, J., & Wenger, E. (1991). *Situated Learning: Legitimate Peripheral Participation.* Cambridge: Cambridge University Press.

Marsick, V. J., & Watkins, K. E. (1990). *Informal and Incidental Learning in the Workplace.* London: Routledge.

Nielsen, K., & Kvale, S. (1999). *Mesterlære – læring som social praksis.* [Apprenticeship learning – learning as social practice]. København: Hans Reitzels Forlag.

Sandberg, J. (1994). *Human competence at work.* Göteborg: BAS, Göteborg University.

Schein, E. H. (1999). *Process consultation revisited – building the helping relationship.* Reading, MA: Addison-Wesley.

Schön, D. A. (1983). *The reflective practitioner – how professionals think in action.* New York: Basic Books.

Schütz, A. (1975). *Hverdagslivets sociologi.* [The sociology of everyday life]. København: Hans Reitzels Forlag.

Wacherhausen, S. (1991). Teknologi, kompetence og vidensformer. [Technology, competence and forms of knowledge]. *Philosophia,* 20(3/4), pp. 81–117.

Weick, K. (1995). *Sensemaking in Organizations.* Thousand Oaks, CA: Sage

Wenger, E. (1998). *Communities of Practice: Learning, Meaning and Identity.* Cambridge: Cambridge University Press.

14
Non-learning in Multicultural Work Communities

Marit Rismark and Jorun M. Stenøien

Why does so little learning take place in multicultural work communities? Experienced and highly qualified Polish nurses working within the Norwegian health system play no vital roles in and barely contribute to developing ward practices.

This chapter provides a case study of a very common situation around the world, namely multicultural staff working together in the joint production of goods and services. It is a study of the dynamics of shared duties in health ward practices, with nurses embedded in two different nursing models working side-by-side. The analysis examines how Polish nurses and Norwegian health personnel have their own socially constructed nursing models – a 'medical' and an 'independent' approach to nursing. The different backgrounds and work experiences become an issue of mutual recognition, and it is evident that the potential for learning is not realized. Rather, we see a non-learning organization and a power-play through which the Norwegian staff preclude themselves from adding to their nursing practice. What does this imply in the wider perspective of international agreements that aim to enhance knowledge exchange and promote mutual understanding between people and nations?

One aim of a major joint-venture agreement between Poland and Norway is to satisfy the demand for nurses in the Norwegian health system by recruiting Polish nurses (*Handlingsplan for Østersjøområdet*, 2001–2002; Kommunal og regionaldepartementet, 2003). Such agreements promote mobile workforces, a phenomenon of which we will be seeing more as Poland and other nations join the European Union and gain access to broader labour markets. This is a situation that calls for deeper understanding of cultural and knowledge exchanges.

In our study we observed two nursing models. It became evident that nursing is not a unified global practice. We identified deviating local practices, each with unique theoretical and practical knowledge bases. The idea of knowledge structures becoming less and less tied to particular national and local working cultures is, moreover, not as straightforward as one might like to assume (Amin & Thrift, 1994). However, the idea that knowledge may apply across cultures is implicit in a global perspective. This also fits well with the expectation that European workforces will become more mobile as a result of the agreements on the free flow of labour. However, this is not the case as it would appear that only quite severe economic or political disadvantages lead people away from the local constraints of kin, language, domestic investments and cultural familiarity (Waters, 1995, p. 89).

The issue of the potential to be found in doing something, for example nursing, differently is by and large an epistemological question. It may be the case that knowledge is not detached from local practices but rather situated in local practice. Our study of two nursing practices is a knowledge–cultural encounter and we explore the dynamics of this encounter and the implications above the local level. This chapter examines how local practices on the wards are sub-cultural sites for negotiation, having policy implications beyond the local level in a world of mobility.

Theoretical framework

Our theoretical framework is based on Vygotsky's (1987) emphasis on the interrelated roles of the individual and the social world. This relation is the basis for developing and maintaining the 'ways' of doing things within a social practice, such as the workplace, encompassing the Polish nurses and the other members of the work communities.

We can see the importance of including social and cultural dimensions, particularly when work communities have workers from other countries with less shared history and less language and culture codes. Knowledge, skills and understanding are created and maintained within the practices, and they are valid according to the particular activity system (Engeström, 1999). Individuals become familiar with the practices through participation. As a result of this, each practice is historically and socially situated and one practice cannot be copied into other times and places (Lave, 1997). With all communication and all actions being situated, according to a sociocultural understanding, these phenomena need to be seen as relative to the context within which they occur. A 'neutral' context does not exist (Säljö, 2000).

To act in appropriate ways within the community of practice requires knowledge of what is valued by the particular work culture. This leaves the Polish nurses in a special situation as they are core personnel and do not have language skills on a par with the other employees and staff, and may not know the general culture so well that this knowledge can guide their actions in the work setting. In general, newcomers do not play a central role in the work community and opportunities to make authentic contributions to the joint enterprise are critical (Cope *et al.*, 2000). Human action is situated in social practice, and individuals act according to their knowledge and experience and to what is required, appreciated or enabled in a particular social situation. At the work site, the immigrant nurses and the work community encounter each other's values, skills and experiences as they participate in daily work activities. One crucial factor is thus the individual's ability to judge the relevance of (i) particular information, (ii) skills and (iii) the understanding of actual situations and the ability to act according to what is valued by the social world. It follows that much knowledge by its very nature is relative so that skills that are valued in one situation may not be relevant for other social partners.

Participation is central to people's lives in general and also applies to workplace learning when workplace practices are seen as jointly constructed (Lave & Wenger, 1991; Billett, 2001). Participation involves the relations between how the work practice affords participation and how individuals elect to engage in the work practice (Billett, 2001). These encounters allow both the individual and the sociocultural environment to be included, as this point of departure encompasses the individuals, their social partners historical traditions and materials and their transformations (Engeström, 1999).

The global within the local

Multicultural work environments reflect local processes for constructing joint work practices. Participants carry with them knowledge, values and skills developed and applied in other sociocultural environments, and their present work culture may be influenced by the participants' prior historical, cultural and social practices. The prevailing work culture is dominant as the newcomers enter the workplace, and immigrants as newcomers are not automatically incorporated into work communities (Waale, 1996; Rismark & Sitter, 2003). Immigrants in work training programmes need to develop a function within the workplace and they have to earn professional acceptance (Rismark & Sitter, 2003).

We identified two nursing models. These work practices most likely come together in several ways. One possibility would be that different practices exist side by side in the same workplace and generally do not come into contact. Another variant is that the local practice dominates and newcomers must adapt to this, and thus a form of forced learning takes place. A third possibility is that new and existing practices meet in a balanced encounter, all of them being recognized so that a new hybrid practice is constructed. The first two possibilities represent non-learning organizations, while the latter represents a situation of learning and change for both the environment and the participants.

Based on these three possible scenarios, we may outline several implications for the importance of recognition of culture and knowledge within a multicultural workforce on a more general level and understand the issues when placed in a deeper globalization discussion (Amin & Thrift, 1994).

The multicultural work environment in our study mirrors the interrelatedness of local and global processes. In multicultural work environments, one can expect to find particular constraints in the ongoing processes of constructing joint local work practices. Participants carry with them knowledge, values and skills developed and applied in other sociocultural environments. When brought together, the workers become part of a multicultural knowledge process.

Large-scale phenomena are often studied in macrosociological perspectives that tend to disregard microsociological processes. However, disregarding the relevance of microsociology to globalization is a misconception of what globalization processes are all about (Robertson, 1995, p. 25). According to Robertson (1995) and Bauman (1998), globalization processes involve a very close connection between the local and the global. Bearing this in mind, the concept of 'globalization' has been introduced to capture the inseparable essence of local and global change processes. This approach is also the basis of our study.

Object of study

This is a case study of how multicultural staff work together to share duties. Our approach is to investigate a contemporary phenomenon within its real-life context. The exploration of the construction of workplace practices means entering into a setting with 'boundaries between phenomenon and context not clearly evident' (Yin, 1994, p. 13), and key themes about nursing cultures that arise within this particular site cannot be easily separated from the context in which they are found.

The theoretical framework suggests that the dynamic contributions from individuals and their social partners, and historical traditions and material and their transformations will be an important focus. We explore the workplace participation through the diversity of interaction involving dynamic contributions from agents in the activities in which they engage. These encounters between agents and activities in the social and cultural environments are captured through studies of units that possessed 'all the basic characteristics of the whole' (Vygotsky, 1987, p. 46) rather than elements of analysis. This allows for a reformulation of the relation between the individual and the social and cultural environments in which each is inherently involved in the others' definitions (Rogoff, 1995, p. 140).

We explore an integrated system of workplace practices with the case study being 'the study of particularity and complexity of a single case, coming to understand its activity within certain circumstances' (Stake, 1995: p. ix). Although we cannot generalize on the basis of one single case, the case study has implications above the local example. As the researcher approaches a specific situation and describes a multitude of details and aspects of this exemplary example, the knowledge that emerges from the example has general application (Josefsson, 1991, p. 82).

Interviewing informants and analysing the material

The data analysis stems from 24 interviews. The Polish nurses were recruited by a Norwegian public job-service centre together with health institutions in need of skilled nurses. Scandinavian institutes at universities in Poland arranged intensive courses in the Norwegian language for these nurses before they headed for Norway. The language training lasted three or four months.

This material has limitations as we do not have direct access to 'study processes, relationships between people and events, the organization of people and events, continuities over time and patterns, as well as the immediate sociocultural contexts in which human existence unfolds' (Jørgensen, 1989, p. 12). Interviews may not always tap the wide range and variety of voices that are also part of the context, and when we encounter hesitation, or an incomplete story, we probe further, but ultimately we can only guess at what remains hidden (Elbaz-Luwisch, 2002, p. 425). Our approach to minimize these limitations was to create a trustful and meaningful interview situation. We did not enter their stage suddenly, hunting for their stories, and then leave as abruptly as we came. We got to know some of the informants in Poland a year ahead of the interviews; we visited and talked to a group of nurses at a time where they were six weeks into the language course (Rismark &

Stenøien, 2002). During the interviews, we were able to understand some of their experiences from that period.

When the Polish nurses tell us about coming to work in Norway, it is not simply a matter of grasping the interpretations and meanings behind the stories they produce. Life as told may or may not correspond to life as lived and life as experienced (Bruner, 1984), and the story will be influenced by the audience and the social context within which it is being told. During analysis, background knowledge may be important. Interpretation depends on knowledge of context and background as one must go outside the text to understand it. Becoming acquainted with some of the nurses in their native country one year ahead of meeting them in Norway provided some background for interpreting their interpretations in creating a 'second-order representation' (ibid.).

Filling the job at the nursing home ward

The analysis of the dynamics of work participation revealed three emerging themes affecting participation on an equal footing within the wards. It became clear that different frames of reference were applied by Norwegian and Polish health personnel when constructing the meaning of doing the job. One theme was the deviating perceptions on the meaning of nursing responsibility. Further analyses elaborate on how the concept of care left the newcomers a blurred sense of responsibility, and with gaps between practices and expectations of appropriate ways of doing the job.

The meaning of nursing

The Polish nurses were not perceived as naturally filling the function as fully qualified nurses once they joined their new work communities. Moreover, the health system does not provide them with authorization. When they started working they were licensed nurses with responsibilities similar to nursing assistants. It is at least six or seven months before they can attend a medical course, pass the examination and achieve full authorization as a nurse.

At the wards, the newcomers were regarded as nurses but with limitations when it came to language and ways of performing the work, such as following ward procedures. When looking beyond the language issues and knowledge of local practices, other differences between the Norwegian and the Polish experience materialized. One such difference involved the contrasting views on what the nursing profession is. These differences may have contributed to the different ways in which work activities were approached. The views differed as to which actions form part of a nurse's job. Among members of the work community, we found the opinion that Polish nurses were not familiar with the concept of 'total nursing responsibility'. A Norwegian nursing assistant provided an example that to her exemplified the different approaches to nursing:

> 'Polish nurses are not used to the idea of total care. They can perform the nursing work, medical care, but they do not look after important social matters, such as taking the patient to the hairdresser etc.'

In other words, as the work community was concerned with providing care for the residents, the meaning of care goes beyond the responsibility of providing medical treatment. It was not adequate nursing to be strictly oriented towards physical health, for instance by observing and providing appropriate medical care. The informant introduced a social dimension into the nursing profession, and spoke of this element as lacking in the Polish nurses' practice. Contrasting this view, the newcomers reported that the Polish experience was to provide total care for patients, as the nurses were responsible for all care: 'In Poland there are only nurses...not care assistants and no other care personnel...we (the nurses) had to do everything'.

The concept of care may have more than one meaning. Bearing these different understandings of care in mind, the Polish nurses described their previous nursing practice as comprising total care and responsibility for patients. Nevertheless, this was not a characterization that was shared by the work community, as they seemed to operate with a different concept of what was in fact total care. The Norwegian work community introduced a social care element as important for nurses working on the ward. The Polish nurses seemed to ascribe a different meaning to care, as they talked about total care in a medical and physical sense. As we can see, the ideas of care capture a different totality within the two approaches to nursing. Both explicit and implicit demands for participation prevail within the wards, and the newcomers have a great deal of difficulty 'grasping together' (Wertsch, 1998) the diverse elements that are part of 'doing a good job'.

When it comes to ways of participating in ward practices, it seemed as if the complexity of demands contributed to a gap between the ways in which the newcomers performed particular work activities and what was seen as appropriate ways of doing the job. When elaborating further on how the practices are understood, the phenomenon of *situational interpretation* emerged. A Norwegian department manager told us about one difficult situation involving the comprehension of ethics:

> 'One Polish nurse just stripped, washed and cleaned the resident. In one way this was very efficient, but the head of ward argued: "these are older persons living here and they have a right to a private life". How one approached one's job in such situations was to her an important ethical question. She had tried to supervise this nurse, but did not appear to have succeeded. When talking to the nurse, she stressed the importance of understanding patients' wishes and how the personnel had to be careful and sensitive to residents' signals. In other words, she stressed the ethics of the situation. To understand these differences, another nurse provided an important piece of information when she said that they were being taught the provisions of the Norwegian Patient Act since they arrived and one difference was that in Norway a patient has the right to say "no" to care and cure. In Poland this is not up to the patient to decide'.

In Norway, care and cure are matters of agreement and understanding between staff and patient. Accordingly, health personnel must act in ways that include the patient in any decision, even when it is difficult to communicate with the patient. These divergent views were a platform for further approaches to work participation. Doing the job in acceptable ways was not straightforward and was not only a question of professional skills (in a medical and physical sense). According to a sociocultural understanding, the participants' skills and practices are situated (Lave, 1997; Engeström, 1999). And as we have seen, a person's prior experiences are not necessarily relevant in a situation with new partners.

As described above, the different meanings ascribed to care for the residents was one element that contributed to unequal platforms. As we elaborate below on the implications of participating in the duties on the ward, we emphasize the ways in which the Polish nurses and the other personnel enter into the working structure of shared responsibility in the joint care for residents.

The limits on nursing

It seemed quite a challenge to interpret situations and act in ways that were valued by the work community. To the newcomers, the many types of health personnel working together represented both potential and challenges:

> 'I find it easier (with several categories of health personnel) but at the same time it's better (when the staff is only nurses) because we know

what we have to do. Here we have to follow what other people are doing and consider other people's work.'

This employee pointed to the potential for support from other personnel, but she also saw challenges with the different categories of health personnel working together. She perceived the situation as complex, as the workers depend on knowing what their share was in the multitude of work tasks to be carried out. It was a matter of 'what to do, how to do it, who is to do it and when to do it'. One aspect that is interpreted differently involves the limits on nurses' tasks:

One example was a Polish nurse who hesitated to do the tasks in the utility room. She did not consider this as part of her job. However, another newcomer overdid the cleaning activities. She actually gave them priority over tending to residents. When invited to go rounds with the other personnel, she refused and claimed she first had to finish the washing. On the one hand, the work community gave her credit for doing an excellent job washing and cleaning the ward facilities. The nursing assistants particularly valued her efforts. But, on the other hand, the nurses in her work community did not consider this activity a priority for nurses. It was described as an activity that should have lower priority than helping and caring for residents.

There was no doubt about this person's eagerness to do a good job. Nevertheless, the work community still interpreted her refusal as a sign of unwillingness to join them in learning the ways of performing nursing duties on the ward. 'She is not willing to learn,' said one of the Norwegian nurses. In this way, as she was not working along with the others, this Polish nurse circulated outside the joint work activities and seemed to lose out on the possibility of constructing a shared understanding of 'how we do the job'.

The personnel lacked shared understandings of nursing, and to the newcomers this meant they faced problems acting in ways that were valued within the wards, with the work community's standards being operative. These standards stood out from a nursing experience characterized by explicit responsibilities within a more defined care area. This became even clearer as independent decision making was in fact a recognized feature of the newcomers' previous practice. Several people in the work community saw the Polish nurses as familiar with independent work. This also contributed to the previous description of Polish nurses providing total care for patients. One Norwegian nurse said:

> 'Polish nurses supposedly are used to a more independent role as a nurse (in a medical sense) than the Norwegians. For example, in their previous job, they had the medical responsibility to decide if medication doses were to be increased. Here this is the doctor's responsibility.'

The newcomers operated independently within a more defined work area. Sticking to their previous nursing experience will mean that they enter into another profession's area of responsibility in their new job. In Norway, nurses observe and report back, while the doctor takes medical action if needed. The division of responsibility between doctors and other personnel was clear and decision making on medical issues was a more restricted area for nurses in Norway than in Poland. One Norwegian nurse claimed newcomers' experiences with a hierarchic health system had affected the ways in which newcomers approached their superiors in their present job.

When working in Norwegian wards, there are no clear-cut limits on which tasks 'belong' to which staff. When staff worked together in shared nursing activities, the vague perceptions of what to do, when to do it and how to do it materialized. Naturally the newcomers participated in the daily distribution of given tasks. The challenge was in the fact that the explicit division of labour comprised far more than a technical distribution of tasks. Clarifying these aspects required active involvement both at the planning level and at the practising level. Many of the newcomers were not aware of the expectation that they take part in the processes of clarifying work content.

In general, workplaces do not afford just any kind of individual commitment (Billett, 2001). In our study, the limits on nursing involved the relation between how the work practice affords participation and how the nurses elected to engage in the practice. To enable the being and growing of a multicultural work practice, participants need to experience each other's practices. One of the main conclusions of this article is that the mutual transmission of knowledge, going both ways between the Norwegian and Polish personnel, is only beneficial when the knowledge is situated in authentic, joint work situations. Learning takes place when the personnel work together in natural joint work situations. It appears to be ineffectual to explicitly 'inform about' the ways work is to be performed outside the work situation. When this is done, the dialogue is not fruitful because the frames of reference are missing in a de-contextualized setting. Participants may have a hard time grasping new elements if they are separated from the natural work activity in time and place. Thus, it is not sufficient to 'tell how' as it is the 'show how' that may bring the experiences together.

Expectations for nursing

As seen above, the diversity of nursing personnel did not operate within clear guidelines with respect to the limits on a nurse's job. One newcomer told us that job descriptions in Poland clarify each employee's tasks, whereas in Norway job descriptions are general and apply to all staff. Thus, there were areas of responsibilities that needed to be discovered, interpreted and acted upon. Although the newcomers were used to working independently, filling a job within the nursing home ward still involved specific expectations for independent action. In the new job, independent action was not a question of acting professionally on an individual basis solely by taking medical and physical responsibility for the residents. They faced expectations of *independency by being a party to co-constructed shared responsibility*:

> *One ward leader expresses particular expectations for the unified group of health personnel. She expects them to solve the distribution of responsibility and to sort out ways of filling the needs, as these are perceived by the full group. They also have to figure out how to develop complementary roles among themselves in ways that make the whole ward run smoothly. In short, they have to find ways of filling the needs together.*

These are expectations for making the ward function as a democratic unit, and this implies a focus on a joint responsibility for tasks, rather than operating explicit and firm limits of individual responsibility. These complex demands on the dynamics between the staff appeared to differ from the newcomers' prior experiences. As mentioned above, there were expectations with respect to playing active roles in the co-construction of the total work situation. One nurse sees it this way:

> 'The Polish nurses are kind, agreeable and in all ways clever in their work, so things go smoothly. But they don't make their own space in the wards in any way. They are hard workers, but they aren't seen or heard because they are so clever. They become invisible in a way. They take responsibility, but they just do the job and set no limits. Sometimes the nursing assistants try to protect them and urge them to take a break.'

The newcomers were active in their work but still played passive roles in the wards. They were hard workers and focused on doing their job. These newcomers were used to playing active roles and handling more medical responsibility in their previous jobs. A paradox emerged as they found themselves playing far more passive roles in the Norwegian system. They did not negotiate what work to do or the ways of doing it. Rather, they initiated work in areas that seemed to be 'free spaces' in the ward.

The expectations placed on active participation in planning and conducting work require closer interaction between the personnel. Knowledge about what is valued by the particular work culture is needed to act in appropriate ways within the community of practice. Communication is central in this situation as it is the key to clarifying responsibility and the premises for participation. This leaves immigrants in a special situation as they often do not have language skills on a par with the other employees and staff. Due to language problems, the newcomers have limited access to enter discussions on an equal footing. Therefore, they may not know the work culture so well and that this knowledge can guide their actions in the daily work. The newcomers make efforts to meet the requirements by incorporating expectations from the work community into their practice. During such processes people experience an 'interpretation collapse' (Horsdal, 1999), as their previous terms of reference do not apply. This 'shift' by no means implies a breakdown of a holistic nature that makes people see their world as totally fragmented. Newcomers, in fact, incorporate the new elements into their existing frames of reference to approach work activities in new ways.

Implications for workplace learning

From a Norwegian perspective, the local wards were seen as more democratic compared to the Polish authoritarian and hierarchic system. Expectations that staff co-construct participation were evident and across all situations; each individual was expected to play an active co-participating role. According to a democratic principle, the implicit assumption of equal participation is crucial. Moreover, individual commitment becomes vital within an organization with few structures of representation. Each person needs to take an active part in the decision-making process, both to protect and promote one's own interests and to be a participant on equal footing. Such involvement is about balancing individual and collective decision making.

If equal participation is to become a reality within the community, the qualities of the community's affordance and the participants' commitment to the ongoing activities is one main issue.

The work community and the newcomers had different ways of observing, interpreting and acting upon situations. The personnel did not operate on an equal footing when constructing the ward's strategies for managing the work smoothly. The newcomers did not play active roles in contributing to ways of doing the work. Naturally, their individual shortcomings were connected to language difficulties and a lack of local cultural knowledge. But there was also little evidence that the work community saw the newcomers' potential as something to be added to the ward practices. Although the newcomers are appreciated as diligent workers, the work community paid little attention to the Polish nurses' culture and knowledge. They were enrolled in work procedures and the existing ways of doing the job. Hence, the newcomers were expected to change their ways – and the work community did not see the Polish nurses as representing a positive potential for changing the existing practice. From these findings it was obvious who the learners were and who were the bearers of valid knowledge and practice. With this dynamic prevailing, we can see that there are constraints on the ongoing processes of constructing a joint local work practice, and the mutual knowledge exchange does not have the desired effect.

As the newcomers and old-timers are starting from separate platforms concerning the premises for participation, there appears to be an untapped potential waiting to be utilized within the work communities. If the personnel are to understand the nature of local practices, it is crucial to make procedures and activities transparent to others, such as immigrants joining the community of practice. One challenge in this picture is for participants to see and describe their own work culture with an outsider's perspective.

In a wider perspective, our findings show newcomers, as learners while the old-timers become non-learners. Organizations with such unused potential may turn into non-learning sites. If newcomers are expected to assimilate local practices, no hybridized 'new' practices will emerge. In these encounters, society loses important knowledge, while the Polish nurses may acquire broad and crucial competence that makes them attractive in the European labour market. As a consequence, we can say that the groundwork has not yet been laid to fulfil the international aim of mutual knowledge exchange through mobile workforces.

References

Amin, A., & Thrift, N. (1994). Living in the Global. In A. Amin & N. Thrift (eds), *Globalization, Institutions, and Regional Development in Europe*. Oxford: Oxford University Press.
Bauman, Z. (1998). *Globaliseringen og dens menneskelige konsekvenser*. [Globalization and the human consequences]. Oslo: Vidarforlaget.
Billett, S. (2001). Workplace pedagogic practices: Participation and learning. Paper presented at Vox, October seminar Workplace Pedagogy, Trondheim, Norway.
Bruner, E. M. (1984). Introduction: The Opening Up of Anthropology. In S. Plattner & E. M. Bruner (eds), *Text, Play, and Story: The Construction and Reconstruction of Self and Society*. St Louis: American Ethnological Society.
Cope, P., Cutherbertson, P., & Stoddart, B. (2000). Situated learning in the practice placement. *Journal of Advanced Nursing*, 31(4), 850–56.
Elbaz-Luwisch, F. (2002). Writing as Inquiry: Storying the Teaching Self in Writing Workshops. *Curriculum Inquiry*, 32(4), 403–28.
Engeström, Y. (1999). Activity theory and individual and social transformation. In Y. Engeström et al. (eds), *Perspectives on Activity Theory*. New York: Cambridge University Press.
Handlingsplan for Østersjøområdet (2001–2002). Det kongelige norske utenriksdepartement. [The plan of action for the Østersjø area. The Royal Norwegian Ministry of Foreign Affairs].
Horsdal, M. (1999). *Livets fortællinger – en bog om livshistorier og identitet*. [Life's narratives – a book about life histories and identity]. København: Borgen.
Jørgensen, D. L. (1989). *Participant Observation. A Methodology for Human Studies*. London: Sage.
Josefsson, I. (1991). *Kunskapens former. Det reflekterade yrkeskunnande*. [The forms of knowledge. The reflecting practitioner]. Stockholm: Carlsson Bokförlag.
Kommunal og regionaldepartementet (2003). *Arbeidskraftsbehov og rekruttering fra utlandet. Rapport fra en tverrdepartemental arbeidsgruppe*. [The Ministry of Local Government and Regional Development. The need for labour and recruitment from abroad. Report from an interdepartmental working group].
Lave. J. (1997). Learning, apprenticeship, social practice. *Nordisk Pedagogik*, 17(3), 140–51.
Lave, J., & Wenger, E. (1991). *Situated Learning: Legitimate Peripheral Participation*. Cambridge: Cambridge University Press.
Rismark, M., & Sitter, S. (2003). Workplaces as Learning Environments: Interaction between Newcomer and Work Community (accepted for publication in *Scandinavian Journal of Educational Research*, No. 5).
Rismark, M., & Stenøien, J. M. (2002). *Tre blikk på intensivopplæring i norsk for polske sykepleiere*. [Three glances into intensive instruction in the Norwegian language for Polish nurses]. Arbeidsnotat, Gdansk/Trondheim: Vox, Forskningsavdelingen.
Robertson, R. (1995). Globalization: Time-space and homogenity-heterogenity. In M. Featherstone, S. Lash & R. Robertson (eds), *Global modernities*. London: Sage.
Rogoff, B. (1995). Sociocultural setting, intersubjectivity, and the formation of the individual. In J. V. Wertsch, P. Del Rio & A. Alvarez (eds), *Sociocultural Studies of Mind*. New York: Cambridge University Press.

Säljö, R. (2000). *Lærande i praktiken. Ett sociokulturelt perspektiv.* [Learning in practice. A sociocultural perspective]. Stockholm: Prisma.
Stake, R. (1995). *The Art of Case Study Research.* Thousand Oaks, CA: Sage.
Vygotsky, L. S. (1987). *The Collected Works of L. S. Vygotsky: Vol. 1. Problems of General Psychology.* New York: Plenum.
Waale, M. B. (1996). *Innvandrernes forhold til det norske arbeidsmarkedet i lys av begrepene 'kulturell kompetanse' og 'kulturell kapital'.* [Immigrants' relations to the Norwegian labour market in the light of the concepts 'cultural competence' and 'cultural capital']. Unpublished manuscript. University of Tromsø: Department of Education.
Waters, M. (1995). *Globalization.* New York and London: Routledge.
Wertsch, J. V. (1998). *Mind as Action.* Oxford: Oxford University Press.
Yin, R. K. (1994). *Case Study Research. Design and Methods.* London: Sage.

15
Working Life Learning: Learning-in-Practise
Elena P. Antonacopoulou

Introduction

If learning is an integral part of living; if working life demands learning as a condition of survival; if learning is an essential human condition, why is it that we have such difficulty engaging with the phenomenon? The intimate relationship between learning, working and living is one that does not easily lend itself to analysis, partly because it is embedded in the dynamics of our human engagement with the challenges of living and working. Learning is both a process and product, a cause, a consequence and context in which emerging life and work patterns co-evolve and in turn organize learning. Therefore, learning is immensely rich and no one perspective is sufficient to capture fully the multiple connections and possibilities that it creates and from which it emerges. Yet, if we seek to move the learning debate forward we must learn to work with and live with the complexity of learning in ways that we can usefully engage and employ it as a driving force, helping us address many of the challenges working and living present us with. Only then can learning become a central feature to our life's journey. Only then can working be lived as a learning journey too.

This final chapter explores these complex interconnections and paves the way for a repositioning of learning, working and living in the context of organizational complexity. This is intended to provide a coherent framework for summarizing the discussion in the previous chapters and at the same time pave the way forward for future research into learning, working and living in work organizations. The discussion begins with a brief overview of our current approaches in engaging with the dynamics of learning, working and living. Attention is drawn to our tendency to look for outcomes like change as evidence of the ongoing co-evolution of learning, working and living. The discussion, however, shows how these modes of thinking are limiting our capacity to fully engage with the complexity of learning as an integral part of living and working.

The section which follows introduces a more dynamic way of engaging with learning complexity highlighting inter-connectivity, diversity self-organization and politics as key neglected dimensions in the learning debate. These dimensions will be analyzed drawing on the main principles of complexity science and a new conceptualization of learning as a complex social system is provided. Based on this re-conceptualization, the notion of *learning-in-practise* will be introduced as a new avenue for future research in learning. The main principles of *practise* and *practising* are discussed in relation to the way learning is enacted in modes of living and working. The chapter concludes with a review of the main implications for future research in learning as a mode of living and working in complex social arrangements such as organizations.

Learning, living, working as change routines

Learning, working and living demand change. This is a message echoed by several contributions in this book (see Elmholdt; Laursen; Wärvik and Thång, this volume, 2005), seeking to capture the dynamic nature of learning as a way of living in work organizations. The need to capture the dynamics of learning is a long-standing challenge in learning research. There has, therefore, been a tendency to equate learning with change and to present them as interdependent (Alderfer & Brown, 1975; Friedlander, 1984). For example, Handy (1989, p. 44) states that, 'if change is another word for learning, then the theories of learning will also be theories of changing'.

In relation to work organizations, the relationship between change and learning has attracted a lot of attention, particularly with the focus on organizations as learning systems (Nevis *et al.*, 1995; Ulrich *et al.*, 1993; Shrivastava, 1983) and the efforts to respond to an ever-changing environment by creating 'learning organizations' (Senge, 1990; Garvin, 1993). Learning is perceived to be important for surviving the challenge of change (Handy, 1989; Heywood, 1989; Clark, 1991; Lessem, 1993; Dixon, 1994; Cunningham, 1994). For effective change to take place, organizations and individuals must first learn (Argyris, 1993; Finger & Buergin, 1998; Fiol & Lyles, 1985; Huber, 1991; Srivastva *et al.*, 1995). Commentators presenting the relationship between change and learning in these terms draw from the laws of ecology and some refer specifically to Ross Ashby's law of requisite variety (Lessem, 1993; Dixon, 1994). The law of requisite variety states that for an organism/system to survive its rate of learning must be equal or greater ($L \geq C$) than the rate of change in its environment (Ross Ashby, 1958).

Very few researchers however, see the relationship, the other way round, that is, learning as leading to change, although some of the definitions of learning do incorporate an element of change (Harris & Schwahn, 1961; Knowles, 1973; McLagan, 1978; Klatt *et al.*, 1985). For example, Cantor (1961, p. 3) argues that 'to learn is to change', while Crow and Crow (1963, p. 1), suggest that 'learning involves change. It is concerned with the acquisition of habits, knowledge, and attitudes. It enables the individual to make both personal and social adjustments'. David King (1964, p. 6), defines learning as 'that which enables the person to adapt to the changing demands of the environment'. However, when reference is made to the content of change in relation to learning, the tendency is to look for (permanent) modification in behaviour (Bass & Vaughan, 1969; Argyris, 1982).

Some commentators, however, also present a counter argument and suggest that the relationship between learning and change aims to enhance stability rather than transformation (Cook & Yanow, 1993; Antonacopoulou, 1998, 1999). Empirical studies by Antonacopoulou (1999, 2004a) confirm this view and show the social, emotional and political forces at play in the process of learning and changing. Maintaining a degree of stability seems to be at the core of learning during turbulent conditions. Interestingly, the tendency to limit learning as a process of preserving than changing the status quo is often dictated by the very organizational systems, which are meant to encourage learning.

These observations would suggest that we have yet a long way to go before we can more fully account for the dynamic nature of learning, living and working. Our modes of thinking about unfolding processes such as learning and changing are still restricted in what Ford and Ford (1994) call a 'formal logic'. As Ellström (this volume) rightly points out, the two dominant logics of learning (focusing on performance or on development) fundamentally affect the space for learning at work. We therefore, need to embrace alternative modes of thinking that permit us to re-conceptualize unfolding processes such as learning and changing. We need to move beyond conceptualizations of learning and changing as stable patterns of routines and practices. We need to embrace more fully the emergent, self-organizing practices that shape learning as both a product and process of diverse activities, structures, artefacts in the way these are interconnected to an equally diverse and disperse group of social actors with multiple identities and agendas.

Orlikowski (1996) argues for the need to approach (organizational) change as ongoing improvization as people in the organization engage with novel and unexpected situations. Likewise, Feldman (2000) suggests that the potential for change is always present as long as social agents perform their routines and respond to the outcomes of previous actions. Therefore, rather than a view of change as a programmatic and punctuated process often to unfold as a grandiose event, change can be explored as a necessary biological condition of living which emerges continually and in an unpredictable way out of ongoing interactions between social agents and their structures.

Tsoukas and Chia (2002), reflect a similar view in relation to organizational change and argue that rather than viewing change as a property of organization, as something that happens inside or in relation to it, our analysis of change should start with the assumption that change is ontologically prior to organization as it is the very condition of possibility for organization to happen. Hence, as Tsoukas and Chia (2002) point out, organization is a secondary accomplishment, in a double sense: organization results from attempting to dominate or order that flux, and is a pattern that comes out of change. As Chia and King (1998: p. 466, original emphasis) put it, 'reality *is* change', there exists a never-ending process of assembling, dissembling and reassembling, through which 'entities' are continually made and remade.

Therefore, accounting for this ongoing process of emergence and evolution is perhaps where our attention in learning research needs to be refocusing. For if changing is an integral part of learning, living and working we need to develop both conceptual and methodological tools for engaging with these unfolding happenings we call learning and change. This also means that our attention needs to move beyond concrete evidence of learning and changing which focus on behaviour or other action outcomes. Instead, we need to find ways of engaging with changing routines as the emerging patterns of connection between different dimensions of learning that create the possibility for learning. In this context, one way of repositioning change in relation to learning is by suggesting that it is in change that changing is possible. The change process enables us to remain open to the multiplicity of possibilities in change and in changing. One could say that a similar view could be applied to our re-conceptualization of learning.

In pursuing this challenge, we need to first carefully reflect on the range of disciplinary backgrounds which inform the learning debate and take stock of their fundamental epistemological and ontological assumptions about learning. A multiplicity of disciplinary perspectives have been documented as informing the learning debate (Easterby-Smith, 1997) drawing predominantly on traditions of psychology, sociology, philosophy and anthropology. These different disciplinary perspectives have coloured and represented learning in different ways drawing attention to different aspects of learning including: behaviour (Pavlov, 1927; Skinner, 1971), cognition (Ausubel, 1985), motivation (Rogers, 1969; Hilgard & Bower, 1975); experience (Kolb, 1984) and action (Revans, 1982; Marsick & O'Neil, 1999).

If we are to come closer to capturing and representing the richness of the learning phenomenon we need to make a concerted effort to integrate these diverse perspectives as they reveal different aspects of learning. Several chapters in this book show the possibilities of connecting diverse perspectives (see Elkjaer & Wahlgreen; Miettinen & Virkkunen, this volume, 2005).

If we are to integrate various perspectives of learning and to fully embrace learning complexity we need to engage with different modes of thinking that enable us to make the necessary connections. Cooper and Law's (1995) 'distal' and 'proximal' thinking modes, provide a useful means of organizing these different perspectives. These modes of thinking explore the implications of emphasizing substance or process and sensitize us to the tensions embedded in processes that seek to connect potentially opposing dimensions.

'Distal' thinking emphasizes outcomes of thought and action and assumes the existence of clear and unambiguous boundaries between perspectives and positions. This logic of differentiation distinguishes process from outcome, learning from working and assumes a hierarchy between the separated categories. Being epistemologically realist, this mode of thinking unproblematically considers that such locatable structures or categories can be measured and represented, provided the 'right' methodologies are used so as to let the facts 'speak out' for themselves.

'Proximal' thinking, however, emphasizes integration and connectivity. It focuses on the unfolding and 'unfinished' nature of events and does not seek closure but strives for the never ending, always partial and precarious process of learning in search of the unknown. Therefore, instead of boundaries or categories there are different possibilities. Antonacopoulou *et al.* (2004) point out that organizational change and renewal conceptualized using a proximal logic can be conceptualized as a process of interpenetrating, interlocking, mobile and non-locatable associations.

Proximal modes of thinking therefore, encourage us to explore interconnections and interdependencies rather than tensions, divisions and differences. Even oppositional dimensions meet in this mode of thinking.

This mode of thinking is consistent with 'trialectic logic' (Ichazo, 1976; Soja, 1997). Trialectics is an alternative logic beyond formal and dialectic logic, which proposes that learning occurs through attraction to different possibilities. Learning, therefore, does not only result from a synthesis of potentially opposing perspectives as suggested in dialectics or formal logics of change. Instead, learning can also emerge as different connections and possibilities are explored. Learning therefore, emerges as a space/context where these possibilities can be contained and it is also a process and product of a multiplicity of connections (Antonacopoulou, 2000a, 2002; Antonacopoulou & Chiva, 2005). Ford and Ford (1994) understand that trialectics as a logic is strongly related to the science of complexity. The science of complexity might provide a new avenue for rethinking learning. We explore this possibility in the section which follows by identifying the key dimensions of learning as a complex social system.

Learning as a complex social system

Although complexity science has its roots in the physical sciences, it is increasingly employed to understand social phenomena, including organizations (Dooley *et al.*, 2003; Ofori-Dankwa & Julian, 2001) and their social complexity (Antonacopoulou & Chiva, 2005), as well as specific management issues such as strategic management (Stacey, 1993), strategic change (Stacey, 1995; Brown & Eisenhardt, 1997), innovation management (Cheng & Van de Ven, 1996), and design management (Chiva, 2004). It is also penetrating into adult education debates (Fenwick, 2003) and more recently organizational learning debates (Antonacopoulou & Chiva, 2005).

It is beyond the scope of this chapter to provide a review of the main principles of complexity science (for such reviews, see Antonacopoulou & Chiva, 2005; Mitleton-Kelly, 2003; Tsoukas, 1998). It is important to clarify however, that complexity science sets out to devise mechanisms to create and maintain complexity, and to produce tools for its description and analysis (Simon, 1996). Complexity science covers many fields of scientific research including chaos theory, the study of fractals and the idea of complex adaptive systems (CAS). The ideas of CAS enable us to understand system behaviour in relation to simple actions that may create multiple effects as interacting 'agents' follow rules and influence their local and global environments (Sherman & Schultz, 1998). One of the most important characteristics of CAS systems is their capacity to learn (Gell-Mann, 1994; Stacey, 1995, 1996). Previous research also shows that CAS ideas are relevant in identifying the essential factors that facilitate organizational learning (Chiva, 2003).

Three key principles of complexity science will be employed here to illustrate dimensions of learning for which the current learning debate does not fully account; inter-connectivity, diversity and self-organization. A fourth and equally neglected element in both complexity and learning debates is politics. The reconceptualization of learning as a complex social system demands that we also pay attention to the socio-political dimension of complexity.

Inter-connectivity

Appreciating the complexity of learning implies a need to understand the inter-connections among parts of the system that constitute learning (Kauffman, 1995; Axelrod & Cohen, 1999). Inter-connections reflect the fractal nature of learning and demonstrate that a number of elements combine to create what we understand learning to be. Learning is clearly not only a cognitive process due to the neural connections it creates as information is connected to create meaning. By the very process of developing meaning, learning is also a highly emotional process that influences how we react and respond to experiences that we encounter. These very responses generate different psychological states that combined with related actions in turn are contained within structures and systems defined and negotiated by social actors. These very social structures by extension provide meaning to social interactions and at the same time provide an understanding that defines one's identity in the context of one's role in different settings. Therefore, learning as a system is embedded within biological, psychological, social, cultural, emotional and other viable systems all of which coexist and co-evolve in relation to internal and external conditions within an ecosystem.

This point suggests that the institutionalization of learning processes within any (social) system are subject to the ongoing institutional transformations that are caused by learning practices that are instituted by social structures. These very social structures, however, are also constantly negotiated as diverse social forces (agents and structures) interact in embracing the heterogeneous nature of self-organization.

Therefore, if learning is about connecting, inter-connectivity implies the coexistence of heterogeneous forces (Gell-Mann, 1994).

Diversity

Heterogeneity and diversity are key dimensions of learning. Diversity is what feeds learning in the way conditions that underpin interactions and connections between systems create tensions. That multiple dimensions exist in tension is to reflect the multiplicity of possibilities each dimension can create by being attracted to different possibilities. Tensions dissolve into the space of possibility and become *ex-tensions* of current reality. These *ex-tensions* reflect the elasticity of processes like learning as multiple possibilities emerge in the way inter-connections are explored. Inter-connections are reflective of the *in-tension* to learn which brings *at-tension* to some specific possibilities, which are more relevant at different moments in time. This ultimately suggests that tensions are not only born out of conflict, power and political differences privileging one mode of reality over another. Instead, tensions are also attractions to different possibilities. It is the way learning space expands to embrace the new space learning creates. Therefore, learning is 'the edge of chaos' in the way the tensions between competing forces drives the possible connections that can be productively created as a result of their interaction. Engaged interaction as opposed to instrumental transaction challenges conditions of power and control in heterogeneous forces. This perspective implies that the learning space embraces different perspectives and engages actants in a reflective and reflexive process of learning. In other words, the inherent diversity need not lead to a synthesis of conflicting perspectives, as per the dialectic logic would suggest. Instead, the diversity needs to be maintained as this is a source of dynamism driving self-organization, which is a basic cause, consequence and context for learning, we frequently refer to as 'understanding'.

Self-organization/emergence

That learning connects heterogeneous forces reflects the ultimate quality of learning; surprise. Learning is not a matter of chance. Learning is part of the stream of practices that constitute organization. Such practices are reflected in routines (Axelrod & Cohen, 1999; Bechky, 2003); models (Stacey, 1996); strategies (Gell-Mann, 1994); culture (Gell-Mann, 1994); or the dominant logic (Bettis and Prahalad, 1995).

Regularities in practices enables a system to determine the nature of further experience and make sense of it (Stacey, 1996). Reconfigurations in practices are a consequence of a process of self-organization and co-evolution. Learning practice therefore, can be reconceptualized as a process and product of the ongoing mutations in relation to the governing practices and the way these co-evolve in time and space in response to endogenous and exogenous forces. Learning does not only arise as a result of noticeable shifts (formal logic) in practices or reintegration of otherwise conflicting perspectives (dialectic logic). Learning emerges from multiple possibilities previously not explored. Such possibilities may be interpreted as *surprise* or *serendipity* depending on whether they are considered relevant or attainable. No single experience determines learning practice, which is unpredictable and uncontrollable (Goodwin, 1994) due to its social nature (Elkjaer, 1999).

Learning, therefore, emerges as a natural condition of creating new order and self-organization as diverse elements within a system co-evolve and provide both negative and positive feedback to support single loop learning (negative feedback) and double loop learning (positive feedback) (Argyris & Schön, 1978; Stacey, 1996). Essentially, self-organization is the process of re-ordering different aspects of learning such that new learning can emerge in a cyclical process of ongoing evolution. Learning is, therefore, not only a mode of connecting, but also an expanse of diverse elements and forces. Learning is also the very foundation of learning. Learning provides the energy for connections to be made and highlights the gaps that exist while it also provides the scope for bridging these gaps. Moreover, learning shapes the emerging models that define the boundaries of action while it also opens up multiple modes of interaction. Modes of interaction are not only the emerging patterns of thinking and action, but also the very social structures that are constantly evolving as social actors become sensitized to new possibilities for learning. These new possibilities are also central to self-organization the inherent nature of social systems to renew themselves. This process of renewal, and ongoing transformation is made possible because learning, like change is endemic to organizing.

Moreover, learning is central to the systemic nature of social evolution because, it highlights the complex (symplegma – fusion) of connecting forces and the conditions that support their interaction. This perspective not only captures the fluidity that is so central to social systems, it also challenges us to explore learning as an integral part of what it means to be a viable system (see Beer, 1972). In other words, self-organization is an inherent mechanism for reaching internal consistency in relation to external forces. This point is critical as it reaffirms the political nature of learning.

Politics and power

The political nature of learning remains one of the biggest challenges in learning research. Researchers who focus on the political nature of learning (Coopey, 1995; Antonacopoulou, 2000b, 2001; Lawrence *et al.*, 2005), highlight mainly the inequalities of power and control, the tensions between individual and organizational priorities in learning or the different perspectives and motives underlying learning and knowledge. The politics of learning clearly illustrate that learning does not take place in a vacuum. Learning is a connection of possibilities stimulated by the signals received within the context in which learning takes place. These signals, however, are subject to multiple interpretations which define the actions one takes to make life and work more meaningful. This point, however, reveals a key dimension of the political nature of learning that we have so far neglected partly because we have paid insufficient attention to the power of learning. The power of learning is at the core of what makes knowing political, hence the common phrase 'I know enough to be dangerous'.[1] Learning entails responsibility and accountability. It is rather common that social actors tend to negate the responsibility learning entails by proposing sad excuses about their inability to learn. These defensive routines as Argyris (2004a) clearly demonstrates in his research reflect the tendency to be reluctant to learn even when the need to learn is obvious. This learning state is what Antonacopoulou (1998) describes as 'mathophobia', which is reflective of the power of learning to steer a whole host of emotions. It is also the powerful connection between learning and what people do in the name of learning.

To learn, therefore, is to make viable connections between a diverse set of emerging dimensions that affect action and interaction with others. To be accountable for one's actions is one of the defining characteristics of those who chose to lead a life of learning (Antonacopoulou & Bento, 2003; Antonacopoulou, 2004b). Responsible action reinforces that learning only gains meaning in the process of interacting with others. This point reasserts the social and political significance of learning which reminds us that learning is not a controllable entity. Rather, learning is better understood as a dynamic complex process, which is embedded in the ways social forces within systems define the conditions of their interaction. Therefore, to say learning is social and political is to appreciate the multiple ways in which learning is manifested in action. How and why people act in relation to their work is defined by their learning and in turn defines their understanding that subsequently guides their actions. In short, political learning is reflective of the emerging tensions as different learning opportunities in life are explored.

All these aspects illustrate the complexity of learning and reinforce the need to explore learning as a complex social system. It is also these dimensions of learning that we can usefully draw from as we develop further our understanding of the patterns, practices and routines that give life to learning-in-practise.

Learning-in-practise

The characteristics of learning as a complex social system renew the importance of embeddedness and situatedness of learning. This is consistent with a growing shift towards a practice-based view which has been marked in recent years in many different parts of social science (Schatzki *et al.*, 2001). In management, this has been reflected in an increasing concern with what do people actually do as a necessary preamble to theorize about organizations and organizing (Barley & Kunda, 2001; Whittington, 2003; Nicolini *et al.*, 2003).

The practice-based view has been particularly prominent in the organizational learning and strategy debates where the focus tends to be on the set of actions or activities (praxis of practitioners) and the mediating objects that constitute part of a practice (Gherardi, 1999, 2000; Johnson *et al.*, 2003). It also emphasizes the importance of communities of practitioners as the space where the social dynamics of learning are negotiated, thus reinforcing principles of inter-connectedness and interdependence between agency and structure, a point which is central both in structuration theory (Giddens, 1984) and in actor network theory (Law, 1999). This is also, of course, consistent with much thinking underpinning the pragmatist framework that Dewey (see Elkjaer, 2004) introduced in the way he has helped us understand participation and experience as integral aspects in the learning process. Therefore, these perspectives encourage us to explore 'learning-as-practice' engaging not only actions and activities in relation to learning, but also the role of language and other cultural and material artefacts, the nature of social interactions and not least the tacit, situated and almost instinctive responses of actors in the socially networked worlds in which they live. Conceptualizing learning as practice (Nicolini *et al.*, 2003), reminds us that practices are influenced by forces that are both inside and outside of the organisation (Bechky, 2003; Gherardi & Nicolini, 2002). The coexistence of multiple adjoining and interlocking practices forms the heart of their evolution. The normal, everyday execution of practice thus, becomes the context of tensions amongst different practices and the groups that embody them. Learning in relation to practice is therefore, conceptualised as an activity but also as a flow, a flexible, ever-changing structure that connects actors, systems and artefacts together. It is from these actions that routines, processes and practices emerge, and thus, it is important to understand the actions themselves if we are to understand learning.

A practice focus is also consistent with (and extending) recent contributions which have stressed that routines (intended as repeated application of a specific practice) can be a source of change and adaptation (Feldman, 2000; Zollo & Winter, 2002; Feldman & Pentland, 2003). This of course adds to their established character as creators of stable order and representations of social truce between different coalitions in the organisation (Nelson & Winter, 1982; Hannan & Freeman, 1984). This clearly only goes to reinforce the socio-political dynamics surrounding these repeated enactments. Modifications of routines have been ascribed to 'slippage' or simple adaptation to new and different situations. While both of these rationales are valid, the actual dynamics of change, with the implied renegotiation of practice, has not been shown.

By focusing on self-organization, we can become more in tune with the tensions among different practices and the groups that embody them. This interlocking of different practices provides scope for engaging with the fluidity of learning as practice and action becomes difficult to separate. This opens the possibility that practices behave fractally.

Therefore, if we are to understand this self-organizing process in the way agents and their practices are inter-connected, two issues need to be further developed. One is the definition of practice, which needs to become more 'elastic' and multifaceted. The existing literature, provides a number of different perspectives on practice as *action* (Bourdieu, 1980); practice as *structure* – language, symbols, tools (Turner, 1994); practice as *activity system* (Engeström et al., 1999); practice as *social context* (Lave & Wenger, 1991); practice as *knowing* (Nicolini et al., 2003). The literature on organizational routines, as a special kind of practice, becomes relevant here, with their conceptions of routines as sources of efficiency, memory and social order (Nelson & Winter, 1982), flexibility (Adler, Goldoftas & Levine, 1997; Pentland & Rueter, 1994), connections (Feldman & Rafaeli, 2002), change (Feldman &

Pentland, 2003) and the creation of resources (Feldman, 2004). A full description of the processes of emergence and self-organization needs simultaneous consideration of many aspects of practice at the same time.

The second issue that needs theoretical development is the dynamics of the practice. Because of the multifaceted nature of practice, the existing conceptualization of institutionalizations (Berger & Luckmann, 1966; Selznick, 1957) are potentially reductive, when talking about practice. Studies of institutionalization processes in fact tend to emphasize the end result, the institutionalized practice. More in keeping with the complex social systems view of learning introduced in the previous section we need to appreciate that there is no end result to this process, only a continuous flow of what could be referred to as *practising*. A trivial but important distinction between practice and practise needs to be made. While practice and practicing refer to the institutionalization of activities and routines, *practise* and *practising* focus on the holistic and emergent nature of practice.

Therefore, practice conceptualized as a dynamic social process that emerges over time entails at its core practising attempts which seek to accommodate endogenous and exogenous forces, brought about by ecological, economic, social and political dynamics. Connections between practices form the core of learning-in-practise as it describes how practices evolve and how learning unfolds through the repeated enactments which configure multiple arenas for negotiations of order, thus involving multiple interdependent stakeholders whose interactions are supported by the degree of learning collaborations they seek to explore (Antonacopoulou & Meric, 2005). By focusing on practise and its emergence, it is possible to map the social network that impacts on the way practices are orchestrated, through practising attempts. By placing learning practise at the centre of the investigation, it is possible to more fully account for the (diverse interests) political forces underpinning learning in time and space. A practise-centred perspective as a new dimension in future learning research can help us potentially develop methodologies for studying fluidity and interconnectivity.

There is a critical need therefore, to refocus attention in future learning research not only on the changes resulting from learning practices, but the *practising* attempts behind those practices and the changes they entail. This view would call for not only a different mode of thinking but a different set of epistemological and ontological positions to engage with such fluidity. Epistemologically this would encourage us to explore the practice of learning and organizing in different working contexts, to pay attention to the dynamics between individual agency, social structures and systems embedded in social systems and the complexity of tasks that shape the focus and orientation of learning and experiences of living in such organized arrangements. Ontologically, in extending process research (Pettigrew, 1989; Langley, 1999; Lewis & Grimes, 1999; Scandura & Williams, 2000), instead of studying processes as objects located in time and space we can embrace the challenge of using the process itself as a foundation for studying the same process. This could be described as a cosmological approach to studying learning (see Antonacopoulou, 2002).

Therefore, in capturing the dynamic nature in which practices, like learning, emerge, we need to also explore how a *practice is practised*, that is, performed, if we are to more fully account for how learning is the condition for learning in the same way as change is a condition for changing. The underlying ethos of practise (i.e. the values, beliefs and interpretations surrounding a practice) is just as critical as understanding the behaviours, activities and actions that constitute a practice. This view implies that learning one's practice is not enough, *practising one's practice* is more important (Antonacopoulou, 2004b). One cannot really master one's practice unless one is prepared to practise it. In other words, by practising one's practice one refines, improves, changes elements of this practice, elements of one's praxis and ultimately elements of one's self (e.g. identity).

In the context of this analysis, practice is not only what one does, what actions they take, but also how one learns to discover the intricate aspects and meanings of one's practice, with the socialization aspects that are implicit in that. Therefore, learning like practice is a constant flow of action, that never reaches the stability and rigidity implicit in some of the institutionally oriented interpretations of practice (e.g., Gherardi, 2000). Instead, as the analysis in this chapter has sought to suggest, learning-in-practise reflects learning as a foundation for learning because at the core of practice is practise. This only goes to reinforce the power of learning as part of living and working and as an extension of learning so that living is purposeful and working can be meaningful.

Conclusions

This chapter outlined the unfinished and ever evolving relationship between learning, living and working. As the concluding chapter to this book the objective was to both provide a summary and integration of the main themes of this edited collection, but more important through this integration to provide a platform for creating new connections and possibilities for linking learning with living and working. This latter point set the foundation for reconceptualizing learning extending the view of learning as practice to embrace the coexistence of multiple adjoining and interlocking practices which forms the heart of learning as part of a co-evolving process of living and working. Learning is therefore, conceptualized as a complex social system where multiple and heterogeneous actants attract each other and create inter-connections that define the emerging purpose of learning in different contexts as self-organizing attempts expose different political agendas. Therefore, learning is not only a practice. It is also a practise; a flow, a flexible ever-changing mode of connecting different practices in ways that enrich learning practice.

This view has several implications for future learning research. For one, the study of learning needs to advance by recognizing the value of viewing and researching the phenomenon as a connecting force between people, systems and other processes that define social complexity it seeks to engage with and represent. Therefore, learning is not only the institutionalization of practices but also a reflection of the self-organizing nature of learning routines, processes and practices. These issues raise a number of methodological implications for future research in learning, particularly in relation to capturing and social complexity underpinning learning. As others (Argyris, 2004b; Easterby-Smith *et al.*, 2004) have recently pointed out in outlining future research directions in learning research, learning needs to describe the universe as completely as possible. For that it is critical that learning scholars reflect on their learning scholarship and constantly renew their learning practices as they practise with their emerging ideas about learning. Unless, learning scholars learn how to learn, learning research will not progress. Hopefully, this edited collection signals the enormity of the task ahead as learning research is driven by its own efforts to support learning about learning.

Acknowledgements

The author would like to acknowledge the support of the ESRC/EPSRC Advanced Institute of Management Research under grant number RES-331-25-0024 for this research. Thanks are also due to Susanne Broekhuizen, Nicola Dragonnetti and Ketu Patnaik at GNOSIS with whom I have been practising some of the ideas presented in this chapter.

References

Adler, P. S., Goldoftas, B., & Levine, D. I. (1997). Flexibility versus efficiency? A case study of model changeovers in the Toyota production system. *Organization Science*, 10(1), 43–68.

Alderfer, C. P., & Brown L. D. (1975). *Learning from Changing: Organisational Diagnosis and Development*. Beverly Hills, CA: Sage.

Antonacopoulou, E. P. (1998). Developing Learning Managers within Learning Organizations. In M. Easterby-Smith, L. Araujo and J. Burgoyne (eds), *Organizational Learning and the Learning Organization: Developments in Theory and Practice* (pp. 214–42). London: Sage.

Antonacopoulou, E. P. (1999). Individuals' Responses to Change: The Relationship between Learning and Knowledge. *Creativity and Innovation Management*, 8(2), 130–39.

Antonacopoulou, E. P. (2000a). Reconnecting Education, Training and Development through Learning: A Holographic Perspective, Special Issue on 'Vocational Education and Training in SMEs'. *Education + Training*, 42(4/5), 255–63.

Antonacopoulou, E. P. (2000b). Employee Development Through Self-development in Three Retail Banks, Special Issue on 'New Employee Development: Successful Innovations or Token Gestures?' *Personnel Review*, 29(4), 491–508.

Antonacopoulou, E. P. (2001). The paradoxical nature of the relationship between training and learning. *Journal of Management Studies*, 38(3), 327–50.

Antonacopoulou, E. P. (2002). Learning as Space: Implications for Organisational Learning, Manchester Business School Research Paper series, No. 443.

Antonacopoulou, E. P. (2004a). The Dynamics of Reflexive Practice: The Relationship between Learning and Changing. In M. Reynolds and R. Vince (eds), *Organizing Reflection* (pp. 47–64). London: Ashgate.

Antonacopoulou, E. P. (2004b). The Virtues of *Practising* Scholarship: A Tribute to Chris Argyris a 'Timeless Learner'. Special Issue 'From Chris Argyris and Beyond in Organizational Learning Research'. *Management Learning*, 35(4), 381–95.

Antonacopoulou, E. P., & Bento, R. (2003). Methods of 'Learning Leadership': Taught and Experiential. In J. Storey (ed.), *Current Issues in Leadership and Management Development* (pp. 81–102). Oxford: Blackwell.

Antonacopoulou, E. P, Graça, M., Ferdinand, J., & Easterby-Smith, M. (2004). Dynamic Capabilities and Organizational Learning: Socio-Political Tensions in Organizational Renewal, paper presented at the *Annual International Conference of the British Academy of Management*, St Andrews, Scotland, September.

Antonacopoulou, E. P., & Chiva, R. (2005). Social Complex Evolving Systems: Implications for Organizational Learning, Paper presented at the *6th International Organizational Knowledge, Learning and Capabilities Conference*, Boston.

Antonacopoulou, E. P., & Méric, J. (2005). From Power to Knowledge Relationships: Stakeholder Interactions as Learning Partnerships. In M. Bonnafous-Boucher & Y. Pesqueux (eds), *Stakeholders and Corporate Social Responsibility – European Perspectives*. London: Palgrave.

Argyris, C. (1982). *Reasoning, Learning and Action*. San Francisco: Jossey-Bass.

Argyris, C. (1993). *On Organisational Learning*. Cambridge, MA: Blackwell.

Argyris C. (2004a). *Reasons and Rationalizations: The Limits to Organizational Knowledge*. Oxford: Oxford University Press.

Argyris, C. (2004b). Reflecting and Beyond in Research on Organizational Learning, Special Issue 'From Chris Argyris and Beyond in Organizational Learning Research'. *Management Learning*, 35(4), pp. 507–9.

Argyris, C., & Schön, D. A. (1978). *Organisational Learning: A Theory in Action Perspective*. Cambridge, MA: Addisson-Wesley.

Ausubel, D. (1985). Learning as Constructing Meanings. In N. Entwistle (ed.), *New Directions in Educational Psychology 1: Learning and Teaching*. London: Falmer Press.

Axelrod, R., & Cohen, M. D. (1999). *Harnessing complexity*. New York: Free Press.

Barley, S. R., & Kunda, G. (2001). Bringing work back in. *Organization Science*, 12(1), 76–95.

Bass, B. M., & Vaughan, J. A. (1969). *Training in Industry: The management of learning* (2nd edn) London: Tavistock.

Bechky, B. (2003). Sharing meaning across occupational communities: The transformation of understanding on a production floor. *Organization Science*, 14(3), 312–30.

Beer, S. (1972). *Brain of the Firm*. London: Penguin.

Berger, P. L., & Luckmann, T. (1966). *The Social Construction of Reality: A Treatise in the Sociology of Knowledge*. London: Penguin.

Bettis, R. A., & Prahalad, C. K. (1995). The dominant logic: Retrospective and extension. *Strategic Management Journal*, 16, 5–14.

Bourdieu, P. (1980). *The Logic of Practice*. Stanford, CA: Stanford University Press.

Brown, S. L., & Eisenhardt, K. M. (1997). The art of continuous change: Linking complexity theory and time-paced evolution in relentlessly shifting organizations. *Administrative Science Quarterly*, 42, 1–34.

Cantor, J. A. (1961). *Delivering instruction to adult learners*. Toronto: Wall & Emerson.

Cheng, Y. T., & Van de Ven, A. H. (1996). Learning the innovation journey: Order out of chaos? *Organization Science*, 7(6), 593–614.

Chia, R., & King, I. (1998). The organizational structuring of novelty. *Organization*, 5(4), 461–78.

Chiva, R. (2003). The Facilitating Factors for Organizational Learning: Bringing Ideas from Complex Adaptive Systems. *Knowledge and Process Management*, 10(2), 99–114.

Chiva, R. (2004). Repercussions of complex adaptive systems on product design management. *Technovation*, 24, 707–11.

Clark, N. (1991). *Managing personal learning and change: A trainers guide*. London: McGraw-Hill.

Cook, S. D. N., & Yanow, D. (1993). Culture and Organisational Learning. *Journal of Management Inquiry*, December, 2(4), 373–90.

Cooper, R., & Law, J. (1995). Organization: distal and proximal views. In S. Bacharach, P. Gagliardi & B. Mundell (eds), *Research in the Sociology of Organizations, Volume 13* (pp. 237–74) Hampton Hill: JAI Press.

Coopey, J. (1995). The learning organisation: power, politics and ideology. *Management Learning*, 26(2), 193–213.

Crow, L. A., & Crow, A. (1963). *Readings in Human Learning*. New York: McKay.

Cunningham, I. (1994). *The wisdom of strategic learning: The self-managed learning solution*. London: McGraw-Hill.

Dixon, N. (1994). *The organisational learning cycle: How can we learn collectively*. London: McGraw-Hill.

Dooley, K. J., Corman, S. R., McPhee, R. D., & Kuhn, T. (2003). Modeling high resolution broadband discourse in complex adaptive systems. *Nonlinear Dynamics, Psychology, and Life Sciences*, 7(1), 61–85.

Easterby-Smith, M. (1997). Disciplines of organizational learning: Contributions and critiques. *Human Relations*, 50(9), 1085–1113.

Easterby-Smith, M., Antonacopoulou, E. P., Lyles, M., & Simms, D. (2004). Constructing Contributions to Organizational Learning: Argyris and the New Generation, Special Issue 'From Chris Argyris and Beyond in Organizational Learning Research'. *Management Learning*, 35(4), 371–80.

Elkjaer, B. (1999). In search of a social learning theory. In M. Easterby-Smith, J. Burgoyne & L. Araujo (eds), *Organizational Learning and the Learning Organization* (pp. 75–91). London: Sage.

Elkjaer, B. (2004). Organizational Learning: The Third Way, Special Issue 'From Chris Argyris and Beyond in Organizational Learning Research'. *Management Learning*, 35(4), pp. 419–34.

Elkjaer, B., & Wahlgreen, B. (2005). Organizational Learning and Workplace Learning: Similarities and Differences. In E. P. Antonacopoulou, P. Jarvis, V. Andersen, B. Elkjaer & S. Hoyrup (eds), *Learning, Working and Living: Mapping the Terrain of Working Life Learning*. London: Palgrave.

Elmholdt, C. (2005). Innovative Learning is not Enough. In E. P. Antonacopoulou, P. Jarvis, V. Andersen, B. Elkjaer & S. Hoyrup (eds), *Learning, Working and Living: Mapping the Terrain of Working Life Learning*. London: Palgrave.

Engeström, Y., Miettinen, R., & Punamäki, R.-L. (1999). *Perspectives on Activity Theory*. Cambridge: Cambridge University Press.

Feldman, M. S. (2000). Organizational routines as a source of continuous change. *Organization Science*, 11(6), 611–29.

Feldman, M. S. (2004). Resources in emerging structures and processes of change. *Organization Science*, 15(3), 295–309.

Feldman, M. S., & Pentland, B. T. (2003). Reconceptualizing organizational routines as a source of flexibility and change. *Administrative Science Quarterly*, 48(March), 94–118.

Feldman, M. S., & Rafaeli, A. (2002). Organizational routines as sources of connection and understanding. *Journal of Management Studies*, 39(3), 309–31.

Fenwick, T. (2003). Reclaiming and re-embodying experiential learning through complexity science. *Studies in the Education of Adults*, 35(2), 123–41.

Finger, M., & Buergin, S. (1998). The concept of the 'Learning Organisation' applied to the transformation of the Public Sector: Conceptual contributions for theory development. In M. Easterby-Smith, L. Araujo & J. Burgoyne (eds), *Organisational Learning: Developments in Theory and Practice*. London: Sage.

Fiol, C.M., & Lyles, M. A. (1985). Organisational learning. *Academy of Management Review*, 10(4), 803–13.

Ford J., & Ford L. W. (1994). Logics of Identity, contradiction, and attraction in change. *Academy of Management Review*, 19(4), 756–85.

Friedlander, F. (1984). Patterns of individual and organisational learning. In P. Shrivastava (ed.), *The Executive Mind*. San Francisco: Jossey-Bass.

Garvin, D. A. (1993). Building a Learning Organization. *Harvard Business Review*, July–August, 71(4), 78–91.

Gell-Mann, M. (1994). *The Quark and the Jaguar. Adventures in the simple and the complex*. New York: Freeman.

Gherardi, S. (1999). Learning as Problem-driven or Learning in the Face of Mystery? *Organization Studies*, 20(1), 101–24.

Gherardi, S. (2000). Practice-based theorizing on learning and knowing in organizations. *Organization*, 7(2), 211–23.

Gherardi, S., & Nicolini, D. (2002). Learning in a constellation of interconnected practices: Canon or dissonance? *Journal of Management Studies*, 39(4), 419–36.

Giddens, A. (1984). *The Constitution of Society*. Cambridge: Cambridge University Press.

Goodwin, B. (1994). *How the leopard changed its spots: the evolution of complexity*. London: Weidenfeld & Nicholson.

Handy, C. (1989). *The age of unreason*. London: Arrow.

Hannan, M. T., & Freeman J. (1984). Structural inertia and organizational change. *American Sociological Review*, 49(April), 149–64.

Harris, T. L., & Schwahn, W. E. (1961). *Selected readings on the learning process*. New York: University Press.

Heywood, J. (1989). *Learning adaptability and change: The challenge for education and industry*. London: Paul Chapman.

Hilgard, E. R. & Bower, G. H. (1975) *Theories of Learning*. Englewood Cliffs, NJ: Prentice-Hall.

Huber, G. (1991). Organisational Learning: The contributing processes and literature. *Organisation Science*, 2(1), 88–115.

Ichazo, O. (1976). *The Human Process for Enlightenment and Freedom*. New York: Arica Institute Press.

Johnson, G., Melin, L., & Whittington, R. (2003). Guest editor's introduction: Micro strategy and strategizing: Towards an activity-based view. *Journal of Management Studies*, 40(1), 3–22.

Kauffman, S. A. (1995). *At home in the Universe*. Oxford: Oxford University Press.

King, D. (1964). *Training within the organisation*. London: Tavistock.

Klatt, L. A., Murdick, R. G., & Schuster, F. E. (1985). *Human Resource Management*. Columbus, OH: Merrill.

Knowles, M. S. (1973). *The adult learner: A neglected species*. Houston: Gulf Publishing.

Kolb, D. A. (1984). *Experimental Learning: Experience as the Source of Learning*. Englewood Cliffs, NJ: Prentice-Hall.

Langley A. (1999). Strategies for Theorizing from Process Data. *Academy of Management Review*, 24, 691–710.

Laursen, E. (2005). Knowledge, Progression and the Understanding of Workplace Learning. In E. P. Antonacopoulou, P. Jarvis, V. Andersen, B. Elkjaer & S. Hoyrup (eds), *Learning, Working and Living: Mapping the Terrain of Working Life Learning*. London: Palgrave.

Lave, J., & Wenger, E. (1991). *Situated Learning: Legitimate Peripheral Participation*. Cambridge: Cambridge University Press.

Law, J. (1999). After ANT: complexity, naming and topology. In J. Law & J. Hassard (eds), *Actor Network Theory and After* (pp. 1–14). Oxford: Blackwell.

Lawrence, T. B., Mauws, M. K., Dyck, B., & Kleysen, R. F. (2005). The politics of organizational learning: integrating power into the 4I framework. *Academy of Management Review*, 30(1), 180–91.

Lessem, R. (1993). *Business as a learning community*. London: McGraw-Hill.

Lewis, M. W., & Grimes A. J. (1999). Meta-triangulation: Building Theory from Multiple Paradigms. *Academy of Management Review*, 24, 672–90.

Marsick, V. J., & O'Neil, J. (1999). The Many Faces of Action Learning. *Management Learning*, 30(2), 159–76.

McLagan, P. A. (1978). *Helping others learn: Designing programmes for adults*. Reading, MA: Addison-Wesley.

Miettinen, R., & Virkkunen, J. (2005). Learning in and for Work, and the Joined Construction of Mediational Artefacts: An Activity Theoretical View. In E. P. Antonacopoulou, P. Jarvis, V. Andersen, B. Elkjaer & S. Hoyrup (eds), *Learning, Working and Living: Mapping the Terrain of Working Life Learning*. London: Palgrave.

Mitleton-Kelly, E. (2003). *Complex systems and evolutionary perspectives on organizations: the application of complexity theory to organizations*. London: Elsevier.

Nelson, R. R., & Winter, S. G. (1982). *An Evolutionary Theory of Economic Change*. Cambridge, MA: Belknap.

Nevis, E. C., DiBella, A. J., & Gould, J. M. (1995). Understanding Organisations as Learning Systems. *Sloan Management Review*, 36 Winter, 73–85.

Nicolini, D., Gherardi, S., & Yanow, D. (2003). Introduction: towards a practice-based view of knowing and learning in organizations. In D. Nicolini, S. Gherardi & D. Yanow (eds), *Knowing in Organizations: A Practice-Based Approach* (pp. 3–31). London: M. E. Sharpe.

Ofori-Dankwa J., & Julian S. D. (2001). Complexifying Organizational Theory: Illustrations using time research. *Academy of Management Review*, 26, 415–30.

Orlikowski, W. (1996). Improving organizational transformation over time: a situated change perspective. *Information Systems Research*, 7, 63–92.

Pavlov, I. P. (1927). *Conditional Reflexes*. Oxford: Oxford University Press.

Pentland, B. T., & Rueter, H. H. (1994). Organizational routines as grammars of action. *Administrative Science Quarterly*, 39(3), 484–510.

Pettigrew, A. M. (1989). Longitudinal Methods to Study Change: Theory and Practice. In R. Mansfield (ed.), *Frontiers of Management Research and Practice*. London: Routledge.

Revans, R. W. (1982). *The Origins and Growths of Action Learning*. Lund: Chartwell-Bratt.

Rogers, C. R. (1969). *Freedom to Learn*. Columbus, OH: Merrill.

Ross Ashby, W. (1958). Requisite variety and its implications for the control of complex systems. *Cybernetica*, 1(2), 83–99.

Scandura T. A., & Williams E. A. (2000). Research Methodology in Management: Current Practices, Trends and Implications for Future Research. *Academy of Management Journal*, 43, 1248–64.

Schatzki, T. R., Knorr Cetina, K., & Von Savigny, E. (2001). *The Practice Turn in Contemporary Theory*. London: Routledge.

Selznick, P. (1957). *Leadership in Administration*. Berkeley: University of California Press.

Senge, P. M. (1990). The leaders' new work: Building learning organisations. *Sloan Management Review*, Fall, 7–23.

Sherman, H., & Schultz, R. (1998). *Open Boundaries*. New York: Perseus Books.

Shrivastava, P. (1983). A typology of organisational learning systems. *Journal of Management Studies*, 20(1), 7–28.

Simon, H. A. (1996). *The sciences of the artificial*. Cambridge, MA: MIT Press.

Skinner, B. F. (1971). *Beyond Freedom and Dignity*. New York: Knopf.

Soja, E. W. (1997). *Thirdspace, Journeys to Los Angeles and Other Real-And-Imagined Places*. Oxford: Blackwell.

Srivastva, S., Bilimoria, D., Cooperrider, D. C., & Fry, R. E. (1995). Management and Organisational Learning for Positive Global Change. *Management Learning*, 26(1), 37–54.

Stacey, R. D. (1993). Strategy as order emerging from chaos. *Long Range Planning*, 26(1), 10–17.

Stacey, R. D. (1995). The science of complexity: an alternative perspective for strategic change processes. *Strategic Management Journal*, 16, 477–95.

Stacey, R. D. (1996). *Complexity and Creativity in Organizations*. San Francisco: Berrett-Koehler.

Tsoukas, H. (1998). Introduction: chaos, complexity and organization theory. *Organization*, 5(3), 291–313.

Tsoukas, H., & Chia, R. (2002). On organizational becoming: rethinking organizational change. *Organization Science*, 13(5), 567–82.

Turner, S. (1994). *The Social Theory of Practices: Tradition, Tacit Knowledge and Presuppositions*. Cambridge: Polity.

Ulrich, D., Jick, T., & von Glinow, M. A. (1993). High Impact Learning: Building and diffusing learning capability. *Organizational Dynamics*, 22(2), Autumn, 52–66.

Wärvik, G., & Thång, P. (2005). Conditions for Learning during a Period of Change. Dilemmas and Disturbances on the Production Floor. In E. P. Antonacopoulou, P. Jarvis, V. Andersen, B. Elkjaer, & S. Høyrup (eds), *Learning, Working and Living: Mapping the Terrain of Working Life Learning*. London: Palgrave.

Whittington, R. E. (2003). The work of strategizing and organizing: For a practice perspective. *Strategic Organization*, 1(1), 117–25.

Zollo, M., & Winter, S. G. (2002). Deliberate learning and the evolution of dynamic capabilities. *Organization Science*, 13(3), 339–51.

Note

1 My thanks are due to Neil Patterson, Divisional General Manager at Hay Consulting Group for reminding me of this powerful point.

Index

Abrahamson, K. 69, 70
Abrahamson, L. 69, 70
activity systems 9, 156, 165–6, 190–2, 198–9
activity thoery 9, 156, 188, 189
adaptive (reproductive) learning 34–5, 62
adult education 6, 16; as deliberate/intentional learning 89–90; and reflection 90–2; returning to experience 90–1
Antonacopoulou, E. P. 1, 10, 44, 236, 238, 239, 243, 246
Argyris, C. xv, 15, 18–20, 21, 33, 53, 77–8, 155, 166, 235, 236, 242, 243
artefacts 7, 154; in activity 157; and boundary setting/crossing 188–9, 191–2, 195–6, 199; intentional/subjective nature of 157; joint creation of 156–8; and labour-protection inspectors' project 158–67; and problem-solving 158; representational 157–8; and shaping of actions 190–1, 199
assessment of practice 129–31

Bandura, A. 55
barriers to learning 131–2
Bartunek, J. 166
Bateson, G. 33
Bauman, Z. xiii, 222
Benner, P. 144
Blästerugn Project 109–10; case studies 110–13; and competence 111; and increased accessibility 110; and integration of individual/organizational learning 112; interest in 111; and organization of learning 110–11; outcomes of 111–12; participant–teacher relationship 110
Boud, D. 15, 70, 85, 89, 90, 91, 107

boundary objects 192, 195–6, 198
Boynton, A. C. 193

Chia, R. 237
Clark, M. L. 86
community of practice 10, 21, 52, 75, 122, 123–4, 211; and division of labour/forms of collaboration 166; interrelations of 124–5; and learning 207–8, 209, 216; learning from above 125; learning from below 125; learning from outside 125; and learning as legitimate peripheral participation 140; and learning resources 124; neighbour learning 125; and responsibilty 126
competence 107–8, 111, 202–3; and adaptation/renewal 208–10; and community of practice 207–8; concept 203–4; development of 102; and development of practical knowledge 206–7; learning connections 216–17; promoted/hindered 217; and sense making 204–5; social workers 210–16
computer-based collaborative learning 140–1
Contu, A. 51
creative learning see developmental (creative) learning
critical reflection 6, 23, 98–9
Crossan, M. M. 177, 180, 181
Crossley, N. 155

Dahlbom, B. 190
Dawkins, R. 156
development activity 171–2
developmental (creative, innovative) learning 34–5, 37–8, 43–5, 62
Dewey, J. 35, 41, 88, 92, 111, 157, 175, 244
Dreyfus, H. 58

education–work gap 104–6
Elkjaer, B. 74
Ellström, P. E. 4, 35, 62, 107, 111, 236
Elmholdt, C. 5, 35, 51, 125
employees 170, 188; individual learning 177–8; and management support 42–3; participation of 42–3
Engeström, Y. 33, 35, 190
experiential learning xvi, 87, 99, 170; individual 177–8; as source of learning at work 175–6; team/group 178–9

family learning 121
feedback 95, 242; adaptive 78
Feldman, M. S. 237
Fenwick, T. J. 40, 45
Fiol, C. M. 75
Ford, J. 236
Ford, L. W. 236
formal–informal learning 24, 86, 189, 203; Blästerugn Project 110–13; and bridging the gap 112, 113; and competence 107–8; complementarity of 106–9; concept 106; effectiveness of 107; and expertise 108; and networking 113–14; and problem solving 108; provision of 108–9; and reflective learning 107; supportive structures 114–15; and top-down/bottom-up strategies 113

Garrick, J. 15
Gustavsson, M. 41

Habermas, J. 212
Hedberg, B. 76
Heidegger, M. 155
Henderson, K. 146–7
Hildebrandt, S. 70
Hirschorn, L. 34
Hutchins, E. 157

identity, development of 133–4, 208
incidental learning 189
information technology (IT) xiii, 69, 139

infrastructure of knowing 78, 79
innovative learning 50, 62–3; background 50–2; case studies 54–5, 56–61; concept 53, see also developmental (creative, innovative) learning

Janlert, J.-E. 190
Järvinen, A. 170
Jarvis, P. 20–1, 24, 86
Johansson, J. 69

Kelly, G. A. 24
King, I. 237
knowedge-based organizations 202
knowing 1; in work organizations 7–11, 139–248
knowledge xiv, xv, 5; access to 69; acquisition 180; collective 180; concept/definition 72, 73; creation 179, 199; externalized 78, 79; facets of 8; growth rate of 70; importance of 69; and intuition 180–1; knowing-what/knowing-how 73, 179–80; necessity of 69; practical 206–7; social organization of 71; transformation of 80; transmission of 7–8, 172–3
knowledge management 154
knowledge society 69
knowledge-based approach 74–5
Kolb, D. A. 20–1, 24, 85, 175–6, 177, 178, 181, 238
Konno, N. 179, 181

labour-protection inspectors, and collective formulation of hypotheses 166–7; and creating new instruments for inspection work 160–5; and database as common memory/organizer of inquiries 162–3; developmental contradictions 158–60; extended hypothesis-driven checklist 163; and informative/epistemic potential of computer-based tools 167; and multi-voiced dialogue 163; new

instrumentality/knowledge production 16; and project report 163–5; and use of shared tools 166
landscape of learning, at work 122–32; background 119–22; in a community of practice 123–6; concept 120–1; and learning barriers 131–2; through assessment of practice 129–31; through participation practice 126–9
Latour, B. 157
Laursen, E. 6, 51, 235
Lave, J. 20–1, 26, 52, 86, 122, 144, 156, 208, 220
Layder, D. 79
Leadbetter, C. 69
learning, as adaptation/renewal 208–10; as change of behaviour/ knowledge 73; as collective investigation/collaborative retooling 7, 8; complexity of 11; concept/definition 71, 72; debates on 1; definitions of 3; importance of 71; as innovative/creative 4, 5; levels/ conditions of 4–5; lower/higher levels 33; necessity of 69; participatory 8; as perspective 81–2; preservation, accumulation, transmission 154–6, 166; separation, initiation, return 86; shared 180–1; as socially based 122; systems 73; theories of 4; as way of living 2, 3–5, 15–64; in work organizations 7–11, 139–248; work/organization link 15; and working 5–7, 69–134
Learning, Bateson level I/II 80
learning organization 1; concept 50; as management tool 69–70; normative assumptions 70
learning outcomes 86, 89; and influence of reflection 92–3; and reflection 96; and transformation of organizational routines 156
learning situations 73, 78–81; and frame of situation 80; relations between learners/teachers 80; and transformation of knowledge base 80
learning-in-practise 11; background 234–5; characteristics 244; as complex social system 239–40, 246; and diversity 241; epistemological/ ontological positions 246–7; focus of 245; and how practice is practised 246–7; implications for future research 248; inter-connectivity 240–1, 246–7; learning, living, working as change routines 235–9; and need for different modes of thinking 246–7; and politics/power 243–4; practice-based view 244–5; and self-organization/emergence 241–3, 245–6
Lektorsky, V. 157
Lewin, K. 175
lifelong learning xv, 6; and bridging the gap between educational/work systems 115–16; failure of 102, 104; and gap with work 104–6; positive aspects 103; problems concerning 103–4; supply-based strategy 102–3, *see also* formal–informal learning
logics of learning, assumptions 35–6; autonomy vs standardization of tasks/work processes 39–40; background 33–4; balancing performance–development 43–5; consensus vs conflict 41; development 37–8; different conditions of learning 38–43, 46; emancipatory potential 46; employee participation 42–3; and improvisation 45; and learning potential of task 38–9; management support 42–3; organizational objectives 41; performance 36–7; reproduction vs development 34–5; subjective/ cultural factors 40; and time 44–5; transformation pressure 41–2
Lyles, M. A. 75
Lyotard, J.-F. 46

Mahoney, 172
March, J. G. 17, 36, 37, 44, 62
Marsick, V. J. 15, 189–90, 208
Marx, K. 156
Meizerow, J. 87, 93–5
Merleau-Ponty, M. 155
Merriam, S. B. 86
middle management 179
Miettinen, R. 190
Moch, M. 166
motivation for learning 119–20
multicultural communities, background 219–20; case study objectives 222–3; and deviating perceptions of responsibility 224; dynamics of participation 224–30, 231; global within the local 221–2; implications for workplace learning 230–1; and individual/collective decision making 230–1; interviewing informants/analysing material 223–4; and learning differences 231; theoretical framework 220–2

national learning process 86
Nielsen, K. 125
Nonaka, I. 177, 179, 180, 181
nursing case study 223–4; challenges 226–7; and concept of care 225–6, 228; expectations for nursing 229–30; filling the job 224–30; and individual commitment 228, 230; limits on nursing 226–9; and meaning of nursing 224–6; and participation in ward practices 225–6; personnel support 227; and responsibility 228; and shared understandings 227–8

organizational knowledge 170
organizational learning (OL) 4, 170; as adaptable learner 75–6; as aggregated learning of employee 74–5; and changes in environment 17; definitions 16, 18, 75, 77; as development of learning opportunities 76–8; as individual development in OL systems 18–20; as individual knowledge acquisition 17–18; infrastructure 78; interactional aspect of 78–81; interest in 69; and Model I theories-in-use 19, 20; origins of 15–16; and participation in organizational practices 21; perspectives on 78; practice-based perspective 22; and processing of information 17–18; similarities/differences with WPL 28–9; social/practice-based perspective 16–17; and theories of action 19; as ubiquitous 20–2
Orlikowski, W. 237
Orr, J. E. 144

participation 126–7, 221; active 127; background 139–41; and child learning 127; hand/body learning 127–8; and imitations/routine work 128; and innovation 128–9; and learning as invisible 127; machine setters on video 141–4; outcomes 150–1; and practical assignments 127; self-produced video/everyday learning 141–7; and tools/equipment 129; and use of technology 140–1; watching a colleague on video 147–50; and workplace learning 127–9
Pedler, M. 77
performativity 33, 36–7, 43–5, 46
personal learning horizon 132; and development of identity 133–4
phenomenology 155–6
Piaget, J. 175
Poikela, E. 170
post-bureaucratic organizations 51, 57–62, 63
problem solving 6, 93–5, 97, 103–4, 108, 158
process model 176–7; challenges 186; cognitive 182–3; implementation 183–5; individual context 177–8;

operational 183; organization context 179–81; reflective 182; shared context 178–9; social 181–2, see also YIT Construction Ltd
production 62–3; analytical concepts 189–92; background 188–9; companies involved 192; control from above vs autonomy 197–8; and dilemma of delay 194–5; logistics agents 195–6; MTM-method 198; planners vs production floor lack of capacity 196; and production-planning meeting 193–8; quality of 129; re-reporting 197–8; replaceable worker vs skilled worker 196–7; run schedule 196–7; substitutes 196; and understanding 'something different' 193
progression 73–4; capability of learning 76–8; competence container 74–5; and quality 75; survival of the wisest 75–6

reconstructive learning, case study 61; concept 53
reflection 177, 204; and adult education 89–92; and attending to feelings 91; benefits of 91; and choice 100; content/process 94; critical reflection 98–9; and decision-making 95; definitions 87–8; embedded in thinking/action 92; *ex post facto* on prior learning 95; and feedback process 95; and individual potential for action 96; initiation 88, 95; and interaction between first-/second-order experiences 99–100; as inward-looking 92; and learning outcomes 92–3; and life perspective/understanding of life/work 96; and motivation 100; and outcomes of learning process 89; perceptual level 95; and personal capability 96; premise 94–5; and problem solving 93–5; and re-evaluating experience 91, 92; and recalling resources 95; return 88, 96; and returning to experience 90–1; role of 95–6; and self-awareness 95; and sense of self/relatedness 96; separation 88, 95
reflection-in-action 97–8, 204
reproductive learning 62–4, 80–1; case studies 54–6, 59–61; concept 52–3, see also adaptive (reproductive) learning
Robertson, R. 222

Sanchez, R. 172
Schön, D. A. 15, 18–20, 21, 33, 77–8, 97–8, 204
SECI (Socialization-Externalization-Combination-Internalization) processes 179; Ba 179, 181
self-awareness 95
Senge, P. M. 15, 77
Shrivastava, P. 74
single-/double-loop learning 80, 242
situated learning 52
social work, development of competences 210–12; development of practice 215–16; dilemmas of 212–13; results of study 213–15; sense making in 204–5
storytelling 80–1
strategic learners 23
System for Depicting the Field of Activity (SDFA) 160–2

Takeuchi, H. 177, 179, 180, 181
Tanggaard, L. 125
Taylor, F. 188
technology, computer-based tools 140–1, 167; video projects 139–51
traditional (bureaucratic) organizations 51, 55–7, 63
training 102, 104
transformative learning 93–5
transmission of learning, and *habitus, habit, routine* 155–6; and individual deposits of experience 154–5
Tsoukas, H. 237

Uusimaa Labour Protection District   160–7

Van Bolhuis-Poortvliet,   88
Victor, B.   193
video projects, intensive care nurses   144–7; machine setters   141–4; as participatory approach   139–41; results   150–1; watching colleagues   147–50
vocational, learning   6; students   119–20; training   23–4
Vygotsky, L.   56, 158, 220

Wartofsky, M.   157
Watkins, K. E.   189–90, 208
Weick, K. E.   57
Wenger, E.   20–1, 26, 122, 144, 156
Westley, F.   57
Wilbrandt, J.   130
Willmott, H.   51
Woerkom, M.   85, 87, 88
Wolfe,   176
workplace learning (WPL)   4, 5–6; case studies   54–62; and change   9–10; characteristics of   24; and competence development   10, 25; concept of   22–3; conditions for   9–10; context/environment   24–5, 27; curriculum   26; experimenting practice   56–7, 58; factors affecting   26; formal/informal model   6–7; individual/collective   9; and informal/incidental learning difference   24; interest in   69; as learning environment   23–5; link with formal education   23; methods of learning   25–8; model for *see* Blästerugn Project; and multicultural staff   10; observation–scaffolding–rehearsal   55–6; observation/imitation   58–9; obstacles to   102–6; origins of   15, 16; practice–observation   57–8; progression   6; psychosocial environment   10; reproductive prior to innovative   59–61; research on   78; retention of learning outcomes   8; shared perspective   9; similarities/differences with OL   28–9; situational   6, 7; skilled support   61–2; support/ guidance from experts   26–7

YIT Construction Ltd, analysis of know-how using process model   174; case organization   171–5; concept-testing phase   174; finding/developing concepts to be shared   174; implementation of process model   183–5; and need for continuous learning/ability to cooperate   172; phases of collaboration   173–5; planning development work   171–2; professional/researcher collaboration   170; recognition of problem   174; remodelling of development activities   174–5; scrutiny of applicability of model   174; and transference of knowledge   172–3; working method   172

Zuboff, S.   15, 179